The Celebration of Death in Contemporary Culture

THE CELEBRATION OF DEATH
IN CONTEMPORARY CULTURE

Dina Khapaeva

University of Michigan Press
Ann Arbor

First paperback edition 2022

For questions or permissions, please contact um.press.perms@umich.edu

Published in the United States of America by the
University of Michigan Press
Printed and bound by CPI Group (UK) Ltd, Croydon, CR0 4YY

First published in paperback January 2022

A CIP catalog record for this book is available from the British Library.

Library of Congress Cataloging-in-Publication Data

Names: Khapaeva, Dina, author.
Title: The celebration of death in contemporary culture / Dina Khapaeva.
Description: Ann Arbor : University of Michigan Press, [2017] | Includes
   bibliographical references and index.
Identifiers: LCCN 2016034791 | ISBN 9780472130269 (hardback : acid-free
   paper) | ISBN 9780472122622 (e-book)
Subjects: LCSH: Death. | Death in popular culture. | Civilization, Modern. |
   Culture. | Death in literature. | Death in motion pictures. | BISAC:
   SOCIAL SCIENCE / Death & Dying. | SOCIAL SCIENCE / Popular
   Culture. | PHILOSOPHY / Movements / Humanism.
Classification: LCC BD444 .K43 2017 | DDC 306.9—dc23
LC record available at https://lccn.loc.gov/2016034791

ISBN 978-0-472-03894-7 (pbk.)

Cover photo: Romeo & Juliet, *Vogue*, 2008. © Annie Leibovitz/Contact Press Images.

Acknowledgments

My thinking about the fascination with fictionalized violent death in contemporary culture continues my investigations into the ways in which the
memory of twentieth-century horrors influences contemporary society.
My interest in this topic originated from my research in historical memory,
which was inspired by Pierre Nora, his seminar at the École des hautes
études en sciences sociales in 1991–1995, and my translation into Russian
of several articles from his *Les Lieux de mémoire*. Over the years, I have had
the privilege of benefiting from his advice, as well as from his suggestions
regarding the first ideas of this book.

Meeting Gabrielle M. Spiegel at a conference in Santiago de Compos-
tela in 1993, where she presented her paper "Orations of the Dead, Silences
of the Living," was another important encounter. Her approach helped me
realize that what I considered my personal feelings about the tragedies of
the past could become a critical intellectual inquiry. I have been exploring
that theme for more than two decades since then. Our discussions with
Jeffrey Brooks were a constant source of inspiration for me throughout
the writing of this book, and beyond. Jeff and Gaby's advice allowed me to
considerably reinforce my argument, and I would like to thank them here
for their generous help and encouragement.

Caryl Emerson, Diana Hicks, Melvin Konner, John Krige, Juliette
Stapanian-Apkarian, and Carol Senf offered me important suggestions on
various parts of the manuscript. It is my greatest pleasure to express my
profound gratitude to them here.

I owe an immense debt to the colleagues who in a variety of ways invigorated my research: Wladimir Berelowitch, Cynthia Blakeley, Alain Blum, Marietta Chudakova, Mikhail Epstein, Boris Gasparov, Sander Gilman, Elena Glazova-Corrigan, Stuart Goldberg, Hans Ulrich Gumbrecht, Catriona Kelly, François Hartog, Nathalie Heinich, Natalia Ivanova, Tamara Kondratieva, Nina Kehayan, Sabina Loriga, Kevin F. M. Platt, Irina Prokhorova, William G. Rosenberg, Ronald Grigor Suny, Laurent Thévenot, Richard Utz, Lisa Yaszek, and Hayden White.

I am grateful to the anonymous reviewers at the University of Michigan Press and to Ellen Bauerle for her support of my project. I am greatly indebted to Liv Bliss, who committed herself to improving my English and has become an intellectual partner and a friend whose suggestions proved important far beyond English style. This book was envisioned during my research fellowship at Helsinki Collegium in 2009–2012, and I thank its former director, Sami Pihlström, for his help, as well as Jackie Royster, the dean of Ivan Allen College, for a research semester made possible through the Dean Research Award in the spring of 2014. Invited Professorship at the École des hautes études en sciences sociales in 2016 provided me with an opportunity to discuss my ideas with my French colleagues, and I am grateful to the EHESS and its Centre d'études des mondes russe, caucasien, et centre-européen for that.

Kate Koposova suggested numerous excellent interpretations of contemporary fiction and film that I have used in this book. Her intellectual contribution to this project is too considerable to be adequately acknowledged here. This book, like my previous publications, would have never seen the light of day without the constant guidance, advice, and critiques of Nikolay Koposov. Nikolay patiently withstood innumerable discussions, offered counseling during frequent writing crises, and endured countless rereadings of this manuscript, which owes so much to his ideas. I would like to thank my dear family for helping me survive this book about death.

Contents

Digital materials related to this title can be found on
the Fulcrum platform via the following citable URL:
https://doi.org/10.3998/mpub.9296915

Introduction

The Paradoxes of Death

This book investigates the cult of death, a distinctive way of engaging with death that crystallized in Western culture in the late 1980s and the 1990s. Three decades ago, Halloween did not rival Christmas around the world; dark tourism was not a rapidly growing industry; death studies were not part of the school curriculum; funerals were incomparably more traditional and uniform; and Santa Muerte, "Saint Death," was a marginal observance, not an international cult. In those days, "corpse chic" and "skull style" did not represent mainstream fashion; Gothic, horror, torture porn, and slasher movies were not conventional entertainment; and vampires, zombies, cannibals, and serial killers did not appeal broadly to audiences of all ages.

I argue that the cult of death reinvents death as entertainment and results from a disillusionment with humanity that renders monsters attractive. The cult of death signifies a rejection of the idea of human exceptionalism and is grounded in a long-standing tradition of the critique of humanism. These philosophical ideas penetrated popular culture, lost their critical potential, and were transformed into commodities. The cult of death says more about attitudes toward human beings than it does about attitudes toward death.

Although an impressive body of research has addressed many aspects of the fixation on death, violence, and the undead, we do not have a convincing explanation of the mounting demand for images of violent death and the dramatic changes in death-related practices. And this is not surprising, since we can hardly explain concrete manifestations of the cult of death without considering them as aspects of a single cultural movement. The main goal of this book is to document, for the first time, the scale and novelty of this cultural movement and to provide an explanation of the specific cultural and historical conditions that triggered the general acceptance of the cult of death.

The extraordinary appeal of death is not limited to the Western world; this is definitely a global phenomenon. My book, however, confines itself to the Western tradition, with an emphasis on American and Russian cultures. My main sources for this book are Anglo-American and Russian fiction, movies, and TV series featuring violent death and idealized nonhuman monsters (*Twilight Saga*, *The Vampire Diaries*, *True Blood*, *Night Watch*, and the Harry Potter series, to name just a few) that I analyze in the context of sociological and anthropological data to explain recent changes in death-related practices. By comparing the American and Russian ways of celebrating the cult of death, this book reveals its common features and variations.

Unspeakable Death

Why indeed, in this time of unparalleled longevity in the West, do we observe the dramatic changes in death-related rituals and practices and an obsessive fascination with death? Why, when our personal encounters with the dead are exceptionally rare compared to previous epochs, are grim reapers and skulls a favorite clothing design for all ages, from newborns to adults? Why do vampires, zombies, and undead monsters enjoy such exceptional popularity? Why has watching movies or reading novels portraying violent death become part of our daily routine?

Since the end of the second millennium, we have been living longer than any previous generation. Medical technology and research are advancing rapidly enough to add a whole year to our lives every half a decade. In the United States, average life expectancy grew from almost seventy-seven years in 2000 to almost seventy-nine years in 2013; in the European Union it had broken the eighty-year mark by the 2000s and has increased by about ten years in the last half a century. But even in less prosperous countries such as Russia, people can expect to live to the age of almost seventy years.[1] The quality of life of the elderly in the West has noticeably improved too, extending active life well into the later years.

To appreciate fully the significance of these numbers, the reader needs to be reminded that a century ago (before the First World War), life expectancy in the United States, Europe, and Russia did not extend beyond the age of forty to forty-nine. Yet compared to the previous demographic regime, even that lifespan was a real achievement. Prior to the eighteenth century, the average age at death in Europe was around thirty to thirty-five. Almost every fourth child died during his or her first year, and only half of all children would survive to marriageable age.[2] It was not until the nineteenth century that a new demographic pattern made possible by the agrarian and industrial revolutions and progress in medicine and science radically reduced child mortality and laid the groundwork for contemporary improvements in longevity.

The successful advancement of life against death, which has made death much less visible in everyday life, ought presumably to have diminished the fear of death. But the mounting anxiety about, and avoidance of, any mention of death-related experience in social interactions remains typical for our contemporaries on both sides of Atlantic.

One of the first attempts to view death denial from a historical and sociological perspective was undertaken by Geoffrey Gorer. In his 1955 essay "The Pornography of Death," Gorer argued that death had replaced sex in contemporary society as the great "unmentionable." He contrasted this attitude to death with its perception by the Victorians in nineteenth-century England, for whom death was a domestic affair.[3]

In 1974, Ernest Becker's book with the telling title *The Denial of Death* (1973) won the Pulitzer Prize.[4] In that study, Becker argued that death denial is an important survival mechanism in that it helps us withstand the terror of death. He believed that the development of culture and civilization were human strategies to minimize the fear of death. His analysis drew attention to death denial as an important feature of his time.

In *The Hour of Our Death*, published in 1977, Philippe Ariès also described the radical change in attitudes to death in the twentieth century as a denial of death. Ariès, who studied attitudes to death in Western society from the medieval period to the 1970s, stated that mass society has revolted against death, denying its very existence. Unlike previous epochs, when rituals and rites surrounding death were a habitual part of everyday routine—which, according to Ariès, helped "tame death"—modern society tries to silence it. As a result, death becomes "untamed" and therefore much more frightening than ever before:

"The old attitude, in which death was both familiar and near, evoking no great fear or awe, offers too marked a contrast to ours, where death is so frightful that we dare not utter its name."[5]

Ariès ends his book by asking if death can be tamed again in the West. He does not, however, seem to hold out much hope that it can. And today, the answer would be resolutely negative.

Demographers and anthropologists agree that since the second half of the twentieth century, Western society, including both the United States and Russia, "shies away" from death. In America, despite some attempts to animate public discussions of death in the 1960s, death is perceived as, and often called, an "unfamiliar," "unnatural," and even "foreign" event:

> Death as such has been described as a taboo topic for us, and we engage in very little abstract or philosophical discussion of death. Public discussion is generally limited to the social consequences of capital punishment or euthanasia. (. . .) Americans are characteristically unwilling to talk openly about the process of dying itself; and they are prone to avoid telling a dying person that he is dying.[6]

International students planning to study at US universities are warned that in this culture, death is an inappropriate subject for conversation. Even a short brochure on cultural orientation takes the time to address the American unwillingness to speak of death: "Americans are notorious for having an especially strained attitude toward the reality of death, often avoiding the whole topic or treating it as if it were something that should not be talked about in polite company."[7] The taboo on speaking about death has impacted studies of American death rituals to the point that "not only is the general population distanced from the dead, but scholarly knowledge about death rites in the United States and Canada is scant."[8]

The denial of death and the unwillingness to admit its inevitability is well reflected in recent surveys: American adults, including those aged seventy-five and older, say they have given either no thought or little serious thought to how their lives might end.[9] Doctors and other practitioners who have to deal with attitudes to death in the United States on a daily basis share this view: "For many Americans, modern medical advances have made death seem more like an option than an obligation. (. . .) [O]ur culture has come to view death as a medical failure rather than life's natural conclusion."[10] Death comes to be seen "not as a natural and inevitable aspect of life, but a preventable evil like polio or measles."[11] This extreme "medicalization" of death equates death to a disease that was not treated correctly or in a timely manner. The presumption that humans would live forever were it not for illnesses is well-documented in death certificates, which do not give old age as a possible cause of death.[12] The process of dying "as a shared set of social exchanges between dying individual and those who care for them" is considered unrecognized in contemporary society.[13] The silence surrounding death is translated into the solitude of the dying.[14]

The idealization of youth is clearly one of the tactics of the "death-denial obsession" in America and globally:

> "Our cultural obsession with youth can be understood as a huge, collective death-denial obsession. Individuals not only hide the deaths of their relatives in nursing homes and hospitals but they also obscure their own mortality, their own aging process, with hair dyes and face lifts."[15]

Denial of death is so profound that it is sometimes regarded as a unique feature of American culture. As cross-cultural studies have shown, however, the inclination to disregard death as an inevitable part of human existence is common in the West: "[P]eople in the West, and many of those in other countries who are now becoming industrialized, are attempting to ignore death."[16]

Contemporary Russia is no exception to this rule: there too, people avoid discussing death, which is considered an uncomfortable topic.[17] Sociologists have observed that it is not customary to talk about death there or even to say the word. Referring to a recent death, Russians use euphemisms similar to those prevalent in the United States: the deceased has "passed away" or simply "left us." Speaking of the deceased as "dead" or referring to "the body" is unthinkable in the presence of relatives. Death denial is also considered part of the doctor's professional ethics. "Devoted relatives" are supposed to prevaricate to the very end, the prevailing idea being that lying is better than acknowledging that the dying person has a terminal illness:

> Death is consigned to oblivion. Asking about the time of one's own death is not customary. Doctors inform only the relatives of a terminal diagnosis, and the dying person, while suspecting that the comforting words of the medical personnel are not a true account of his or her condition, still prefers to find solace in those lies since "hope dies last." (. . .) Death is almost completely expelled from the everyday life of Russians.[18]

Even adult children are not supposed to discuss mortality or anything related to the death of their parents: mentioning a will or discussing the parents' preferred death rituals is considered heartless. Often, this prevailing attitude discourages people from making a will, which ordinary Russians tend not to do anyway.

The tendency to silence death in Russia is even more striking than it is in the United States, since recent Russian history, especially in the first half of the twentieth century, might have been expected to make reflections on, and public discourse about, death a major preoccupation. The First World War, the Red Terror, the Civil War, the Great Purges, collectivization, and the Second World War had devastated the country. According to available estimates, twenty-seven million people died in the Second World War, and around ten million perished during the political repressions only two generations ago.[19] Even today, young adult and child mortality is higher in Russia than it is in any Western country.[20] Life expectancy there is almost ten years less than in the West, and the issue of mortality reduction became a subject of lengthy and heated political debate in the 1990s.[21] Yet in contemporary Russia, death has no more of a voice than it does in the United States.

Death as Entertainment

Expelled from social life on both sides of Atlantic and silenced in mundane conversations, death has instead found its way into fiction and movies. It triumphs in virtual reality; it appears on screen in its most violent forms; its terrifying descriptions haunt readers. This apparent paradox—anxiety about death leading to death denial and a fascination with violent death—has repeatedly drawn the attention of scholars, especially with respect to American culture.[22] "[M]any Americans express a great deal of death anxiety. On the other hand, many Americans also have an obsessive fascination with death, dying and the dead. (. . .) Nowhere is this paradox more apparent than in our popular culture. Television programs, movies, songs, the print media, games, jokes, and even recreational activities are fraught with thanatological content," says Keith Durkin in his study of the representations of death in popular culture.[23]

The same could be certainly said about Russians: the allure of movies featuring violent death is not at all exclusive to Americans.[24] "Moreover, there can be no doubt that this phenomenal appeal is not limited to audi-

ences in the Western world, but is universal. The attraction of supervio-
lent entertainment is evident cross-culturally," Dolf Zillman affirms.[25] An
escalating fascination with death is a hallmark of the past decade: "Though
death has been around since the beginning of humankind, in recent years a
near fascination with death has evolved," conclude Michael R. Leming and
George E. Dickinson.[26] The desire to view the agonies of fictional death
represents a peculiarity of contemporary popular culture. From the late
1970s, "thanatological entertainment"—representations of death as a widespread source of amusement—has become a "prominent and integral part
of contemporary popular culture."[27] In the media, violent death established
itself in the 1980s and 1990s as something to be avidly witnessed.[28] At the
beginning of this new trend, the frequent appearance of death in the news
was noticed and explained away as a reflection of the tragic reality of life. By
the 1990s, however, there remained little doubt that the trend had acquired
a dynamic of its own, given that the occurrence of violence in prime-time
programs on American TV was far more frequent than in real life.[29] This
tendency continued, and by the mid-1990s the rapidly growing numbers
of cartoons and movies featuring violent death and attacks on humans was
puzzling observers. Critics commented on the growing incidence of violent death in the media: "Sadistic maiming and killing are on the rise."[30] By
the 2000s, death-related content had acquired such prominence on television that researchers were speaking of death as a public spectacle.[31] Now
commodified, death entered the entertainment mainstream.

The 1990s saw a Gothic renaissance and the explosion of the horror
genre. But by the 2000s, the horror genre alone was no longer horrific
enough to deliver the desirable dose of agonizing deaths. "Torture porn,"
BDSM, and "slasher" movies featuring extreme violence began to separate
themselves from the horror genre. By the mid-2000s, torture porn and
slashers had invaded genres other than horror, generating a great deal of
controversy over the past decade.[32] Critics point out that films of this kind
are fixated on "extreme graphic violence. Scenes that dwell on the victim's
fear and explicitly portray the attack and its aftermath are the central focus
of slasher films."[33] The rapid expansion of Gothic motives has also contributed to this tendency. Although researchers may disagree as to the exact
time when violence took over the entertainment industry, no one disputes
that media and fiction are much more bloodthirsty today than they ever
used to be: "Comparing modern horror films with their classic counterparts, or contemporary gangster movies with the originals of the 1930s, it
is clear that screen violence has become much more graphic and spectacu-

lar."[34] The significant increase in torture and violence in fiction since the 1990s surprises scholars: "[G]ratuitous violence seems to be so much on the rise that one could even speak of escalation."[35]

This escalation of violence was especially apparent in young adult literature (YAL). Back in the 1990s, the reactions of several intellectuals, journalists, and academics on both the right and left of the political spectrum betrayed astonishment regarding the extent to which YAL has violated what was previously considered appropriate for children. A *New York Times Magazine* reviewer fretted in 1998:

> Somewhere in America tonight, in a delicious rite of childhood, a teen-ager will curl up in a window seat or overstuffed sofa to devour a young-adult novel . . . about murder, incest, rape or drug addiction. These are the subjects of a spate of recently published young-adult novels.[36]

Nowadays, the state of the art in YAL is best reflected in the secrets of success that are being proposed to neophyte authors. Among "The 8 Habits of Highly Successful Young-Adult Fiction Authors," high priority is given to the slogan "It's Okay for YA To Get Dark." The idea that "there's nothing off-limits when it comes to YA fiction, which frequently dives into unsettling territory like death, drugs, and rape across all of its genres and styles" appears to be one area of common ground shared by those who labor in this field.[37] "Pathologies that went undescribed in print 40 years ago, that were still only sparingly outlined a generation ago, are now spelled out in stomach-clenching detail," says Meghan Cox Gurdon in an article that invigorated the debates on violence in YA literature in the 2010s.[38]

Images of violent death, both real (in news reports, historical films, etc.) and imaginary, are a much-sought-after mass entertainment for audiences of all ages. And the obsession with violent death goes beyond the virtual world: the celebrity culture of serial killers and cannibals competes for popularity with a vampire subculture and communities known as "vampire churches." The public debates on media violence, violence in young adult literature, the aestheticization of violence, the correlation between the escalation of violence in entertainment and violent behavior, and the related question of censorship occupy an important place in contemporary politics both in the United States and in Russia.

Three striking paradoxes are apparent. First, the anthropological and sociological data demonstrate that the denial of death is a salient feature of present-day culture in both America and Russia. Yet the obsession with images of violent death contrasts with the taboo on mentioning death in everyday social interactions. Second, the fascination with death has taken over our society at a time when life expectancy is the highest in human history and continues to rise. Third, the political culture of Western democracy that protects individual rights and the value of human life would seem to stipulate a predominance of humanistic aesthetics. Instead, there is an extraordinary disconnect between the politics in a democratic society and an aesthetic that is fixated on violent death. What do these paradoxes tell us about our present cultural juncture? What are the reasons for our rising fascination with violent death?

Violent Entertainment Explained

Attempts to explain violence in entertainment have produced a significant body of research. Here I will limit myself to studies dealing with the reasons for the rise of violent entertainment in contemporary Western society, predominantly discussed in research on media violence and violence in YAL because the majority of novels and movies analyzed in this book target a young adult audience. Researchers are, understandably, concerned primarily with the potential sociopsychological impact of violent entertainment, which leads them to focus predominantly on "why we watch."[39] Scholars, who are usually mindful of the heated political debates on media violence and violence in YAL as well as of the related debates on censorship, split into two opposing camps on the impact of media violence, some holding that violent entertainment has positive effects and that its role is "therapeutic," while others consider that exposure to both media violence and literary brutality is damaging to the individual psyche and apt to result in negative social effects.[40]

The mainstream "therapeutic" explanation of the fascination with violent death in contemporary culture stems from the idea that we live in a death-denying society, in which representations of death in the media, movies, and fiction substitute for the absent experience of observing real death in our lives. The death-denying society makes us "crave some degree of information and insight concerning death, and we feed that craving through popular-culture depictions of death and dying."[41] Since Vicki Goldberg's 1998 study "Death Takes a Holiday," the idea that the spectacle of violent death substitutes for the actual experience of dealing with death in everyday life has become prevalent in media studies. According to her, media representations of death, though "removed to some degree from actual experience," "offer more and more realistic or exaggerated versions of how we die."[42] The internal contradiction of this position was less apparent in the late 1990s, when the upsurge of media and fiction violence was not yet as overwhelming as it has become over the past decade. Death is as displaced from the daily experience today as it was back in 1998, while the intensity of media violence continues to grow exponentially and to an unprecedented level. In addition, the escalation of violence in the entertainment cannot be explained as a substitute for "the absence of real experience of death and dying," simply because a natural death is not usually accompanied by scenes of graphic carnage. In fact, as indicated above, death in the West increasingly takes place in the sterile setting of hospitals and hospices, and with greater palliative care than any previous generation could have imagined.[43] How then can it follow that we are obsessed with images of a violent death accompanied by the most excruciating agonies?

Some argue that exposure to violent entertainment provokes compassion and hones its audience's moral sensibilities.[44] Hence, media horrors—war atrocities, murder, etc.—while presenting sufferings as entertainment, at the same time restrict voyeurism "in the name of respectability" and even support democracy.[45] These claims are, obviously, highly controversial. In her book *Compassion Fatigue: How the Media Sell Disease, Famine, War, and Death*, Susan D. Moeller argues that on the contrary, the superficial and sensational American media coverage of atrocities tends to desensitize the audience.[46] The quest for "excitement in an unexciting society" is another psychological reason invoked.[47] But if the fascination with gore in movies and fiction were related to that factor, resurgence of the Gothic and the horror genre would have coincided with periods of peace throughout history, and that would be hard to demonstrate.

Targeted arguments have also been advanced to address the rise of violence in young adult literature. When YAL first conceptualized itself as a new genre in the 1970s,[48] it contested the previously prevailing ideas of pedagogical theory, namely, that sadistic impulses should be tamed in children by education and culture. Roald Dahl, a major contributor to the invention of YAL, argued that the torments of suspense are more apt to cast "a narrative spell on readers" than would moralizing tales about "good little children":

> By creating suspense, the writer is simply playing upon the subconscious masochistic instincts of the reader. He is torturing him. And if the torture is expertly applied, the reader will cry out: 'I can't stand

it, not for another moment! Oh, isn't it wonderful!'—and he will read on.[49]

Dahl justified the use of the "macabre" in the interests of moral retribution, following a prevailing trend in YAL of the 1980s:

Children love to be spooked [. . .]. They like a touch of the macabre as long as it's funny, too. [. . .] And my nastiness is never gratuitous. It's retribution. Beastly people must be punished.[50]

But one can hardly apply Dahl's ideas of moral retribution to contemporary YAL. Therefore, another chain of arguments in defense of violence in YAL has tapped into the idea that children should face the truth about the world.[51] YAL writers justify the abundance of naturalistic descriptions of violent death and other types of mayhem as "giving voice to tortured adolescents who would otherwise be voiceless. If a teen has been abused, the logic follows, reading about another teen in the same straits will be comforting."[52] But it could be argued that instead of showing victimized children a different world and other realities and values, violent YAL tends to confine them to a universe of the mind in which violence is inescapable.

The argument that violent entertainment can have therapeutic effects may actually carry ambiguous implications. Let us suppose that the spectacle of virtual violence is a remedy against real violence (although no available data show any direct observable correlation between violent entertainment and a drop in violent crime). Then we must ask why contemporary society needs this remedy, and why in ever larger doses? And what if the unprecedented escalation of violent entertainment is actually a symptom of a serious social malaise? The proponents of the "therapeutic" understanding of the role of violent entertainment argue that there is no reliable correlation between violent content and violent behavior.[53] Several experts point out that while media content has become more ferocious over the past few decades, the incidence of violent crime, especially among young people, has decreased.

While real-life violence was a major cause of death for young adults in the United States in the early 1990s, it has declined in the 2000s. This might seem to argue in favor of the idea that increasing violence in the media may actually have served to reduce violence in the real world and that the consumption of violent content provides psychological relief and may help to prevent crime.[54] Following this line of reasoning, thanatological content "socially neutralizes death" and is therefore legitimately entertaining and enjoyable.[55] Media death diminishes our "primordial terror." Since media and fictional death is less frightening than real death, the argument goes, we readily indulge in it: "It appears that the thanatological themes in U.S. popular culture function as a mechanism that helps Americans to deal with death."[56] According to this view, violent entertainment can bring catharsis by offering liberation from pathogenic emotions or by producing emotions of excitement and pleasure in a viewer who is not exposed to any risks.[57] The catharsis doctrine, formulated by Aristotle, is widely used to justify the lure of violent entertainment on the grounds that through it the audience acquires moral lessons and experience while witnessing the sufferings of protagonists confronted by tragic life circumstances. To apply this theory to torture porn or slasher flicks, however, may require a considerable stretch of the imagination: catharsis, after all, traditionally entails moral retribution that is not accentuated by these genres. The question remains, though: If fake violent death is offered as gratuitous pleasure, are the feelings experienced by those who empathize in any way with murderous monsters also fake? Or is the pleasure gained from viewing a fictional victim's sufferings a *real* emotion?

Scholars who hold the view that the emotions produced by violent entertainment are unpleasant and potentially harmful to the psyche argue that media violence is a risk factor for violent behavior.[58] They state that "[r]esearch evidence has accumulated over the past half-century that exposure to violence on television, movies, and most recently in video games increases the risk of violent behavior on the viewer's part just as growing up in an environment filled with real violence increases the risk of violent behavior";[59] that viewing violent death promote "macabre enjoyment in the misfortunes of others";[60] and that media may add to the spread of self-hatred and suicide.[61]

While violence against others may be down in the US due to all kind of social factors, the statistics on suicide in fifteen- to forty-five-year-olds, who have inevitably had substantial exposure to media violence in the past decades, are less reassuring. The World Health Organization estimates that each year almost one million people die from suicide, which represents one death every 40 seconds. It is predicted that by 2020 the suicide rate will increase to one every twenty seconds. In 2012, suicide became the second leading cause of death in fifteen- to twenty-nine-year-olds globally.[62] That rate is much higher in the developing countries than in the developed world, and no one argues that media violence is solely responsible for the rise in suicides worldwide. Yet it would be equally hard to prove that the boom in depressing media content has played no role whatsoever in this trend.

To conclude, as human beings have presumably been haunted in various ways by fear of death since the beginning of time, psychological explanations, despite their importance, have shown a limited capacity to address the escalating fascination with violent death, which is a concrete historical and cultural phenomenon. There is no reason to believe that modern man should feel any greater insecurity in the face of death than people did when, say, the bubonic plague was running rampant. And by definition, a constant psychological factor cannot explain historical change.

Some observers consider violence an immanent feature of pure art and just another form of self-expression. For them, the upsurge of violent entertainment is a natural manifestation of this particular aesthetic experience. Supporters of this idea trace their intellectual genealogy to *On Murder Considered as One of the Fine Arts*, by Thomas de Quincey, and to the antiheroes of classical literature and to the Gothic novel. According to this view, representations of violence craft a specific aesthetic understanding. Hence, an act of murder can be regarded as art and the murderer as an artist.[63] What remains unanswered, then, is the question of why the unprecedented demand for this "aesthetic experience" has hit popular culture so hard in the past two or three decades.

Alongside psychological and aesthetic explanations, political explanations are often put forward as a reason for the growth of violent entertainment. Terrorism in general and September 11 in particular, as well as other political events that may provoke anxiety among the general public, are considered responsible for the interest in violent content.[64] But this whole trend in entertainment dates back to the late 1970s and early 1980s, when terrorism was perceived as much less politically important in the United States than it is today. In addition, the fascination with death is truly international and cannot be explained by American political conjecture alone. Besides, it remains unclear why watching carnage and brutality should help in overcoming political anxiety and insecurity.

Other supposed causes of the rise of simulated violence over the past two decades include technological and economic factors.[65] But however important the role that technology and the economy may play in the development of deadly entertainment, their advancement and commercialization alone cannot explain the choice of content. Even if the upward trajectory of Halloween spending were to correlate with economic growth (which it does not, as we will see in chapter 2), why would those who have contrived to recover some of their lost funds in the wake of a financial crisis opt to spend it on ghastly costumes and fake corpses?

Attempts to relate these recent tendencies in entertainment to the rise of skepticism and secularization in Western culture are also less than satisfactory: skepticism and secularization date back at least to the eighteenth century and can hardly be regarded as a proximate cause of the recent cultural change. And finally, although the fascination with violent entertainment may bear some relationships to the rise of Wicca, this factor alone is also insufficient: violent entertainment is much more popular and influential than paganism.

However much one may agree that any or all of the factors discussed here could play a role in the rise of violent entertainment, none of them in particular, nor all of them taken together, satisfactorily explains why this obsession with violent death is taking place right here, right now. By failing to address the specificity of today's cultural and historical conditions, they raise more questions than they answer.

Over the past three decades, violent entertainment was not the only topic discussed in relation to death. An immense body of scholarship focused on death as a real-life event explores attitudes toward death, dying, and bereavement, death-related rituals and practices in different cultures, the question of euthanasia, and the impact of contemporary advancements of medical research on the physical, cultural, and philosophical meaning of death. This proliferation of research can itself be interpreted as an indication of the powerful appeal of death in contemporary culture. Changes in funerals and other death-related rituals, in Halloween celebrations, in worship of "Saint Death," the role of death in education, dark tourism, and the serial killer celebrity culture, as well as popularity of the dead—vampires, zombies, ghosts—have been intensively researched, and we will discuss some of the relevant findings in later chapters.

The Cult of Death

My approach differs from the studies discussed above in several respects. In this book, I consider the cult of death from a historical perspective, as a distinct cultural phenomenon emerging at a particular moment in time and under specific cultural, intellectual, and aesthetic conditions. A historical comparison with other epochs enables me to identify the specificity of the current situation. In my analysis, I seek to establish the concrete historical and cultural junctures of the past decades that laid the groundwork for the commodification of fictional violent death in popular culture and conditioned the current widespread acceptance of the cult of death.[66]

To locate the cult of death in history, it is crucial to clearly distinguish it from traditional cults of the dead. Scholars who study death cults—from the veneration of ancestors in ancient Rome to the Mexican Day of the Dead—define them as a system of beliefs that unites the deceased and the living in a single community. A cult of the dead affirms the bond between the world of living descendants and the world of dead ancestors. Funeral and mourning rituals are intended to re-establish the harmony of a social entity that has been destroyed by the death of a member, as Robert Hertz was one of the first to demonstrate:

> Thus, when a man dies, society loses in him much more than a unit; it is stricken in the very principle of its life, in the faith it has in itself. (. . .) It seems that the entire community feels itself lost, or at least directly threatened by the presence of antagonistic forces: the very basis of its existence is shaken.[67]

Reinforcing the sense of belonging to a larger social whole and reinstating the harmony of the social organism is a primary function of the cult of the dead. The contemporary cult of death is not relatable to remembrance of the dead or ancestor worship. It does not reinforce the cohesion of either real or imaginary society. Its true heroes are fictionalized monsters— vampires, zombies, and other representatives of the living dead—and not the dead relatives.

Although, as I argue, the contemporary cult of death has to do with the experience of horror and atrocities of the twentieth century, it is not related to the phenomenon of state-organized rituals of remembrance that prompted Pierre Nora to call our times "the era of commemoration."[68] Equally, it has no association with a "heroic death for the Fatherland" or various cults of national heroes, a central element of the political or civic "religions" that have proven so important to the nation-state and the ideology of nationalism.

As a popular culture movement, the cult of death has no articulated sacral or religious meaning, although worship of violent death or vampires as sacred beings can be regarded as one of its manifestations. While irrational mysticism plays an important role in contemporary culture, the cult of death also cannot be reduced to belief in magic[69] and cannot be explained away by antireligious secularization of society. At present, it relies upon no rationalized dogma.

Attitudes toward real death as a personal, social, or existential event, whether rendered through the prism of media or not (clearly the province of death studies, anthropology, philosophy, and media studies), are of lesser concern to me than the cultural and historical phenomenon that has emerged from the commodification of fictional death as entertainment.[70] To interpret the cult of death as a distinct feature of current cultural conditions, I apply the concept of the culture industry and the theory of the commodification of cultural products developed by Theodor Adorno and Max Horkheimer, to the contemporary cultural situation.[71] The commodification of ideas—the appropriation of philosophical ideas or works of art by the culture industry—denies their autonomy and entails mutation of their meaning.[72] I am interested in investigating how the double rejection of humanism and the human exceptionalism, which originally emerged as a complex philosophical idea has been appropriated by popular culture and has triggered the cult of death.[73] Through the concept of commodification, my approach reveals the linkages between fictional world and life and the way their intersection has given rise to a new cultural movement. I consider the cult of death that redefines our understanding of humanism and humanity in the secular value system[74] in the context of the changing attitudes about the place of humans in the spectrum of species. The commodification of violent death as entertainment symbolizes popular culture's rejection of human exceptionalism. A focus on attitudes toward human exceptionalism is critical to my analysis of contemporary cultural production, in both movies and fiction.[75]

The cult of death manifests itself in a constellation of changes in popular culture alongside the changes in social practices: burial rituals, holidays, cults, language, education, and commercial ventures. I interpret those social and cultural facts through an analysis of the profound shift in the representations of the human being. Changes in the attitudes toward humans reflected in popular fiction and movies help us understand the meaning and the nature of changes in these social practices.

Yet violence per se and the complex relations between death and sex that have been much scrutinized since Freud and Gorer will not be part of my research: I believe that the shift we are observing today has much more to do with a redefinition of the attitudes toward human beings vis-à-vis other species, which cannot be reduced to just another vicissitude of the sexual revolution.

Like several other contemporary cultural trends, the cult of death does not fit in terms of existing political antagonisms, and it corresponds to no political divide. Despite persistent attempts to appropriate some meanings related to the cult of death—the left's claims that the images of violent death, monsters, or apocalypse expresses "revolutionary protest" against capitalist exploitation, gender, racial inequality, and American imperialism, or the conservatives' declarations that the "death culture" is a result of a centuries-long "leftist conspiracy against Christianity and traditional American values"—its manifestations transcend political divides and its meaning sidesteps the rifts of the culture wars. Primarily a cultural and a historical phenomenon, the cult of death must be analyzed in its own terms if it is to receive the serious attention it undoubtedly deserves.

Gothic Aesthetic

To explain the cult of death I rely on several concepts I have developed in my previous research.[76] In this section, I will briefly introduce the concept of Gothic Aesthetic and explain why I prefer to use it instead of the more familiar notions of the Gothic and horror genre.

Until now, the horror genre has been something of a metaphorical concept. Studies of the horror genre stress that it has Gothic elements, "escapes categorization," and evades any conclusive attempt to explain the reasons behind the growing interest in its multiple manifestations.[77] Due to this broad definition, the horror genre has been held to cover diverse texts from blood-and-gore thrillers to vampire sagas, from mystical spine-chillers to dystopian fantasy. In addition, over the past decade, the horror genre has exploded and diversified wildly.[78] As for the Gothic genre, scholars trace it back to the Gothic novel, which evokes images of gloomy ruins, death, and destruction and focuses on darkness and the horrors of the underworld.[79] Researchers accentuate the role played in its formation by an interest in monstrous and supernatural forces, the desire to look at the dark side of the human psyche, and a protest against rationality. Among countless attempts to define the Gothic genre, and especially to establish the difference between it and horror, David Punter emphasizes that unlike the classical Gothic novel, the contemporary Gothic has acquired new meanings.[80] These narratives feature worlds "infested with psychic and social decay," where "violence, rapes and breakdown are the key motifs" and "the crucial tone is one of desensitized acquiescence in the horror of obsession and prevalent insanity."[81] Punter accentuates the blurring of horror and the Gothic in contemporary culture and emphasizes the problems of distinguishing between the two.[82] In his later works, Punter goes on to consider indeterminacy of meaning as a characteristic feature of the Gothic.[83] Fred Botting, another scholar of the Gothic, adds to the roster of the genre's features "tortuous, fragmented narratives," mysterious villains, and the castle or old house as the setting.[84] He holds that the Gothic spreads like a disease, implying that it is able to "infect" other genres.[85] The fusion of the Gothic and horror over the past decade has been a constant complaint of the critics. In fact, it has become almost impossible to distinguish horror from Gothic, prompting Luis Gross, for example, to speak of fear—which one would consider a feature of horror by default—as the essential feature of the contemporary Gothic.[86] In this broad interpretation, both Gothic and horror are all-embracing concepts that are of little help in understanding the works that are important for my analysis.

The genre concept itself has a significant restriction relative to my purposes: it has a strong formal and technical aspect that limits its application in the context of a study whose primary interest lies in the interconnection between intellectual ideas, aesthetic principles, and social practices.[87] I think that the notion of an aesthetic trend offers a better opportunity to relate particular features of fiction or cinematographic works to the historical and ideological context from which they have grown, on the one hand, and the social practices and popular culture phenomena they have informed, on the other.

I therefore propose the concept of Gothic Aesthetic, which allows us to single out those cultural products that are relevant for an understanding of the cult of death but are usually categorized as part of the Gothic and horror genres. Gothic Aesthetic manifests itself in fiction and movies through a combination of two features. First, the prime selling point and principal goal of those literary texts and visual arts products is to convey the experience of nightmare to its audience. Since the turn of the millennium, nightmare has become a highly desirable state for millions of readers, viewers, and gamers. The imitation of nightmare determines the framework of the respective narratives, their artistic devices, and their plots.[88] Second, the undead—a vampire, zombie, or their ilk—performs as the novel's or movie's first-person narrator and/or main protagonist, with whom the audience is expected to identify and who represents an unassailable aesthetic ideal. Undead monsters were ideally positioned to take over from human characters because they are the perfect protagonists for a manmade nightmare.[89]

Unlike Gothic or horror, Gothic Aesthetic does not form an all-inclusive category. However horrifying a bloody thriller or mystical spine-tingler might be and however savage cyberpunk might become, if the protagonists and narrators of those texts are not murderous monsters and if their actions in the plot are not conditioned by the aim of immersing the audience into a nightmare trance, they are no part of Gothic Aesthetic.

The monster-centered narratives of Gothic Aesthetic can be seen as part of a larger questioning—if not outright rejection—of the idea of human exceptionalism. The vampire is a perfect symbol of those new attitudes toward human characters. When these imaginary monsters not only kill human beings but also consume them as food, that act becomes a radical expression of disenchantment with humanity as an ultimate value. The act of murder alone is apparently deemed insufficient to articulate the denial of the unique value of human life: humans are to be degraded to the level of animals in the act of consumption, and this is the most important message of Gothic Aesthetic. Gothic Aesthetic conveys those nightmarish emotions to its audience, rejects the relevance of human life, and promotes the cult of death.

Dark mysticism is the only ontology that Gothic Aesthetic allows, which makes irrationality its other important feature. The present-day vampires or zombies are not servants of the devil, nor are they sinners condemned by God for making deals with the devil, nor are they mortals whose corpses were buried contrary to Christian custom, as was the case with their literary and cinematic predecessors.[90] Gothic Aesthetic is equally hostile to rationalism and religion, since it postulates that the origins of evil cannot be known or explained, least of all in terms of Christianity. The literary devils of Christian mythology that are so plentiful in all of Western literature and whose nature is fully explained by Christian dogma are of no concern to Gothic Aesthetic. They embody the temptations that torment the human protagonists, as in the case of Goethe's Mephistopheles and Dr. Faustus, and contribute nothing whatsoever to the idealization of nonhuman monsters.[91]

While monsters have no religious explanation, they are also not the result of scientific experiment: the science fiction agenda is not even applicable to works impacted by Gothic Aesthetic. Since the beginning of the new millennium, the fascination with vampires has produced several attempts to inject vampires into science fiction and explain their origins by "natural causes."[92] But science fiction's explanation of the vampire's existence is so "rational" that those works have been unable to enter the mainstream of Gothic Aesthetic and therefore remain marginal. Once again, this demonstrates the empirical power of the concept: the ontology of the narratives influenced by Gothic Aesthetic holds that the nature of monsters and the origin of evil are, in general, irrational, mysterious, and unknowable.

Gothic Aesthetic is an expression of disillusionment with rationalism and religion, with faith and scientific reason, and with civilization. The addiction to nightmare and the undead that has grown out of Gothic Aesthetic has greatly facilitated the rise and spread of the cult of death. Man-eating monsters and fatal nightmares have been instrumental in promoting the commodification of violent death.

Manmade Nightmare as a Literary Device

Today, one can hardly imagine a horror movie or novel not attempting to bring its audience as close as possible to a living nightmare. Offerings such as the Harry Potter series, *Twilight*, *Night Watch*, *The Vampire Diaries*, *True Blood*, *Snow White and the Huntsman*, *Charmed*, *Van Helsing*, *Avatar*, the *X-Men* franchise, and *The Walking Dead*, among hundreds of others, have several features in common insofar as their framework and plot structure are concerned. We see flying monsters chasing after the hero or heroine, monsters exercising dreamlike magical powers, and a pursuit accompanied by horrifying atrocities and violence. We witness trancelike experiences that the protagonist—and the audience—confuse with reality. Prophetic nightmares come true, flashbacks disturb causal relations, eerie sounds and spinning sensations unsettle the normal perception. Most often the protagonist acts in an altered state of mind (either drugged or delirious) that underscores his or her weakness and unsteadiness. The overall intention is to disrupt our sense of time and space in order to create the impression of being fully disconnected from reality.

The tradition of depicting nightmares is not a recent phenomenon in Western literature: many eighteenth- and nineteenth-century writers used nightmares in their works. Literary scholars, however, have paid almost no attention to the study of nightmare as a literary device and as an important creative project that defined the works of several classical writers. In my book *Nightmare: From Literary Experiment to Cultural Project*, I show that experiments with nightmare played a crucial role in the development of the intellectual and artistic agendas of Charles Robert Maturin, Nikolai Gogol, Fyodor Dostoevsky, and Thomas Mann, among others.

In order to convey and recreate the nightmare in literature—a mental state that is resistant to the standard linguistic ploys—authors needed to invent special expressive devices. I propose to use the term *hypnotics* to describe the set of artistic tools required to plunge the audience into a sense of nightmare. The concept of hypnotics is necessary, since the term "poetics," developed by the Russian formalists and especially by Mikhail Bakhtin in his famous work on Dostoevsky, is insufficient here, implying as it does that the author is not entirely aware of his own reasons for writing in a particular way and employs various literary devices unconsciously.

Unlike poetics, hypnotics points to the author's conscious efforts to reproduce the nightmare state in the reader's mind.[93]

Hypnotics encompasses several devices, such as depictions of the dizziness of a protagonist with whom a reader tends to identify, by means of a rotating motion or a glimpse into an abyss. Sudden breaks in logic and chronology, doppelgangers acting as protagonists, repetitions of words and events, instances of déjà-vu, lighting that distracts the readers' attention—all these tools of hypnotics serve to make the reader feel that "time is out of joint," diminishing the reader's critical ability and dislocating his sense of identity. Flight, chase, and falling—frequent plots of our nightmares and of fictional offerings—are the simplest ways for our consciousness to represent what happens in a nightmare as a distinct image. Over the course of thirty years, a mistrust of "the real" and contempt for "the human" created an atmosphere highly conducive to the rise of nightmare as a prime plot premise that prepared and facilitated the formation and spread of the cult of death.[94]

ONE

_____

The Intellectual Origins of the Cult of Death

The Last Man of French Theory

The fascination with fictional violent death represents a new stage in the durable tradition of the denial of humanism and rejection of the idea of human exceptionalism. In this chapter, we will observe how critique of humanism has transitioned in recent decades from a philosophical concept to a product of popular culture, and has created conditions favorable to the rise of a cult of death.

Since the Italian humanists and the philosophers of the Enlightenment, humanism has held that humans have a unique sense of morality, along with free will and creative intelligence. These qualities make them capable of creating society, culture, and art. Humanism is bound to the idea of human exceptionalism, which holds that humans are profoundly different from any other species and are therefore to be uniquely valued. It is certainly beyond the scope of this book to address the history of the centuries-long debates on humanism in any detail.[1] Rather, in this overview, I will focus on the commodification of antihumanism that laid the groundwork for the rising cult of death and stimulated the idealization of monsters in popular culture. To this end, we will discuss the constellation of diverse ideas that emerged in the 1960s and 1970s. Analysis of the intellectual premises of the cult of death will help us better understand the origins of that movement.

The intellectual influence of the heritage of French Theory[2] in the cri-

23

tique of humanism can hardly be overestimated; its rejection of human exceptionalism has in many respects determined the contemporary intellectual climate. The rise of the animal rights movement in England contributed to the creation of a political context wherein the radical denial of human exceptionalism became widely accepted. In this zeitgeist, the aspiration to transcend humanity voiced by transhumanism and posthumanism became the next logical step.

The most influential French intellectuals—Claude Lévi-Strauss, Michel Foucault, Roland Barthes, Jean-François Lyotard, Jacques Derrida, and Jean Baudrillard—announced "the death of man" as an important premise of their critique of capitalist society. The philosophical and theoretical considerations that drew them to a persistent critique of humanism were linked to their rejection of the transcendental subject and the dichotomies of classical philosophy, including those of human versus animal and culture versus nature.[3] This led the principal proponents of French Theory to adopt a radical stand against human exceptionalism. The oppositions of language and mind and the notion of the subject as a central theme in philosophical inquiry were to be excised from their conceptual apparatus.[4] In Jean-François Lyotard's words, "the humanist obstacle" needs to be removed from philosophy in order to "make philosophy inhuman."[5] The concepts of the subject and of individual thinking were discounted in favor of the deep structures of language.[6] These propositions predisposed the leading thinkers of French Theory to rebuff the traditional humanist understanding of the differences between humans and other living creatures, which created an important common ground for their otherwise distinct philosophical systems. The critique of humanism was arguably subordinate to French Theory's major goals of overthrowing the Kantian transcendental subject and overcoming the dichotomy of European philosophical thinking. But for the purposes of this book, their stand on humanism is of foremost importance.

In their critique of humanism, the French thinkers were influenced by Karl Marx and Friedrich Nietzsche. Marx considered traditional humanism to be the very epitome of dehumanization. The Marxist critique labeled humanism "false," "bourgeois," (or "petty-bourgeois") and opposed the idea of class struggle against "hypocritical capitalist humanism." A class struggle leading to the revolutionary destruction of the exploiting class was the only way to achieve a "true humanistic society" based on the absence of social classes, private property, and exploitation. In 1965, Louis Althusser continued to pursue the Marxist critique of humanism, which contributed

greatly to the success of his book *For Marx* (*Pour Marx*, 1965) among the
French left:

> Marx, Engels and Lenin, to refer only to them, ceaselessly struggled
> against ideological interpretations of an idealist, humanist type that
> threatened Marxist theory. Here it will suffice to recall Marx's rup-
> ture with Feuerbach's humanism, Engels' struggle against Dühring,
> Lenin's long battle with the Russian populists, and so on.[7]

Althusser further develops this understanding of Marxist humanism with
reference to what he called "proletarian humanism":

> So revolutionary humanism could only be a 'class humanism', 'pro-
> letarian humanism'. [. . .] For more than forty years, in the U.S.S.R.,
> amidst gigantic struggles, 'socialist humanism' was expressed in the
> terms of class dictatorship rather than in those of personal freedom.[8]

The concept of "proletarian humanism" articulated by Maksim Gorky,
a "proletarian writer" famous in France and Italy, was fundamental to
Soviet ideology. For Gorky, forced labor was an example of the consistent application of proletarian humanism to society, in that it helped "the
enemies of the people" rid themselves of their "deadly bourgeois mental-
ity." In his article "Proletarian Humanism," published in two major Soviet
newspapers, *Pravda* and *Izvestia*, in May 1934, Gorky says the following:

> In our times, there is no need to prove the mendacity and hypocrisy
> of bourgeois "humanism," in which the bourgeoisie, by organizing
> fascism, itself discards its humanism like a worn out mask, revealing
> the fangs of a predatory beast. . . . This revolutionary humanism
> gives the proletariat a historically founded right to combat capital-
> ism without quarter, a right to destroy and annihilate all the foul
> foundations of the bourgeois world.

He pursued this line of argument thus:

> A time approaches when the revolutionary proletariat will step, like
> an elephant, on the mad, the frantic anthill of shopkeepers—will
> step on it and crush it. This is inevitable. Humankind cannot perish
> because it has an insignificant minority that has grown creatively

decrepit and is decomposing from the fear of life and from a morbid yet incurable thirst for gain. The demise of this minority is an act of great justice, and this act history commands the proletariat to carry out. This great act will be followed by the peoples of the world working together in friendship and fraternity to create, in beauty, a new life.[9]

Gorky's article received the enthusiastic endorsement of Joseph Stalin, who co-opted the concept of "proletarian humanism" for his own speeches.[10] Emerging as it did on the eve of the Great Terror (1936–38), this concept proved helpful in legitimizing the coming repressions. The disillusionment with Soviet communism and Stalinism was a formative experience for the French thinkers and for the Western intellectuals in general. The Twentieth Soviet Communist Party Congress in 1956 had only started this long process. Yet the concept of "proletarian humanism" and especially the idea of "false bourgeois humanism" outlasted the condemnation of Stalinism and retained its importance among French thinkers in the late 1960s and early 1970s.[11]

Another strain of the nineteenth-century critique of humanism that profoundly influenced French Theory harks back to Friedrich Nietzsche, whose impact on French thinkers is difficult to overestimate. His criticism of morality became an important source of inspiration for many French thinkers, in particular Michel Foucault and Jacques Derrida. Nietzsche's complex heritage and the appropriation of his critique of morality by French thinkers is a well-researched subject that we cannot adequately deal with here. Let me instead briefly remind the reader the main direction of his criticism of humanism, which he too considered an artificial and counterproductive philosophical idea. In his *Genealogy of Morals*, Nietzsche argued that the notion of humanism was invented only to help the weak coerce the strong, which he considered profoundly unnatural. He famously articulated the case against mankind in philosophy that resonated with French Theory:

> So that we, my friends, can actually defend ourselves, at least for a while yet, against the two worst epidemics that could possibly have been set aside just for us—against great nausea at man! Against deep compassion for man![12]

To appreciate the effect of the Marxist and Nietzschean critiques of humanism on French Theory, one has to bear in mind the several theoretical attempts that were made to rehabilitate the notion of humanism in the second half of the twentieth century, since the misappropriation of humanism by totalitarian regimes played an important role in the disillusionment with that concept. Stalinism was not the only regime that misused the notion of humanism; Fidel Castro also declared Cuba a "humanist country." At the opposite end of the political spectrum, Benito Mussolini and some of Adolf Hitler's supporters described the fascist and Nazi regimes as the "New Humanism." Attempts to design communist or fascist versions of nontraditional "humanism" offered palpable examples of how this concept could be abused to justify crimes against humanity.

In *Humanism and Terror* (1947), Maurice Merleau-Ponty reflected upon the possibilities of establishing a humanist society fundamentally opposed to communist totalitarianism while Karl Jaspers attempted to recover the concept from fascist misuse in his "Premises and Possibilities of a New Humanism" (1952).[13] This advocacy plus the general political discourse created an intellectual atmosphere that French avant-garde thinkers found paralyzing for critical reflection and were proposing to challenge. Michel Foucault describes this atmosphere in a 1981 interview:

> One cannot imagine into what a moralistic pond of humanist sermons we were plunged in the post-war period. Everyone was a humanist. Camus, Sartre, Garady were all humanists. Stalin was a humanist too. . . . This does not compromise humanism, but simply allows us to understand that at that time I could no longer think in the terms of that category.[14]

A pivotal moment that made humanism a systematic target of French Theory was the controversy that erupted between Jean-Paul Sartre and Martin Heidegger. Sartre considered himself a Marxist, and Heidegger believed Nietzsche to be one of his predecessors in being the first to point out certain "new beginnings for the West."[15] Sartre denied "bourgeois humanism" and claimed in his article "Existentialism Is a Humanism" (1946) that this is so because existentialism is based on what man makes of himself. Martin Heidegger's response to Sartre in his "Letter on Humanism" (1947) stated that the understanding of the essence of man is a metaphysical—and hence unprovable—claim.

The representatives of French Theory perceived existentialism as their chief rival for intellectual domination; they admired Nietzsche's philosophy and appreciated Heidegger's contribution against existentialism. And the pessimism of Nietzsche and Heidegger with respect to the future of

Western civilization was a sentiment widely shared in Paris, especially after the events of 1968.[16]

In his struggle against existentialism, Claude Lévi-Strauss made the criticism of humanism an important point in his polemic with Sartre. Lévi-Strauss considered the "dissolving of man" as a focal point of knowledge to be the main goal of the human sciences. He proceeded from the idea that the opposition between nature and culture is misleading. Tracing the genealogy of his critique of humanism back to Jean-Jacques Rousseau, Lévi-Strauss, according to some of his commentators, regarded traditional humanism as "harmful to the extent that it promotes the myth of the exclusive dignity of the human, valorizing human nature over all other forms of being and all other forms of life."[17] Moreover, he states that the human dissociation from nature, in which human beings establish themselves in "an absolute reign," thus separating "humanity and animality," generated a "vicious cycle" of dissociation between self and Other: "The one boundary, constantly pushed back, would be used to separate men from other men and to claim—to the profit of ever smaller minorities—the privilege of a humanism, corrupted at birth by taking self-interest as its principle and its notion."[18] Lévi-Strauss developed the concept of "democratic humanism" in his essay "Three Humanisms." Marcel Hénaff characterizes his version of humanism as "good not only for humanity but for all living things and the whole of the living world."[19] Indeed, in his controversy with Sartre, Lévi-Strauss affirmed that the human being cannot enjoy any privileged status, even as a subject of scientific inquiry, that would differentiate humans in any respect from other living beings: "I believe the ultimate goal of the human sciences to be not to constitute, but to dissolve man."[20] Most importantly, in *The Savage Mind*, Lévi-Strauss proposed to challenge the idea of uniqueness of human culture and civilization and "undertake the resolution of the human into nonhuman."[21]

Michel Foucault contested the belief that "human nature" or "man" should be seen as the center of all knowledge and the prime preoccupation of philosophy and morality.[22] Both the Marxist critique of humanism and Nietzsche's critique of morality were important to Foucault's deconstruction of the transcendental subject.[23] As Hayden White shows, humanity and man are for Foucault "a hypostatization of the fictive subject of discourse," which will inevitably "come to an end."[24] According to Foucault, man is a subject formed by discourse as a result of the arrangement of knowledge over the prior two centuries. All periods of history have been characterized by underlying epistemological assumptions, epistemes (discursive practices or paradigms) that delineate scientific discourse as a system of knowledge in a given period of time.[25] Man is regarded as one such episteme, and one that is not atemporal but historically grounded:

> [M]an's mode of being as constituted in modern thought enables him to play two roles: he is at the same time the foundation of all positivities and present (. . .) in the element of empirical things. (. . .) it is not a matter of man's essence in general, but simply of that historical a priori which, since the nineteenth century, has served as an almost self-evident ground for our thought [. . .]"[26]

Hence man would disappear as the apex of our knowledge and thinking, to be replaced by another episteme: "[N]ew gods, the same gods, are already swelling the future Ocean; man will disappear."[27] Foucault traces this preoccupation with the death of man back to Nietzsche:[28]

> [B]y means of a philological critique, by means of a certain form of biologism, Nietzsche rediscovered the point at which man and God belong to one another, at which the death of the second is synonymous with the death of the first, and at which the promise of the superman signifies first and foremost the imminence of the death of man. In this, Nietzsche, offering this future to us as both promise and task, marks the threshold beyond which contemporary philosophy can begin thinking again. . . .[29]

Foucault reiterated the "imminent death"[30] of man repeatedly and in various ways: "As the archaeology of our thought easily shows, man is an invention of a recent date. And one perhaps nearing its end." Man will soon be "erased, like a face drawn in sand at the edge of the sea."[31] According to Foucault scholars, this historization of man was rooted in the Marxist critique:[32]

> Like Marx, Foucault regards humanism as a contingent phase in Western history that is on the verge of surpassing itself. (. . .) After humanism there will be the "death of Man," or rather the dissolution of "the subject" into preconditioned habits and reactive responses, in which concepts like "reason," "consciousness," and "right" as humanism understands them will cease to exist.[33]

Foucault's critique of humanism, which is quite often taken metaphorically,[34] has been the subject of intense discussion.[35] Some of his critics gave serious consideration to his antihumanistic stance.[36] Others sought to contrast the "early Foucault" with the "late Foucault" and to distinguish between his "French" (i.e., Nietzschean) and "American" (i.e., more liberal and more oriented toward multiculturalism and identity) philosophies, as Richard Rorty does, trying to reconcile him with John Dewey.[37] But no attempt to dissociate Foucault from the Nietzschean heritage can mitigate the rigor of Foucault's attack on humanism.[38]

Roland Barthes continues this denial of humanism. In his essay "The Death of the Author," he symbolically rejects individual thinking and creativity, which for centuries had been considered the essential expression of genius and of human exceptionalism. For Barthes, the death of a literary creator's subjectivity is indispensable to assure the existence of intersubjective discourse. The individuality of the author is here sacrificed to the anonymous readership that represents the nonindividual and collective nature of discourse.

> [T]he reader is without history, biography, psychology; he is simply that someone who holds together in a single field all the traces by which the written text is constituted. Which is why it is derisory to condemn the new writing in the name of a humanism hypocritically turned champion of the reader's right. Classic criticism has never paid any attention to the reader; for it, the writer is the only person in literature. [. . .] we know that to give writing its future, it is necessary to overthrow the myth: the birth of the reader must be at the cost of the death of the Author.[39]

The sacrificial death of the author is required if the process of interpretation is ever to begin.[40]

Inspired by the Marxist critique of capitalism, Jean Baudrillard postulates the absolute commercialization, and hence the aestheticization (an attempt to turn everything into an attractive and saleable image) of every sign in "capitalist Western society," including "anti-images" such as death and violence. In *Symbolic Exchange and Death*, he offers a radical semiological critique of capitalism.[41] Proceeding from the autoreferential nature of the sign, he argues that in a society dominated by the logic of digital code, nothing can escape the code but death, because only death can halt an exchange of codes and exchange of values: "Perhaps, death and death alone, the reversibility of death, belongs to a higher order than the code. Only symbolic disorder can bring about an interruption in the code."[42] And further:

The only strategy against the hyperrealist system is some form of pataphysics, "a science of imaginary solutions" (. . .), a reversible simulation in a hyperlogic of death and destruction. (. . .) All that remains for us is theoretical violence—speculation to the death, whose only method is the radicalisation of hypotheses.[43]

This chain of argument ultimately leads him to the special role of death articulated in his *Fatal Strategies*.[44] Death offers the only escape from a miserable existence for the consumers and victims of the omnipotent codes of capitalistic exchange. Death becomes the only path to freedom and the only meaningful choice to be made. It should be noted that in another book, *The Transparency of Evil*, Baudrillard was among the first to give close attention to the rising phenomenon of media violence as well as to the growing presence of death and horror in contemporary mass culture.[45]

Among other French thinkers, Jacques Derrida also contributed to the critique of humanism, but we will consider his impact later on in this chapter. Let us just point out that Derrida also proposed a presentation titled "The Ends of Man" for a conference held in New York in October 1968.

In his *History of Structuralism*, François Dosse notes that French structuralism was a self-contestive movement:

Structuralism was contestatory and corresponded to a particular moment in Western history. It expressed a certain degree of self-hatred, of the rejection of traditional Western culture, and of a desire for modernism in search of new models.[46]

The psychological and cultural motivations behind the French theorists' stand on humanism may be interpreted as their reaction to the tragedy of the recent past. In her article "Silence of the Dead, Orations of the Living," Gabrielle M. Spiegel points out this connection between deconstruction and the experience of the Holocaust:

Deconstruction is often falsely accused of nihilism. But since it is elaborated in the shadow of death and annihilation, perhaps it bears the unconscious trace of its own absent origin. (. . .) Deconstruction, I have argued, at its most fundamental level is a philosophy of rupture and displacement. Insofar as the emblematic figure of the postmodern world is the displaced person—and I believe that it is—then we are all displaced persons in some profound sense.[47]

In other words, the modern conception of man contradicted the experience of horrors and atrocities that, on a deep psychological level, informed French Theory and made intellectual honesty its battle cry. In this same line of argument, may we also suppose that the French thinkers felt profound disgust with the self-indulgent and self-congratulatory society of the 1950s and 1960s that had emerged from the catastrophe of the Holocaust and the Second World War? The shadow of death and violence loomed over the sunny landscape of the postwar prosperity.[48] The eagerness to forget the tragic past—as Tony Judt argues, the reconstruction of Europe was based on consigning the crimes committed during the war to oblivion[49]—left a profound mark on the "thirty glorious years" of postwar economic growth. It may even have been this "business as usual" attitude in the consumption-driven society that radicalized the French intellectuals' thinking about humanism.

The catastrophes of the first half of the twentieth century left little hope for humanism and little admiration for humanity. The disturbing realization that unspeakable crimes committed in living memory could disappear without trace, leaving successive generations to celebrate their life and prosperity as if neither was built upon mass graves, may well explain the investment that several French avant-garde intellectuals subsequently placed into dismantling the concept of humanism and human exceptionalism. The critique of the Enlightenment may have been experienced as an expression of deep disenchantment with humankind and with ideals focused on the glorification of human nature. Denying humans the status of superior beings may have been conceived as a gesture of intellectual justice and philosophical retribution, and probably more so than a merely moral irresponsibility.[50]

The intellectual heritage of French Theory has conditioned the views of academia on both sides of the Atlantic, including my own. Yet the condemnation of humanism has developed into a recurrent trope far beyond the confines of French Theory, as many prominent intellectuals have adopted "the death of man" into their ideological agenda.[51] But most important for the purpose of this book is that since the 1970s, French ideas on humanism have provided an intellectual framework for a wide variety of antihumanist trends in contemporary popular culture.[52] Once critique of humanism was adopted by popular culture, however, it lost its critical potential. François Cusset depicts this transgression with special reference to American culture:

The trend of shrinking bits of theory into productions of the cultural industry, such as the press and the cinema, for the sake of its subversive sheen or its intellectual backing, generally resulted in completely emptying the theoretical reference of its content—as well as its philosophical implications.[53]

No longer a critical tool but a commodity, antihumanism has acquired a new cultural role and a new cultural meaning.

Animal Rights after the Death of Man

In the book *French Philosophy of the Sixties. An Essay on Antihumanism* (1985), Luc Ferry and Alain Renaud sarcastically ask:

> Why was it declared by the sixties generation that the valorization of man had to be disturbed or denounced? It goes without saying that the opposition of '68 philosophy to humanism never meant that it intended to defend barbarianism and plead for the inhuman. In fact it is because of the supposedly catastrophic effects (for whom if not for man?) of modern humanism that it must have appeared to be the enemy of philosophy.[54]

Today, the question "For whom if not for man?" which seemed obvious to Ferry and Renaud in the 1980s is no longer as self-evident. Monsters and animals are readily and routinely chosen over humans in contemporary discourse, both in academia and in popular culture. At the end of the 1970s, the rise of the animal rights movement[55] had reinforced the denial of humanism. For those thinkers concerned with animal rights, the eagerness to overcome dualistic thinking and to break free from "binaries" such as culture/nature, human/animal, etc. was as important as it was for the French intellectuals. The point of crossover between French Theory and the anglophone thinkers who theorized the animal rights agenda was the rejection of human exceptionalism. The concept of the nonhuman animal and the monster was equally important for both trends. The deconstruction of humanism, the rejection of human exceptionalism, and the assertion of the "death of man" are apt to evoke monsters.

This connection between the notion of the monster and the rejection of human exceptionalism goes back at least to Jeremy Bentham (1748–1832), who revolted against human exceptionalism in the early nineteenth century. He also invented the Panopticum, a perfect prison whose inmates live with the impression of being under constant surveillance (the prototype of the totalitarian state). Bentham derived "Panopticum" from ancient Greek *Panoptes* ("all-seeing"), a sobriquet of Argus, the hundred-eyed monster of Greek mythology. Bentham's Panopticum and the idea of the monster also occupied a prominent place in Michel Foucault's writings. The concept of the monster proves efficient in dismantling human exceptionalism and, ever since Foucault's *The Order of Things*, has been viewed as a way of overcoming "binaries." The sharp opposition between humans and other species is overcome if the monster becomes the vehicle of an evolution.[56] For Foucault, monster and fossil create a continuum between human and nonhuman in the general picture of evolution and break down the opposition between the two by emphasizing the difficultly of distinguishing the various stages of evolutionary development, because "they form a shady, mobile, wavering region in which what analysis is to define as identity is still only mute analogy; and what it will define as assignable and constant difference is still only free and random variation."[57] The monster is understood as a hybrid creature, both human and nonhuman, a dual "breach of law and nature"[58] that maintains the continuum between humans and other species and dissolves the boundaries between humans and animals. This idea of a monster can be related to the importance of the discourse on madness for Foucault starting from his doctoral thesis *Folie et déraison: Histoire de la folie à l'âge classique*, where he shows the extent to which the idea of European normality was based on cruelty and oppression.

Jacques Derrida's works offer a powerful example of the intimate connection between French Theory and the discourse of animal rights. The persistent critique of humanism in Derrida's early work[59] led him to his ideas about animality.[60] As Patrick Llored demonstrates in his book on Derrida, the question of animality is central to his theoretical thinking and to deconstruction in general.[61] It is especially present in Derrida's works "The *Animal* That Therefore I Am (More to Follow)" (1997) and *The Beast and The Sovereign*, the two-volume publication of his lectures and seminars at the École des hautes études en sciences sociales (2001–2003). According to Llored, the most important concepts for understanding Derrida's thinking on animality are "carnophallogocentrism" and the idea that humans are inseparable and undistinguishable from animals. As Derrida claimed, neither culture nor philosophy could establish with any degree of certainly "the proper of man" "[e]ither because some animals also possess such traits, or because man does not possess it as surely as is claimed."[62] For Derrida, the animal as category is absolutely central and indispensable to the definition of everything human, including philosophy. Killing animals and devouring them is "displaced cannibalism," which Derrida declares fundamental to Western consciousness. Therefore, Western subjectivity, which is based on killing animals, is nothing more than a "massacre." Interestingly, Derrida does not consider this a common trait of the evolution of humans into an omnivorous species. According to him, it is specifically typical of the "West." The idea that "in fundamental ways, the oppression of human over human is rooted in the oppression of human over nonhuman animal" is deeply ingrained in the reasoning of Derrida's followers as well as in that of the defenders of animal rights.[63]

Adherents of deconstruction advance the argument that human history, permeated as it is with an unwillingness to acknowledge the equal status of humans and animals, is "a process infused with human vanity."[64] Attacks on humanism have therefore become an indispensable part of their discourse, which speaks of the "animal turn" and "Animal Manifestos"[65] and blames humanism for "its patently false insistence on the autonomous, willful human subject who acts independently in the world."[66] The defense of animal rights has a long history. Since Jeremy Bentham first posed the question "Can they suffer?" the defense of animals has been inspired by a desire to end human cruelty and violence against animals. Animal rights advocacy was therefore viewed as the ultimate moral stand for people of conscience who wished to achieve utilitarianism's goal of "the greatest good for the greatest number." By contrast, the advocacy of humanism and human exceptionalism is perceived as an immoral assertion that only justifies, in words of historian Joanna Bourke, a "systemic violence."[67]

The central argument for the philosophically minded defenders of animal rights is that humans should not be deemed uniquely to possess moral rights. The group of ethical philosophers and social scientists concerned with animal rights, which formed in the 1970s and included Richard Hare and Richard Ryder, claimed that animals also have moral rights and should therefore not be used in animal research. Furthermore, they sought to sustain this argument without appealing to humanism or humanistic values. Contrary to Kant, who condemned cruelty against animals due to its negative effects on human morality, they desired to make their case without reference to human feelings or sentimentality. They wanted to assure the equality of humans and animals even at the epistemological level and therefore maintained that humans are fundamentally indistinguishable from animals.[68] The term "speciesism" was coined by Ryder in denunciation of the desire of human beings to consider themselves essentially different from other mammals.[69]

The trajectory of this thought is well-illustrated by the views of philosopher Peter Singer, whose book *Animal Liberation: A New Ethics for Our*

Treatment of Animals (1975) was instrumental in winning a great deal of political support for the animal rights movement. Singer compares the feminist movement and animal liberation, claiming that animal liberation is the next step in the program of total liberation. He states that the boundary between animals and humans is arbitrary, and, grounding himself in utilitarianism, he dismisses the notion of the exclusive sanctity of human life as outdated and unscientific: "[W]e are intimidated into uncritically accepting that all human life has some special dignity or worth."[70] Or as he puts it elsewhere, "[W]e should recognize that the fact that a being is human, and alive, does not in itself tell us whether it is wrong to take that being's life."[71]

Consistent with these views, Singer supports the idea of a hierarchy of human lives, which is based on the presumption that an objective point of view can determine which life makes more sense and hence which life is more worthy of being preserved.[72] For Singer, who sees no major difference between the slaughter of people and of animals, the comparison drawn between the Holocaust and the mass confinement and butchery of chickens is legitimate and plausible:

> The conclusion Peta wants us to reach is that both the Holocaust and the mass confinement and slaughter of animals are horrific. A free society should be open to discussing such a claim.[73]

This statement is an example of the clouded boundaries between the extreme left and the far right over the issue of human exceptionalism. It should be emphasized that historically, the support for animal rights is by no means an inherited feature of leftist discourse. The Nazi regime, in fact, was consistent in its implementation of animal-protection legislation. As Boria Sax documents in *Animals in the Third Reich*, from its very first days, care for animals was high among the Reich's priorities; an animal-protection law introduced to regulate the treatment of animals in 1933 was just the beginning.[74] Several Nazi Party leaders, including Hitler, were more or less consistent vegetarians who consciously avoided eating animal flesh. Himmler, head of the SS and therefore responsible for the concentration camps, was reported to have argued against hunting, calling it "pure murder."[75] Sax persuasively shows that animal-protection laws had a perverse effect on the treatment of people by the Nazis. Indeed, those laws encouraged a denial of human exceptionalism and of the ultimate value of human life: "[T]he strategic blurring of the boundary between animals and people helped the Nazis extend these extreme controls to the lives of the human beings."[76]

The legislation protecting animals may have helped reduce cruelty to animals in Nazi Germany,[77] but, more importantly, it also assisted in degrading people to the level of animals and permitted humans to be treated as nonhumans. As Sax points out, Jews, Roma, and Slavic prisoners were actually transported in wagons labeled "meat" or "animals,"[78] and "many Nazi practices made the killing of people seem like the slaughtering of animals."[79] The history of the Nazi defense of animal rights does not compromise the idea that cruelty to animals should be legally prohibited. Rather, it shows the potential dangers of undermining the idea of human exceptionalism.

The Uploaded Future

We should now discuss two other trends that have greatly contributed to the popularity of antihumanism in recent decades: transhumanism and posthumanism. Both transhumanism and posthumanism have been promoted by renowned scientists in the fields of artificial intelligence, bioengineering, and biocomputing and have acquired great prominence in popular culture and public debate. They have directly influenced the attitudes to humans and humanity.

The concept of transhumanism was invented by Julian Huxley, brother of Aldous Huxley, the author of *Brave New World*, who was one of the first to anticipate the social and ethical problems that could ensue from advancements in genetic engineering and human conditioning. Julian Huxley conceptualized transhumanism in the following way:

> The human species can, if it wishes, transcend itself—not just sporadically, an individual here in one way, an individual there in another way, but in its entirety, as humanity. We need a name for this new belief. Perhaps transhumanism will serve: man remaining man, but transcending himself, by realizing new possibilities of and for his human nature. 'I believe in transhumanism': once there are enough people who can truly say that, the human species will be on the threshold of a new kind of existence, as different from ours as ours is from that of Peking man. It will at last be consciously fulfilling its real destiny.[80]

Transhumanism aims to enhance human nature and transcend humanity in its current form through science and technology. As a movement, it is mainly concerned with the extension of life by all possible means. The final goal of transhumanism is immortality, since transhumanists have no doubt that eternal life can be attained through technology.[81] Transhumanists envision several scenarios for the future of humanity. One such scenario, the singularity, is endorsed by transhumanists such as Raymond Kurzweil.[82] Once technological and scientific progress has exceeded the human ability to understand it, artificial intelligence, infinitely greater than human, will come into being. And that is when the singularity occurs: superpowerful computers will "awake" to become the universe's new actors, and humans will give way to self-programming intelligent machines, which will radiate reason until it saturates the universe. Humans are considered by transhumanists as nothing more than a transitional stage to a "strong AI," and their destiny after the advent of technological singularity is of no further interest, since at that point humans are likely to be fully under the control of those intelligent machines. These views are supported by theories of "mutation meltdown" and "genetic death," which predict the human race's inevitable genetic degeneration. According to this theory, mutations in the human genome are detrimental, the process is unstoppable, and the human species is destined to proceed on an irreversible downward spiral. These theories imply that the transhumanist vision of a nonhuman future is the inevitable outcome of scientific progress and evolution.

From transhumanists' viewpoint, the future after "the end of man" is bright. The proponents of the posthuman future—Hugo de Garis, for example—are on the side of intelligent machines against humans in the event of global conflict between them. For de Garis, the human species is only a link in the evolutionary chain and will eventually become extinct, at which point reason will rule the universe through AI.[83] In one of his publications, de Garis uses primitive forms of life as an analogy to describe the future relations between humanity and AI. He argues that the preferencing of younger but more promising forms of life over the one that "was there first" is obvious. In his reasoning, humans are on a par with primitive organisms:

"Personally, as a human being, I don't want humans to be swatted like mosquitoes," he said. "But humans should not stand in the way of a higher form of evolution. These machines are god-like. It is human destiny to create them."[84]

More perceptive than many of his fellow transhumanists, de Garis also confesses in the same interview that his work does keep him up at night with nightmare thoughts: "'I love my work during the day,' he said. 'But I lie awake at night, feeling terrified that my work may lead to gigadeath.'"[85]

The concept of posthumanism unites different trends.[86] The word "posthumanism" is much acclaimed by those natural scientists who dream of a future free of humans. Posthumanism, which is understood as a technological culture compounded by medical enhancement, is more radical in its views than transhumanism.[87] Indeed, posthumanists "have treated technology as an ideology, a particular kind of instrumental attitude that shapes the world" and that holds, among all else, that the future needs to be freed from the human species.[88] Unlike transhumanists, who limit themselves to solving technological problems associated with the achievement of eternal life and for whom the destiny of human civilization is a peripheral issue, the end of the human race is a matter of principle for posthumanists: "Within thirty years, we will have the technological means to create superhuman intelligence. Shortly after, the human era will be ended."[89]

The appeal of the term "posthumanism" is a measure of how attractive anything that surpasses, bypasses, or simply contributes to the deconstruction of the concept of the human being is to contemporary thinking. It is not, certainly, a coincidence that another version of posthumanism, a powerful trend in the humanities and social sciences, is rooted in French Theory.[90] In her *Cyborg Manifesto* Donna Haraway pioneered "cyborg studies" and advocated for transformation into a machine to bypass the limitations of human nature and thinking.[91] Neil Badmington and Katherine Hayles,[92] among others, are active adepts of this trend. Along with Cary Wolfe, they are highly invested in the idea of removing any inkling of "anthropocentrism" from thinking and argumentation in the humanities. Wolfe, for example, considers posthumanism "a historical moment in which the decentering of the human by its imbrication in technical, medical, informatic, and economic networks is increasingly impossible to ignore [. . .] a new mode of thought that comes after the cultural repression and fantasies, the philosophical protocols and evasions, of humanism as a historically specific phenomenon."[93]

Nowadays, the modification of the human species is no longer a mere figment of the imaginations of quirky scientists or eccentric writers. Practical steps are also underway. For example, Kevin Warwick, who believes that humans and machines must merge, is actively transforming both himself and his wife into cyborgs.[94] Henry Markram, who has received a billion-

Fig. 1. "Modifying Mankind," an *Our Weekly* cover story

euro European Flagship Initiative grant from the EU, is building a full cellular simulation of the human brain that he plans to construct within ten years. He is inspired by his success in building a cellular rat brain; he and his colleagues estimate the human brain to be technologically equivalent to one thousand rat brains.[95] In Markram's experiments and others like them, the human brain is going to be "emulated," even though researchers acknowledge that they still do not understand how the brain gives rise to mind.

Immortality is the major attraction for the transhumanist and posthumanist proponents of "mind uploading" or "strong AI":

One of the core concepts in transhumanist thinking is life extension: Through genetic engineering, nanotech, cloning, and other emerging technologies, eternal life may soon be possible.[96]

Transhumanists believe that if the information in the brain could be wholly or partially transferred into a computer, it could exist indefinitely, which would qualify as the achievement of eternal life. This is how Kurzweil, known for his predictions of immortality, describes the immortality of the uploaded mind:

> However, if we are diligent in maintaining our mind file, making frequent backups, and porting to current formats and mediums, a form of immortality can be attained, at least for software-based humans. Later in this century it will seem remarkable to people that humans in an earlier era lived their lives without a backup of their most precious information: that contained in their brains and bodies.[97]

Similar ideas are expressed by biogerontologist Marios Kyriazis, who believes that humans will stop procreating and dying and will be able to live for centuries, developing their brains to their full potential through advancements in artificial intelligence and synthetic biology.[98] Technocritic Dale Carrico is already concerned about "morphological freedom," which entails the proposed civil right to maintain or modify one's own body at will to achieve immortality.[99]

Transhumanism and posthumanism's views on immortality differ strikingly from any previous religious or cultural tenets. Immortality is no longer seen as eternal happiness in paradise attained through living a pious life or as a secular ideal of postmortem glory achieved by noble deeds. In fact, it is completely divorced from any religious, moral, or meritocratic meaning. It is about escaping death by purely technical means. Zoltan Istvan's "Three Laws of Transhumanism" straightforwardly formulate this idea that survival is above any ethical concerns for transhumanism: "A transhumanist must safeguard one's own existence above all else."[100]

Both transhumanism and posthumanism are eager to dispose of humanity and transcend human nature. The hedonistic understanding of immortality is every bit as powerful among post- and transhumanists as it is among vampire fans.[101] As we will see, there is a traceable connection between transhumanist and posthumanist ideas of immortality and the idealization of monsters. The replacement of humans by monsters as the main protagonists in literature and arts, and the popularity of transhumanism and posthumanism, attest to the profound influence that antihumanism has exerted on contemporary culture.

A main point of agreement between the posthumanism and transhumanism is that technology should help humans abandon their nature and merge with machines.[102] The very genealogy of transhumanism relates the rejection of humanism to the utopian tradition, making the denial of humanism, rather than the apotheosis of human rights, the truly "Last Utopia."[103] But once the rejection of humanism and human exceptionalism becomes a discursive routine and mainstream mood not only in philosophical or scientific debates but also in popular culture, they acquire new implications.

Welcome Apocalypse?

The broad acceptance of antihumanism and the rejection of human exceptionalism in contemporary popular culture manifests itself in the immense popularity of apocalyptic themes.[104] The strong connections between critique of humanism and the anticipation of the end of humanity are clearly evident to critics and biographers of the French avant-garde's leading figures. "Apocalyptic pronouncements are common enough in the writings of recent avant-garde French intellectuals. They go along with that strain of theoretical anti-humanism which heralds an end to all traditional (anthropocentric) philosophies of language and interpretations,"[105] says Christopher Norris, a biographer of Derrida. It is also argued that Foucault's discourse "always tends towards the oracular and intimations of apocalypse."[106] But while the apocalyptic predispositions of the French thinkers can be explained by a revolutionary "desire for radical endings and transformations,"[107] attempts to rationalize the mounting popularity of the apocalyptic genre in the 2000s as an expression of social or political critique of contemporary society do not appear entirely persuasive. Today's apocalyptic genre most often has no connection with the biblical themes of moral redemption or glorious future that have nourished apocalyptic thinking for thousands of years.[108] Krishan Kumar sees the contemporary apocalypse, rather, as an expression of a deep cultural pessimism that emphasizes only "endings without new beginnings."[109]

Indeed, the apocalyptic and postapocalyptic movies and fiction of the past decade persistently describe the extinction of the human race in favor of some other intelligent species. This new vision of apocalypse may, in fact, be the reason for the genre's huge popularity. *The Planet of the Apes* reboot,

Rise of the Planet of the Apes (Rupert Wyatt, 2011), one of the most popular movies of the past decade, offers an illustration of this point, as morally superior intelligent apes ride roughshod over worthless human beings. The extinction of the human race is depicted as a natural, unproblematic course of events. This greatly distinguishes representations of apocalypse in contemporary novels and movies from the classic apocalyptic offerings. Plague in Mary Shelley's *The Last Man* (1826), the comet slamming into the earth in Edgar Allan Poe's "Conversation of Eiros and Charmion" (1839), and the unfriendly intelligent machines in the Wachowski brothers' *Matrix* franchise (all of which either threaten or end human civilization) presented humanity's end as the ultimate catastrophe. The message of the majority of these works is that humanity must be guarded against any horrible unforeseen mischance that may be fatal to the species. Twenty-first-century productions, by contrast, regard apocalypse as the inescapable future and a normal evolutionary process, not at all as an existential catastrophe. The sheer number of apocalyptic movies, novels, and short stories may even have dulled the sensibilities of both creators and audiences. An ultimate manifestation of global death, apocalypse is the anticipation of the death of man in its supreme form and can be interpreted the ultimate denial of human culture and civilization.[110]

Apocalypse and the end of humanity are sometimes even welcomed as a desirable scenario for the future. One source of the endorsement of this scenario springs from the deep conviction that antihumanism is an indispensable expression of the political and social critique. For example, academics and reviewers alike perceive zombie apocalypse fiction and movies as a uniquely productive criticism of capitalist society, American foreign policy, etc. The idea that brain-eating monsters may signify something other than a protest against capitalism or American imperialism does not even occur to these authors. Nor are they prepared to acknowledge that once an idea becomes a popular culture commodity, it loses its critical potential.

Deprived of its cultural and political context of origin and taken to extreme, the message of French Theory is reduced to a caricature. For example, some critics conflate acts of cognition and acts of murder, and they bill serial killers as "idealist truth seekers."[111] Others, in keeping with their assertion that "Western culture and/or late capitalism" is inherently cannibalistic, go so far as to equate tourism with man eating. Richard King concisely covers the gamut of such statements:

> Crystal Bartolovich playfully glosses consumerism as the cultural
> logic of late capitalism; Bell Hooks speaks of the Euro-American

desires for and incorporation of things ethnic as "eating the other"; and Rosalind Morris suggests that cannibalism is the essential metaphor for late capitalism. Dean MacCannell, in an exciting exploratory review of the documentary Cannibal Tours, makes explicit what O'Rourke left unsaid, that we are cannibals, and contemporary capitalism is neo-cannibalism. Perhaps more radically, Jack Forbes argues that Western civilization fosters cannibalism as an embodied, psychosocial condition or psychosis rooted in exploitation and consumption. Inspired at least in part by Forbes, Deborah Root rethinks Western civilization as cannibal culture.[112]

There are also attempts to present the proliferation of violence in entertainment and the rising appeal of death as primordial features of Western culture, "the nature of capitalist society," "the logocentrism of the Western discourse," and so forth. Grace Jantzen's argument can be taken as an illustration of this viewpoint. She maintains that "the choice of death, the love of death and of that which makes for death, has been characteristic of the west from Homeric and Platonic writings, through centuries of christendom, and takes particularly deadly shapes in western postmodernity." According to Jantzen, this existential characteristic of the Western culture is rooted in its male drive, which has resulted in a "gendered necrophilia," and "violence and the love of death has been sedimented in layer upon layer in western history."[113] Her arguments would be better grounded had she demonstrated that the histories of other known societies are violence-free or that there is no gender inequality outside the Western world.

Most significantly, theories of this kind cannot explain the rapidly changing cultural landscape; they eclipse the specificity of our present cultural juncture and conceal the uniqueness of the contemporary cult of death. They add as little to our understanding of the fascination with cannibalism, violent death, and apocalypse in popular culture as do statements from the opposite side of the political spectrum that blame the left for creating a "death culture" that prevents its adepts from "rediscovering a benevolent God" or claim that the feminist/Left elites are conspiring to destroy "the values of our civilization."[114] The cult of death, like many other contemporary cultural trends, cannot be described in terms of existing political oppositions. Its cultural significance and its manifestations transcend political divides and exemplify that the concepts of the left and the right are in profound crisis and are becoming increasingly inapt to describe contemporary culture.[115] As Richard Wolin has shown to good effect, the failure of the notions of both left and right is an inevitable consequence of the contradictions inherent in the discourse of the epigones of French Theory:

> Paradoxically, whereas a visceral rejection of political modernity (rights of man, rule of law, constitutionalism) was once standard fare among counterrevolutionary thinkers, it has now become fashionable among advocates of the cultural left.[116]

TWO

The Commodification of Death

The Social and Historical Perspectives

In this chapter, we will explore the unprecedented and rapid invention of the new rites and death-related commodities in recent decades. The cult of death is not a phantom of the imaginary world limited to philosophical ideas, novels, and movies. It is a social and cultural phenomenon that manifests itself in various social practices. The meaning of these social practices, however, is best revealed and interpreted through the analysis of popular culture.

In the first part of this chapter, I will review anthropological and historical research to identify some rapid changes taking place in funeral rituals, the spread of death symbolism in fashion, recently established death-related industries (such as dark tourism and the marketing of murderabilia), newly emerging educational initiatives, the proliferation of new words related to death, and the stunning popularity of Halloween and of Santa Muerte, the worship of "Saint Death." In the second part, I will discuss whether the current celebration of death finds any parallels in previous historical epochs or represents an exceptional way of engaging with death.

The Social Life of Death: Holidays, Cults, Rituals, Language and Fashion

Death Rites

As a child back in the 1970s, I used to spend my summer vacations in Gomel, a provincial Belorussian city. In the apartment building where my grandmother lived with a view over the large green courtyard, funerals were frequent. The building was old and so were its inhabitants, mainly elderly women of Jewish and Belorussian origin.

Under the Soviets, nationality and religion were supposed to have little relevance to funerals. In the cities, rites were strictly secular unless the deceased's family was brave enough to openly declare its faith. Since such courage was rare, funerals tended to be quite uniform and follow the state-imposed model, even in the cities with an ethnically and religiously mixed population, as was the case in Belorussia. An open casket holding the flower-strewn corpse was placed in the courtyard so that neighbors could come and say goodbye to the departed. Obituaries were lengthy and cliché-ridden. Because the old women in my grandmother's building were usually alone in the world, I do not recall any dirges being sung or any wailing; the funerals were by and large for the neighbors rather than for family. Once the visitation was over, a procession escorted the coffin through the city to the cemetery. A band playing loud funeral marches usually accompanied the cortege, so that no one in the general vicinity could fail to know that a funeral was taking place. After the burial, the procession returned to the deceased's apartment for a meal that could last for several hours and that usually featured special kinds of food and drink, often *kisel'*, a cranberry beverage, and *kut'ya*, boiled rice mixed with raisins. I was always very frightened by funerals because I feared that my beloved grandmother might also die like that one day. I was glad that in Leningrad, the Soviet Union's second largest city and my hometown, nothing of the kind existed. Funerals, except for those of the state officials, were not intended to attract much public attention, and in the 1970s, death denial was actually more typical of funerals in the big cities.

Soviet burials involved either interment or cremation. There were no private funeral agencies, and the state ones were highly centralized: the egalitarian spirit of Soviet society ruled the dead even more than the living. The chronic shortages affected goods for the dead too. The rough wooden coffins, the poor-quality monuments, were identical from end to end of that huge country. The state funeral agency dictated what was going to happen and when and how, with few variations permitted.[1]

In an effort to divest death rituals of their religious connotations, cremation had been introduced as an alternative to the traditional Orthodox interment. The first crematorium was built in Moscow in 1927 at Novo-Danilov Cemetery. By the 1970s, cremation had become the standard procedure in the large cities, especially among the poor and recent migrants. In the cities, which were easier to regulate centrally, the majority of funerals were secular, although some elements of the Orthodox tradition—transfer of the corpse to the mortuary soon after death, an open casket, and disposition on the third day—were integrated into the state-imposed rites.

Despite active atheist propaganda and serious repressions, however, the Soviet success in desacralizing funerals was uneven. Since the vast rural areas of provincial Russia and Belorussia were the hardest for the communists to control, funerals in villages and small communities preserved, to end of the twentieth century, all the major elements of Orthodox rituals, including visitation at the deceased's home, a church service, an open-casket funeral accompanied by dirges and wailing, and burial on the third day. Refusal of an autopsy, avoidance of the mortuary, and rejection of cremation remained the norm.[2]

Back in the 1970s, American funeral practices were also quite stable. Studies of funerals conducted in the United States concluded that practices and rites were uniform, controlled more by funeral directors than by American religious institutions. As Huntington and Metcalf pointed out in their classical cross-cultural study of death rituals in the late 1970s, the American way of interment was uniformly conservative:

> Given the myriad variety of death rites throughout the world, and the cultural heterogeneity of American society, the expectation is that funeral practices will vary widely from one region, or social class, or ethnic group, to another. The odd fact is that they do not. The overall form of funerals is remarkably uniform from coast to coast. Its general features include: rapid removal of the corpse to a funeral parlor, embalming, institutionalized "viewing," and disposal by burial.[3]

American death rituals were typified by embalming, which became acceptable even for Christians after Abraham Lincoln's death, and interment after an open-casket funeral. Additionally:

> The usual rites are relatively simple (. . .) As a society, we emphasize the expression of personal feelings but not the public expression or sadness or grief. (. . .) We do not require mourning, although the absence of tears can be taken to signal denial in someone. (. . .) We interact minimally with the dead, having buried them in places removed from centers of commerce and residence. Too much speaking of or with the dead is considered deviant. Although we fear death and it is considered impolite or morbid to talk much about it,

we have little fear of the dead. Although we do not think of death or the dead as polluting, we nevertheless have a hands-off approach to death and hire professionals to handle the dead for us.[4]

In the United States as in Russia, institutionalized funerals handled by professionals, which was the norm prior to the 1990s, can be regarded as the translation of death denial into death-related rituals. In the early 1990s, the evidence that death rites had begun to evolve in America was reflected in two novelties, namely the growing acceptance of cremation and the establishment of hospices.[5] These initially revolutionary innovations today seem as ordinary as a jazz funeral in New Orleans.[6]

By the early 2000s, it became clear that death rituals were being reinvented in America and that the traditional funeral was becoming exposed to a wide range of challenges. Even the titles of the books describing this process—*Final Rights: Reclaiming the American Way of Death*, *Transforming the Culture of Dying*, etc.—are indicative of the change.[7] Beginning in the new millennium, "green funerals," home funerals, and the home death-care movement have all "worked [their] way into American culture."[8] The most distant from all traditional rites known in the West is "green" or "natural" funerals. The landscape is modified by grave markers as little as possible, if at all. Often these sites are privately owned, but sometimes cemeteries make accommodations for funerals of this type. The main idea is not to inhibit the natural decay and decomposition of the body. Since the body is to recycle naturally, no preservatives, embalming fluids, or disinfectants are used in its preparation, and the grave is shallow to ensure better contact between the body and the soil.[9] The growing popularity of green funerals resulted in their institutionalization in the late 1990s. The United States' first "green cemetery" was opened in 1998 in South Carolina, but, all clichés about "the hidebound English" notwithstanding, it was the United Kingdom that spearheaded those innovations. Another nontraditional way of burying the dead, which has yet to become as popular as "green funerals," is "promession," a technique that allows the freeze-drying of the body so that the remains decompose quickly in the soil. Although the concept of promession, developed by Swedish biologist Susanne Wiigh-Mäsak, has yet to be widely implemented, it represents an additional radical challenge to the traditional notion of burial in the West.[10] The cryonization of bodies in hopes that some future technology will enable their revival is another recently developed approach to coping with death, although it is not really a burial in any form. This practice is particularly widespread among adherents of transhumanism and posthumanism. This new way of handling

the deceased explicitly demonstrates how transhumanist and posthumanist ideas of future immortality owing to the progress of technology are
engendering new social practices. Cryonics offers a prime example of the
link between changing ideas about death and immortality and changes in
posthumous traditions. New death rites are also becoming established in
US hospitals to accommodate dying nonbelievers "without compromising
the faith statements of the normative burial rite."[11] Scholars place some of
these emerging rituals among the "many ongoing adaptations and evolu-
tions occurring in official death rituals today" and surmise that "the next
generation of adaptations may draw on different cultural experiences and
concerns of piety in a rapidly evolving church in the United States."[12]
Home funerals, which are also fast-growing in the United States, are
derived from the growing support for a family's right to care for its dead.
Today, specialized agents offer assistance to families that would like to have
a home funeral but do not know how to go about it.

But America is not alone in facing challenges to its funeral traditions.
Funerals in Russia after the fall of communism have also undergone profound changes, some of which resemble their American counterparts while
others do not. Although changes in funeral rites in Russia could be at least
partly explained by the collapse of communism and the profound economic and political transformations in that country since 1991, the fact
that the chronology of these changes coincides quite closely with changes
in American death rites suggests that there may be some common reasons
behind them. To the astonishment of Russian anthropologists, who seem to
have been caught off guard by the scale and rapidity of the transformations,
what Soviet propaganda and repressions failed to achieve in the country-
side in seventy years has happened there in a single decade absent any
ideological intervention.[13] Cremation has become common in the coun-
tryside, while an autopsy is now performed in the majority of deaths, under
pressure from local law enforcement, which places a strong emphasis on
ensuring that the death resulted from natural causes, especially if the dece-
dent was elderly. Embalming has always been considered a gross violation
of Orthodox tradition, much as it is for many other Christian denomina-
tions. (Orthodox believers perceived the embalming of Lenin in 1924 as a
just punishment for the dictator, who was now visibly damned for eternity,
just "like the pharaohs of Egypt.") Embalming was in any event unavail-
able to ordinary people under the Soviets. But it was promptly adopted
by everyone, atheist and Orthodox alike, as soon as it became available in
post-Soviet Russia.

Paradoxically, this dramatic change in funeral rituals occurred at the same time as the Orthodox Church was staking its claim as supreme moral authority in a multidenominational society. But to the same extent as it proved unable to fill the moral vacuum left by the collapse of communism,[14] the Orthodox Church has also failed to create a mass-appeal model for funeral rites in post-Soviet Russia. Much as in the United States over recent decades, funerals in post-Soviet Russia have become whatever a client wants them to be. The privatization of funeral services has given rise to a great variety of customized options that depend entirely on the client's ability or willingness to pay for them.[15] Private agencies boast of providing "elite" individualized services that address their clients' specific needs. Russian scholars have even given these new approaches the name of "spontaneous burials" due to their totally innovative character and their disconnection from any tradition, be it Orthodox or Soviet.[16]

In both countries, cremation is undergoing transformations of its own. Based on the research of Russian scientists, the technique has developed to turn the ashes of the deceased into "jewels," and these "objects full of emotion" (as one website described them) have become increasingly popular over the past decade, not only in Russia but also in Europe and the United States. This new invention seems to be particularly emblematic of the commodification and the aestheticization of death. The custom of accompanying the coffin all the way to the crematorium furnace is also becoming more common in the United States, bringing yet another change to a ritual that has itself not been around for very long.[17] In Russia, Europe, and the United States, the options of scattering the ashes[18] or sending the ashes into space are readily available to those who can afford them.[19] Although in general Russians, especially city dwellers, resemble Americans in their preference for an arm's-length approach to death, entombing the family dead on a private lot near the home has also become permissible in the post-Soviet period. Nothing of the kind existed before: in tsarist Russia being buried anywhere other than in consecrated ground was considered a sin, a great misfortune, and the final destination of criminals and suicides; under the Soviets the practice of placing a private memorial to the dead anywhere other than in a cemetery was also quite unusual.

Today, driving along Russian roads, through miles and miles of uninhabited forest, one is struck by the number of roadside memorials of various sizes, styles, and complexity. Simple wooden crosses decorated with artificial flowers, huge monuments in marble and iron stakes are erected at the sites of fatal accidents. Some are soon abandoned, while others are well-tended for years. Roadside memorials at the site of fatal accidents are also seen in the United States and in Europe. Only some of those memori-

Fig. 2. Highway Memorial Crosses.   *(Copyright constantgardener, from iStock.)*

als are temporary; others, often in the form of a cross or a secular tombstone, become permanent, and their numbers are growing.[20]

The virtual world has certainly not been excluded from these newly emerging death rites and practices. According to researchers studying them, web "memorials" represent "a new ritual to commemorate the dead," creating not only a memorial space but also a community of social support.[21] These memorials demonstrate how those who construct them are struggling to make sense of death: "Though traditional eschatological beliefs are vague there remains a sense of bridging the living with the dead through newly devised rites."[22] Overall, scholars studying funerals in the United States conclude that the "diversification of our ways of publicly remembering and commemorating the dead" is growing fast.[23] Researchers of post-Soviet funeral traditions also hold that funeral practices in post-Soviet Russia are far from stable even now and will continue to evolve.[24]

To conclude, in the United States, Russia, and in Europe more broadly, death rituals, both secular and religious, are becoming increasingly individualized and are losing their prevailing traditional uniformity: "While professionals still have a substantial role [in determining the form taken by the ceremony], recently, from the 1980s and onwards, the authority is increasingly also ascribed to the individual mourners creating their own death rituals."[25] The tempo of change is such that this most conservative of all rituals has suddenly come to involve the mastery of a fairly steep "learning curve": "But because our modern society has lost the common knowledge of how to care for the dead, it may be particularly difficult for many people to go through that learning curve at a time of immense grief."[26]

The inventions of new death rites before our very eyes clearly indicates that there is a compelling mass interest in death and that the established rituals are falling short of fully and accurately reflecting newly emerging ideas on death and dying.[27] Anthropologists have argued that the changes in funeral rituals may be related to a paradigmatic shift in the understanding of death.[28] Archaeologists and historians who study past societies consider a change in burial rituals to be a prime indicator of a civilizational shift. These changing burial rituals may in fact be evidence of the huge cultural change that our society is currently undergoing, in particular, as I argue in this book, with regard to ideas about death, humans, and immortality.

A Language for Death

To fully appreciate the scale and diversity of the multiple manifestations of the cult of death in America and Russia, we will have to look beyond changes in death rites. The fascination with death has generated a slew of new words and terms to be used in discussing these newly emerging death-related practices. The remarkable conceptual productivity of the cult of death may be fully appreciated once the reader is reminded that the times we live in are marked by "the silence of the intellectuals."[29]

In contrast, taphophilia, thanatourism, thanatography, thanatosensitivity, thanatechnology—words that the cult of death has recently made available to us—did not even exist twenty years ago. The abundance of such words is evidence of new social, educational, and cultural practices encouraged by the allure of death. It points to the creation, in recent decades, of new services, activities, and fields of study that are flourishing amid an increasing demand.

Previously, death and mortality were studied by demographers alongside other demographic processes. Sociology, psychology, and philosophy were traditionally responsible for investigating the social, psychological, and philosophical aspects of death. Over recent decades, however, death studies, mortality studies, and thanatology have surfaced as independent academic fields.[30] (The researchers may feel compelled to stipulate that death studies, as a new area of specialization, might be "a strange thing to people."[31]) Numerous colloquia and symposia are held to discuss death and dying, and death studies associations vie with thanatology associations for members. Studies of death have also been high on the agenda of philanthropic foundations around the globe.[32]

The impact on education of these new developments has been profound. "Death education" had entered secondary school curriculums in the United States by the end of the 2000s.[33] Tertiary education is now offering "certificates in thanatology" designed to lead to "thanatology jobs" and "thanatology careers." Thanatechnology, the communication technology used to provide death education and grief counseling, has also recently entered the educational market.[34]

Thanatourism ("dark tourism") is a whole new segment of the tourist industry that involves travel to sites historically associated with murders, mass crimes against humanity, and other tragedies.[35] Popular destinations advertised on dark tourism websites include, among many others, the site of the Kennedy assassination, former prisons in Europe, the Hiroshima Peace Memorial Park and Museum in Japan, the Chernobyl site in Ukraine, and the Auschwitz concentration camp in Poland. In his 2003 study, Keith Durkin emphasizes the novelty of the term "dark tourism": "Some scholars have adopted the term dark tourism to refer to 'the presentation and consumption (by visitors) of real and commoditized death and disaster sites.'"[36] And since that time, it has become a mainstream notion both in the tourist industry and in the death studies.

Another rapidly growing death-inspired industry is the marketing of "murderabilia," collectibles related to violent crimes and serial killers including the artwork of serial killers. According to Ricarda Vidal, this market offers a way of participating in the transgression of the murder.[37] The fascination with death has also initiated several other new activities with broad appeal. Thanatography—the recounting of symptoms and thoughts by a dying person—has developed into a new narrative genre in recent years.[38] And the "popularity" of death is traceable even in humor. A strain of dark humor overwhelmed America in the 1980s, unlike in Russia, where black humor has always been an important part of a culture.[39] In the United States as in Russia, the fixation on death resonates with a large variety of subcultures. The Goth and Emo youth subcultures in particular are focused with dark, grisly, suicidal, and pessimistic death-related themes. The role-playing game subculture and contemporary rock (and especially Gothic rock) also come naturally to mind in this regard. Death motifs have always been popular in songs, though, making it difficult to locate evidence of a rising cult of death there. Gothic rock, heavy metal, and rap, which all originated in the 1970s, however, do appear to be specifically focused on death.

The high incidence of new words, the development of the new industries, etc. do not run counter to the death denial discussed above. Although death is denied as part of a person's social and general life experience, this does not hinder an increased interest in death as entertainment and commodity. The fascination with death in its every manifestation correlates with a profound disarray and confusion as to what death is, what it means, and what happens after death. The lack of a coherent system of references that would explain the meaning of death is painfully felt, as Colin Murray Parkes, a famous English psychiatrist and a specialist in traumatic bereavements in childhood, remarks:

> When real death forces itself on our attention, we become greatly distressed, for we have no schema, no system of belief that can make sense of it. The bereaved experience this as a breakdown in the meaning of life.[40]

Halloween

Rotting corpses, mutilated body parts, skulls and crossbones, and, most importantly, skeletons—skeletons of all sizes, standing, sitting, hanging, carrying coffins. Welcome to a residential area in any American city on Halloween night. Already by late September, the homes in the neighborhood had been well on their way to becoming bogus graveyards. The Grim Reaper smiles cynically on every corner in these wealthy enclaves that never observe a funeral cortege passing by or ever hear a funeral dirge. But there is nothing truly playful about these images of death and the dead; on the contrary, most of them are there to scare, and they are about as realistically revolting as they can be. These representations of death outnumber the more traditional Halloween decorations—the spider webs and the pumpkins—many times over. What motivates Americans to fill their homes and yards with horrifying images of death?

According to surveys, more than 157 million Americans planned to celebrate Halloween in 2015.[41] For Americans, Halloween is second only to

Christmas in terms of decorations purchased and displayed. Adults are as enthusiastic as children over the celebration, and that enthusiasm translates directly into numbers: the billion dollars spent on Halloween represents a near doubling over the past decade.[42] This trend, which began in the early 2000s, has observers wondering why Halloween has evolved from a small-scale festival into the second-largest seasonal marketing event after Christmas.[43] The answer to that question may shed light on the reasons behind the unprecedented escalation of the "popularity" of death, and I will consider it at the end of this chapter. The ascent of Halloween affects other dates on the American calendar in a most interesting way. Retailers are now promoting Halloween along with their back-to-school events; in full Harry Potter mode, "wizardly" merchandise is offered to help usher children into the new school year. This cultural expansion of Halloween has led some researchers to consider it not a holiday but a full-fledged subculture movement.[44]

Looking back, it is fascinating to see how this holiday was perceived in the late 1980s and 1990s, when the Halloween "craze" was just beginning.[45] The success of a holiday whose meaning was so obscure for Americans puzzled observers: "Why do we celebrate Halloween? No one gets the day off, and unlike all other major holidays it has no religious or governmental affiliation."[46] Back in the 1990s, even liberally minded onlookers expressed their discomfort with the success of Halloween, emphasizing that there was "something ironic and unsettling about the immense popularity of a holiday whose main images are of death, evil, and the grotesque."[47] Halloween was viewed as a remarkable case of Americans "inventing a tradition": "Halloween has become one of the most important and widely celebrated festivals on the contemporary American calendar, and it is not even officially a holiday. Interesting, isn't it?"[48] Back then, local festivals— for example Guy Fawkes Night (November 5) in Great Britain—were still considered as alternatives to Halloween.

But why did Halloween, this remnant of the death-centered agrarian rituals of the druidic Celts, come back into vogue at the turn of the second millennium? The symbolism of the holiday is not particularly relevant to postindustrial and postmodern society. It is alleged that the Celts celebrated Samhain, the "end of summer," either as a holiday consecrated to the dead or as a celebration of the god of death, with human sacrifices to ensure fertility and a good harvest.[49] Halloween then persisted through the Middle Ages, especially in northern Europe, including Britain, Ireland, and Scotland. It is supposed that human sacrifices were eventually replaced by the burning of black cats in cages.[50] Although Halloween survived in England and Ireland well into the twentieth century, in the 1950s its future, in Europe as well as in the United States, was not looking at all bright. Anthropologists were expecting it to lose all meaning and eventually die out.[51] It is therefore far from obvious why the marginal and ultimately juvenile ritual of "trick or treat," which was brought to the United States in the 1840s by Irish immigrants, should have become one of the largest American holidays in the third millennium. The growing attraction of Halloween is undoubtedly a global phenomenon that thrives today in Western and Eastern Europe and places farther afield, such as South Africa and Hong Kong.[52] In Mexico, Halloween—a commercial holiday with no sacral meaning—is actually perceived as a rival to the traditional Dia de los Muertos, the Day of the Dead. Its spread across Mexico has been interpreted as "symptomatic of U.S. imperialist aggression."[53]

This association of Halloween with "American aggression" or "Americanization" also mirrors anti-Western mindsets in Russia, where the Orthodox Church opposes Halloween as "alien and hostile to Russian traditions and culture." Yet this hostile reaction did not prevent it from developing into one of the most popular Russian holidays in the 1990s and gaining even more popularity in the early 2000s. The irresistible lure of Halloween for Russians is even harder to rationalize by a desire to "rediscover one's ancient Celtic roots" than is the case for Americans. The majority of Russians who celebrate Halloween learned about the holiday from the news, from Hollywood vampire sagas, or from the Harry Potter books. Russians are even more unclear than Americans about the meaning and origins of the holiday. If asked, people refer to all kind of supernatural monsters, including vampires, witches, ghosts, zombies, the dead, and Harry Potter, or they retell the plot of the most recent vampire movie they have seen. Halloween is an urban holiday in Russia, celebrated mainly by school and college students, young professionals, Goths, Emos, and certain other youth subcultures. As in the United States, the Russian Halloween is highly commercialized. Russians try to keep their celebrations as close to the Hollywood model as they can afford, buying zombie or vampire costumes, skulls, skeletons, and certainly pumpkins to decorate their apartments.[54] Death symbols are, in fact, as popular in Russia as they are in the West. In the era of economic growth and relative stability ushered in by the 2000s, Halloween has been eagerly received by Russia's city dwellers as a new pastime and, like many other Western novelties, has become something of a status symbol. The anti-Western propaganda that swamped Russia in preparation for the war in Ukraine had a peculiar effect on Halloween. Right-wing nationalists supported by the Orthodox Church began criticizing it along with several other "Western evils." Halloween-related activities were banned by schools in some areas.[55] Yet exotic locations accommodating huge crowds remain a signature of Halloween in Moscow and St. Petersburg.[56]

The Day of the Dead and Santa Muerte

Despite the popularity of Halloween and its undeniable success in Russia, Americans still outmatch Russians in their devotion to death-related festivities. For some states, a once-yearly celebration of death is no longer enough. In Alabama, Arizona, and California, death is feted beyond Halloween, on the Day of the Dead (November 1).[57] Celebrants of the Day of the Dead go to the cemetery to "share" a meal with dead ancestors, constructing a small altar at the gravesite. Initially associated with Mexican immigrants in the United States, it is now winning over the non-Hispanic population.[58]

The current devotion to death, though, extends beyond the "deathly" holidays. The cult of Santa Muerte (also known as Saint Death, the Skeleton Saint, or the Bony Lady), which also originated in Mexico, is currently sweeping the United States. Unlike the male Grim Reaper, this female saint is represented as a skeleton dressed in colorful robes of silk, velvet, and organza. The worship of Santa Muerte was traditionally performed privately at home, as a marginal observance, until the early 2000s, when it experienced meteoric growth. Despite being banned by both the Catholic and the Protestant churches, the cult has expanded over the past decade from its humble beginnings on the outskirts of Mexico City to several million followers on both sides of the border and overseas. It thrives today in Central America, Canada, Spain, and the United States, where it is spreading beyond the Latino population of Northern California and New Orleans and is now found in New York, Chicago, Houston, San Antonio, Tucson, Los Angeles, and other major metropolitan areas.[59]

The roots of the cult are unclear. Attempts to trace it back to Catholic imagery as well as to Mexican and even Aztec beliefs are not entirely convincing.[60] Its origins are said to be found in Mexico's criminal underworld, where Saint Death is worshiped by drug lords and contract killers.[61] (Some observers even believe human sacrifice to be part of the ritual, which may have prompted the idea of its Aztec roots.) The obscure set of beliefs associated with this cult, which grew largely due to Santa Muerte's reputation as a miracle worker, is fully in line with its asocial origins.[62] The FBI experts even suppose that this cult endorses criminality and "condones morally corrupt behaviors (. . .) rewards personal gain above all else, promoting the intentional pain and suffering of others, and, even, viewing killing as a pleasurable activity."[63]

The rapid growth in the number of Santa Muerte devotees and the international triumph of Halloween may be related to the fact that they express new attitudes rather than reinterpreting old beliefs. The fact that the holiday and the cult are both sustained by nonexistent (Halloween) or very imprecise (Santa Muerte) beliefs supports this assumption, as does the fact that they do not feed into already existing death-centered occult practices, such as Satanism.[64] Satanism implies an acknowledgment of the entire gamut of Christian mythology and morality. The cult of Santa Muerte, on the contrary, expresses an untrammeled devotion to death, which requires no rationalization and seeks no metaphysical explanations. The lack of any articulated doctrine or set of dogmas other than the unrestrained adoration of death correlates the cult of Santa Muerte closely with a larger death-centered cultural movement prompted by Gothic Aesthetic. Its epidemic spread is illustrative of the rising cult of death, an obsessive desire to see death walking among the living.

Fashion to Die For

We shall now consider daily consumption and fashion. For all the popularity of Halloween, the Day of the Dead, and the cult of Santa Muerte, the excitement over death extends far beyond them. Death's conquest of minds and hearts is not limited merely to rituals, cults, and holidays.

Probably the most visible but also the most astonishing of all our new ways of engaging with death is the eagerness to see death symbolism in everyday life, in home decor and fashion.[65] The images traditionally associated with death across cultures—skeletons, skulls, bones, the Grim Reaper, corpses, and so forth—have penetrated every aspect of our daily routine on both sides of Atlantic, making representations of death one of the most desirable objects of consumption.[66] In previous epochs, toxic items were marked by skulls and crossbones; today those markings are found on supposedly "kid-friendly" candies. The largest retailers sell clothes, bedding, and furniture with death symbols all year round, not only at Halloween.

"While death as a theme was once at the periphery of the style world, explored by avant-garde photographers and by experimental fashion designers who staged and designed it to call attention to socio-political problems, it is now at its center," fashion critic Jacque Lynn Foltyn asserts, comparing the current situation with the trends in 1980s.[67] New trends

Fig. 3. Everyday skull style.   *(Copyright hiphunter, from iStock.)*

in photography, advertising, and fashion design actively embrace death by presenting images of beauty models as the dead victims of violent crime, usually highlighting the naturalistic details of a jarringly violent demise.[68] The model has "typically suffered a heinous 'death' at the hands of a murderer, serial killer, sexual sadist, paedophile, animal, or even demented toy." Foltyn has termed this fad "corpse chic" and has pointed out that the imagery of dead beauties is "staged for public amusement and aesthetic enjoyment, and covered as an infotainment phenomenon." Tim Burton's *Corpse Bride* movie spawned a line of "collectible" dolls, jewelry, and casual clothing for women and girls.[69] This death imagery seems to have no specific associations with political parties or movements or occult connotations, but it certainly expresses changing attitudes toward human life.

But corpses are not alone in representing the fashion industry's veneration of death; skulls and crossbones also enjoy huge popularity. Apart from cavemen and the Aztecs, it is hard to think of other cultures that were equally enthusiastic about using skulls and bones to decorate their homes. The skull, for centuries a dreadful reminder of mortality, has been made over as "a contemporary figure of fashion" and a "much-desired decoration by the trendsetters of tomorrow." As one fashion-related site tells us, "At nearly any store today one can find items embellished with skulls." No longer for Halloween but year-round, "from clothing to house wares to bedding and furniture, skull imagery is tremendously popular and in high demand."[70] Skulls are emblazoned on T-shirts, sneakers, keychains, pajamas, wallpaper, baby clothes, and pet outfits. Stripped of all philosophical or Christian connotations of mortality and the transience of human life, the skull has become "the Happy Face of the 2000's."[71] No efforts to tie the skull's popularity to pirates, to protest symbolism, or to "outlaw" antilogos, or to explain its celebrity though romantic associations with the swashbuckling Jolly Roger have been entirely persuasive. Even if they may have initially contributed to the rising cult of death, they alone are insufficient to explain the enormous scope of this phenomenon.

The death trend in fashion and furnishings is the most recent of the challenges presented by the cult of death. "Corpse chic" dates to the past decade. We can even pinpoint the year of "skull style" birth: 2003, when Alexander McQueen created a scarf covered with skulls and artist Damien Hirst became famous for decorating a skull with diamonds.[72] What was once an extravagant artistic experiment has now become mass fashion's most popular trend, spreading the imagery of death across the globe. Commercialized death now claims a market of millions. Few major fashion houses and even fewer fashion magazines have been able to avoid death themes entirely. In the fall of 2014, even the Metropolitan Museum of Art opened an exhibition devoted to mourning attire.

The spread of deathly fashion has perturbed several observers. In 2008, a special issue of the journal *Mortality* dealt with the wholesale devotion to death. To what may we attribute the eye-popping success of this "deathly" fashion trend? The most widespread explanation is psychoanalytical. As readers may remember, Geoffrey Gorer's "The Pornography of Death" argues that our culture has reached a point at which two most powerful cultural taboos—death and sex—may both be violated with few or no repercussions. Following this chain of reasoning, the novelty of death fashion is that it flouts both of those cultural taboos at once by substituting death for sex: in our society "oversaturated with sex, death has become 'the new sex' (. . .) the corpse and its simulated versions is the new fetishized body to be voyeuristically explored."[73]

The most recent developments in fashion seem to support none of these explanations. It is not "sex as death," nor "death as sex," nor even their interconnection, but the proliferation of images of the Grim Reaper and the skeleton that represents the current trend in mass fashion. The Grim Reaper stands for death in its most threatening and asexual form. It has no associations with the philosophical message of memento mori or the outlaw connotations of the skull and crossbones, and it is free of the necrophilic overtones of the beautiful corpse. Death symbolism that perplexes our everyday life manifests an unprecedented yearning for the images of ultimate destruction of human life.

Death: A Historical Perspective

A brief sketch of the Western historical past will help us see if images of violent death have ever before functioned as a diversion devoid of any moral, didactical, or philosophical meaning and as a fashionable commodity for the masses. For this purpose, we will compare some of the most harrowing and dramatic periods in the history of the West, whose unprecedented mortality affords them a dire distinction with our relatively untroubled times. We will review studies on the use of the representations of death in everyday life during the periods of the Black Death, the American Civil War, and the Russian Revolution. We will also examine representations of violent death as part of official ideology under Soviet and Nazi regimes. How widespread was the commodification of violent death in those deadly epochs?

The Art of Dying in the Age of Plague

During the fourteenth and fifteenth centuries, the Black Death, the Hundred Years War, the climate change known as the Little Ice Age, and famine rivaled one another in their contribution to an unparalleled level of mortality. In only four years, from 1347 to 1351, the Black Death (a combination of several plague strains) killed, according to various estimates and depending on the country, from 25 to 50 percent of Europe's population.[74] In 1348, around a half of Florence's population died.[75] "And no one could be found to bury the dead, for money or friendship"; these famous lines by Angelo di Tura, a chronicler from Siena, recreate for us the doleful world of the Black Death. This was just one of several related pandemics that reoccurred at intervals well into the eighteenth century. The last major recorded outbreak was in Marseille in 1720, when some fifty to sixty thousand people died.[76] In Russia too, the bubonic plague surfaced at intervals from the twelfth century on. The most destructive episode came at the end of the eighteenth century, from 1770 to 1772, when Moscow was essentially depopulated, with more than twenty-one thousand people dying of plague there in the single month of September 1771.[77] Historians are inclined to compare the devastation caused by plague in Europe with the carnage of the First World War.[78]

Even aside from the Black Death and other "horrors of the Apocalypse," seeing death and the dead was daily routine. Pandemics were just one of the multiple causes of death in medieval and early modern Europe. To quote Emmanuel Le Roy Ladurie, a French historian of *Annales School*, it was a Malthusian world, in which population growth surpassed the economy's ability to sustain so many people.[79] Wars were constant. The underdevelopment of agriculture caused periodic harvest failures that brought famine. Primitive medical knowledge and technological backwardness made the most trivial disease fatal. Every person observed death at firsthand from early childhood on, knowing that her or his own chances of survival were poor at best. "[T]he man of the late Middle Ages was very acutely conscious that he had merely been granted a stay of execution, that this delay would be a brief one, and that death was always present within him, shattering his ambitions and poisoning his pleasures," Philippe Ariès concludes.[80]

As Ariès and Johan Huizinga show to great effect, death was not only a public affair but also a social event. There was the concept of a "good death," which involved dying at home, surrounded by family and friends. Dying was highly ritualized and was as central to social life as any other important rite of passage. *Ars moriendi*, an instructional manual on the art of dying, or how a good Christian should face the hour of his death, was a bestseller—by medieval standards—for two centuries. In fact, Roger Chartier demonstrates that *Ars moriendi* was as popular in the fifteenth and sixteenth centuries as were *Le roman de la rose* and Gilles de Rome's *De regimine principum*, respectively one of the most popular medieval novels and a highly influential political treatise. The success of *Ars moriendi* is attributed not only to its textual content (the precepts of a good Christian death) but also to the eleven illustrations, many of which depicted the struggle between angels and devils for the soul of a dying man. According to Chartier, those woodcuts, originally from Bavaria, were in wide circulation during that troubled time.[81]

Another reason for the ubiquity of death has to do with premodern penal system. The spectacle of public execution was supposed to combine entertainment and education, making a permanent gallows with dangling bodies a familiar part of many landscapes, both urban and rural:

> For several centuries, and down to the Revolution, hanging was the most common mode of execution in France; consequently, in every town, and almost in every village, there was a permanent gibbet,

which, owing to the custom of leaving the bodies to hang till they crumbled into dust, was very rarely without having some corpses or skeletons attached to it. (. . .) The gallows, the pillars of which varied in number according to the will of the authorities, were always placed by the side of frequented roads, and on an eminence.[82]

The medieval experience of death, "hideous and threatening"[83] to use Huizinga's words, found expression in literature, poetry, philosophical reflections, and painting, making "death and with it necromania a veritable organizing principle, a central allegory" in the late Middle Ages.[84] The "religion of death," as Alberto Tenenti calls it, ruled late medieval Europe. Realistic images of death and decomposition gave rise to an artistic style that graphically depicted the various stages of the body's decay. The ossuaries that were established in several churches during the Black Death created yet another dreadful symbol of death. Johan Huizinga, in his classical study of medieval culture, has interpreted the appearance of the cadaver and the mummy in iconography and painting as a signal of the deep moral crisis that beset "the waning of the Middle Ages."[85] And Ariès, for his part, has argued that bodily decay was associated with the failure of man and the idea of eternal sin.[86] This concept that the body of a saint cannot decay survived in the Russian Orthodox tradition to the end of the nineteenth century, as we know, in particular, from the description of the Elder Zosima's funeral in Feodor Dostoevsky's *The Brothers Karamazov*.

In painting, images of skulls, crossbones, and skeletons complemented by Latin proverbs—such as *Memento mori*, *Vita brevis*, etc.—emphasized the temporary and transitory nature of life and the inevitability of death. They symbolized the Christian idea of the afterlife and salvation for the pious. Works by Breughel, Bosch, and Cranach, reflecting on the experience of the Black Death, feature the danse macabre that first appeared in French poetry in the late fourteenth century and became a popular theme in art. In the premodern Netherlands and Flanders of the sixteenth and seventeenth centuries, the *vanitas* art movement created a specific way of expressing on canvas the idea that worldly joys and wealth are impermanent and that death is inevitable. Hamlet's "poor Yorick" best summarizes those reflections, which until recently were inseparable from an image of a skull or a skull as a physical object.

Religion's all-encompassing domination of spiritual life also strengthened the fixation on death. The inevitability of death and the belief in the finality of the Last Judgment were critical to the religious experience.[87] That is why the images of death—in painting, sculpture, and literature—

were inseparable from their religious meaning and were created as religious objects. None of those symbols were intended for use other than in a religious or moralistic context and symbols of faith. In the Middle Ages—an era of omnipresent death—images of death never found their way into fashion or interior décor. Garments, furniture, food, and everyday goods, which may be reconstructed in exquisite detail from paintings and artifact collections, never displayed symbols of death, nor were skulls, bones, skeletons, or images of the Grim Reaper used as secular decorations. Had such items ever made an appearance, the Church would certainly have frowned on them as evidence of witchcraft. Death was not to triumph over the living but "to be tamed," using Ariès word, by belief in the immortality of the soul. This "nonproliferation" of the representations of death in daily life may also be explained by Mikhail Bakhtin's notion of carnival culture.[88] The essence of carnival, which was central to medieval culture, is eternal rebirth and renaissance. Death does play an important role, but only insofar as it is coupled with life. Carnival represents the eternal struggle of life and death in a never-ending circle, a continuation of life re-emerging victorious after death. In essence, carnival is rooted in pagan fertility cults, which, according to Bakhtin, explains its risqué symbolism and its desire to turn the world upside down. The lure of death was therefore contained by rebirth, fertility, and a belief in resurrection and life after death.[89] For people in the medieval and early modern world, unlike today, death was all around and was much feared, yet its place in the system of beliefs was well-determined and confined.

The revival of the interest in the medieval epoch proved a potent stimulus to the use of macabre and grim symbolism and motifs in literature and the fine arts several centuries later. Among the eighteenth- and nineteenth-century aesthetic movements that have shown a considerable interest in death, the English Gothic novel, which opposed the Enlightenment's radiant rationality and had many prominent devotees in both Russian and American culture, clearly stands apart. In the second half of the eighteenth century shadowy castles (with hidden dungeons where tortures and other atrocities were committed) and a fascination for grisly mysteries haunted the imagination. For the authors of the Gothic novel, the medieval epoch was no longer regarded as the dark ages of European civilization. Instead, it was positively re-evaluated against humanism and Enlightenment philosophy. The irrational and supernatural themes associated with the Middle Ages developed a powerful appeal. Plots involving the mysterious death of the protagonist heralded by mysterious music, creaking doors and howling winds, and stories rife with ghosts and vampires, caught the fancy of the reading public. Readers of Gothic novels, however, were far more taken by miracles, monsters, and romance than by death itself. Simultaneously, though, a desire to communicate with the world of the dead was reviving an interest in the occult. But even in its heyday, and its importance as a source for contemporary Gothic Aesthetic notwithstanding, the Gothic novel can hardly be considered in any way comparable with the present-day obsession with violent death as entertainment. Even the Gothic writers, however much they strove to horrify their readers, would never have proffered the suffering and death of their protagonists as amusement or as a "party" (as death is described in the Harry Potter series, as we will see in chapter 4). Still, despite all its popularity, the Gothic novel failed to produce a comparably robust trend in the visual arts. The Enlightenment rationality still dominated the cultural atmosphere and the aesthetics of the period. The images of death used to depict the terror of the French Revolution and the Napoleonic Wars were instruments of political propaganda but certainly not sources of entertainment.

Romanticism continued this interest in the macabre and the mysteries of death, although the creators of that movement distanced themselves quite emphatically from the Gothic novel's monsters and other excesses. A serious and tragic—and not at all playful or voyeuristic—attitude to death characterized the members of this movement.[90] Even so, one could hardly call death the central or even the most important idea of Romanticism. The periodic flashes of interest in the macabre, occultism, and mysticism during the eighteenth and nineteenth centuries, which became a conventional form of reaction against the optimism of modernism, never resulted in a commodification of violent death that in any way resembles the contemporary situation.

Death Goes Public

The development of new media such as the penny press and the rise of illustrated magazines and photojournalism in Europe and the United States played an important role in bringing death to the forefront of public attention. By the mid-nineteenth century, images of death, including obituaries and depictions of the deceased, were common in the popular periodicals. American, English, and Russian history of the nineteenth and early twentieth centuries contains episodes in which images of violent death invaded the everyday life. Those episodes may be referenced to highlight the differences between the representations of death at that time and in our day.

In Victorian England, when violent crime began to occupy an important place in the news, gruesome pictures flooded the penny press, which was gaining in popularity over the more sober weeklies.[91] Yet even if one agrees with Vicki Goldberg that these representations of death were the actual precursors of contemporary media violence, they had in any event disappeared from the penny press by the end of the nineteenth century.[92] One reason why violent images of death, oriented toward a not-yet-mass audience, had faded from the "gutter" press may be that the general readership considered such graphic details inappropriate and repugnant.[93] Indeed, those gross images stood in sharp contrast with the lifestyle and fashion of the time, dominated by *art nouveau*. Yet they were as distant from today's "pornography of death" as could be; even in that context, death was approached with all due decorum.[94] A prime example of this is the Victorian custom of photographing the deceased, carefully posed as if still living and often in the company of their living relatives. The clearly commemorative purpose of those portraits once again distinguishes them dramatically from current trends in photography discussed earlier. Yet it is still claimed that the Victorians were exceptionally obsessed with death and that they had a thorough-going "cult of death":

> Evidence of the Victorians' obsessive interest in death is as widely available in the imaginative literature of the period as it is in the theology. The deathbed scene, for example, was a familiar literary convention not only in prose fiction but also in narrative poetry and biography (. . .) Deathbed scenes and anthologies of poems for mourners are features of the "Victorian cult of death," together with mourning costume and jewelry, the elaborate plumes and other trappings of the Victorian funeral, black-edged mourning paper and envelopes, the gravestone and the pious epitaph and "God's acre," whether small country churchyard or vast urban necropolis.[95]

People have certainly been obsessed with death since prehistoric times, and the Victorian culture was no stranger to an acute awareness of and interest in death.[96] The Victorian "cult of death," though, has little in common with the contemporary practices that interest us here, except for the way it has been labeled by a modern scholar. For the Victorians, with their burgeoning sentimentalism, death signified an emotional and spiritual experience, and the veneration of death was never close to being regarded as entertainment or commodity. Furthermore, the Victorian upper class constituted the "happy few" of English society with the leisure and means to indulge itself in the commemoration of death; the bulk of the population exhibited no heightened interest whatsoever in what was known at the time as "the heavenly birthday."[97]

In America, death began to receive wide media exposure during the Civil War. Modern photography allowed the war to be directly depicted and to create an imagery of its horrors. The newspapers documented images of the battlefields and described the corpses of soldiers killed in action. Pictures also helped families learn what had happened to their relatives and to identify their dead. But as many researchers have pointed out, these pictures normally contained no mangled corpses; more often than not, the bodies of the dead were shown intact. Those photographs were "elegantly composed, most purposefully mediated," and in some cases were even staged. The premier photojournalists of the time—Mathew Brady, Alexander Gardner, and Timothy O'Sullivan—consistently created a "picturesque unity" of associations for viewers and readers.[98] Obviously in all these cases, the images of death had little in common with the voyeuristic images of the fictionalized dead that are so common today; their function was completely different. They carried a serious political, informational, or emotional message, and their goal was anything but entertainment.

In most Western countries, representations of death were widely used in nationalist discourse for various purposes, including the fostering of patriotic feelings.[99] War monuments that have become extremely popular since the end of the nineteenth century illustrate this point quite well. This use of death was powerfully developed later in the twentieth century. Symbolism, Decadence, and the Fin-de-siècle movement showed a great interest in physical decay and the supernatural. The preoccupation with the cult of Dionysus and the Eleusinian mysteries, the Gothic revival and the centrality of death in Nietzsche's philosophy, the nascent social sciences' fascination with suicide and death rites—all of this attests to the great significance of death as a theme in the intellectual life of the time.[100] Much like occultism and spiritualism, however, those trends enjoyed only limited circulation outside the cultural elite and the "educated" public. Decadent, pseudo-satanic entertainment venues such as the *Cabaret du Néant* or the *Cabaret de l'Enfer* in Paris would be the closest analogy to the death-focused entertainment of the present day were it not for their clear antireligious agenda: Satan and representations of hell dominated the imagery there, while, as we discussed in the introduction, today's death-centered entertainment may be many things, but it is not related to disapproval of Christian dogmas.

Prerevolutionary Russia is also illustrative of how easily images of death may intrude into daily life, in a way that may parallel the contemporary sit-

uation. Imperial Russian culture was profoundly influenced by the French
Fin-de-siècle, Decadence, and Symbolism. Explorations of the occult and
death-related imagery in literature, poetry, and art were immensely popular with the Russian elite: "Russian cultural elites of the turn of the century
followed European modernism in questioning positivism and rationalism.
Orthodoxy, forms of spiritualism, mysticism, and occult practices, including Satanism came into favor."[101] Spiritualism (also known as "spiritism"
or "table turning") was so fashionable among the Russian aristocracy and
the "educated" public in the last third of the nineteenth century that Leo
Tolstoy was moved to mock high-society séances in his play *The Fruits of
Enlightenment* (1889). And so ardent was the belief in spiritism that Dmitry
Mendeleev, author of the periodic table, set up a commission to critically
assess the issue and to counter it with scientific data.[102]

At the end of the nineteenth century, the mystical mindset overtook
several prominent intellectuals, including Vladimir Soloviev, a Russian philosopher and a Christian religious mystic who influenced Feodor Dostoevsky, the poet Alexander Blok, as well as the Russian Symbolists, among
many others.[103] A religious philosopher, Nikolay Fedotov, offered a doctrine that searched for the physical resurrection through religious belief.[104]
The theosophy of Helena Blavatskaya, the first attempts to establish a
theosophical society in Russia dating back to 1907, also resonated with
Russians. The scandalous influence that Grigory Rasputin, an illiterate
charlatan and mystic, had over the family of Nicholas II, Russia's last tsar, is
also symptomatic of the atmosphere prevailing there at the time. Rasputin's
influence with the royal family began with his apparent ability to stem the
bleeding of the severely hemophiliac crown prince Alexei, but his shocking
private life became a perpetual theme of antimonarchist propaganda.

The preoccupation with death grew into a mass phenomenon at the
very beginning of the twentieth century, a perilous time in Russian history
when the country was still reeling from its defeat in the Russo-Japanese
War and was roiled with social and political unrest. A plethora of skulls,
skeletons, and crossbones appeared in the "yellow" press, which targeted
the mass readership. These images, though, unlike those in the English
and American penny press, were not photos of war casualties, portraits of
heroic soldiers, or images of the victims of accidents or crimes. They were
satirical drawings that used death-related symbolism as political caricature.
Jeffrey Brooks, a prominent historian of Russia, asserts:

> The use of the occult and images of death distinguishes the satire
> of this period most clearly from its predecessors. When humor took

center stage in the 1860s and the 1880s, satirists used the occult playfully if at all. In contrast, the satirical magazines of 1905–1907, in the era of the First Russian Revolution were filled with truly foreboding harbingers of death. Among the most potent was the skeletal grim reaper.[105]

Images of death proliferated in low-cost satirical magazines and on wall posters, where death would be variously presented as a woman, an avenging angel, or any one of Russia's various nemeses.[106] Images of vampires and other nonhuman monsters also appear occasionally in those posters. This may seem to hint at a Russian version of the Gothic revival. Yet during that same period, literature was surprisingly free of representations of monstrous nonhumans.[107] The death symbolism was primarily engaged to sap the prestige of the ruling elite and call for the Revolution. The Grim Reaper expressed a radical rejection of moral limitations: nothing was considered out of bounds in undermining the authority of the tsarist regime and voicing political or social discontent. The intense application of death symbolism, which clearly functioned as political propaganda, is quite exceptional within the Modernist context:

> The magazines are not only decorated with skulls and demons; they are visually defined by them. The skeletal figure of death appears in a third of the left-leaning magazines in a sample of 277 issues from the larger University of Southern California collection. Monsters appear in about a third, and devils with claws or tails in almost fifteen percent. Skulls, ravening birds, splotches of blood, and corpses are too numerous to count.[108]

Death imagery, as Brooks has persuasively shown, played an important role in the radicalization of public opinion in Russia, a country on the road to a disastrous military defeat in the First World War, a ruthless Bolshevik coup d'état, and a bloody civil war. Pointed ideological propaganda and not entertainment were driving this deadly satire. The Bolsheviks employed the demonization and dehumanization of the "enemy" in their propaganda, since it offered them an important ideological tool for the mobilization of millions in the mass murder and havoc of the Red Terror, the Stalinist repressions, and the Second World War.[109]

As all these episodes show, representations of death were present in various ways in the daily life of previous centuries, but they never became an object of everyday consumption and routine entertainment for millions. Food, fashion, home décor and commercial advertisements remained untouched by death symbolism.

The Veneration of Death in Soviet Russia and Nazi Germany

Soviet communism and German fascism provide examples of cultures in which not only the elites but also the masses were involved in the veneration of death. Those regimes destroyed millions in a dramatically brief period of time, and millions were directly implicated in their crimes. As François Furet emphasized, both regimes were rooted in the unprecedented carnage of the First World War. Indeed, the Great War was gravid with revolution and the destruction of the existing social order.[110] The First World War formed a new attitude toward death and a new representation of it. The parallels between the Nazi and Soviet endorsement of "heroic death" rites, which originated in that agonizing experience, are numerous. German Nazis as well as Russian Bolsheviks were obsessed with memorializing "for eternity" the "sacrificial deaths of fallen soldiers" and with the glorification of military heroism that took extreme forms under these extremist regimes.[111] In both systems, funerals and rituals conducted on the graves of heroes provided far more important channels for state propaganda than was ever the case in the United States, the United Kingdom, or France. For Nazis and Soviets alike, the cult of the war dead and the political martyrography of deceased party leaders served to establish new expectations with regard to the sacrifices that the state could demand of its citizens.[112] In both cases, loyal subjects were expected to prepare themselves for a role in the violence, as either victims or perpetrators.

While the intellectual roots of Nazism and Bolshevism were very different,[113] both regimes took as their point of departure the radical critique of traditional humanism, which they utilized to justify extreme state violence (as discussed in chapter 1). For the Bolsheviks, the Marxist attack on traditional humanism was critical to the establishment of "proletarian humanism" and "proletarian morality." In Nazi Germany, the attack on traditional humanism was linked to mysticism. The cultish veneration of death was an important component of Nazi ideology. Saul Friedlander, for example, famously terms this ideology a "death cult," perceiving it as the "redemptive" motivation behind Hitler's drive to rid the world of Jews.[114] He demonstrates that the obsession with death manifested itself in various aspects of the Nazi culture, from mass murder to state-staged public funerals: "The important thing is the constant identification of Nazism and death; not real death in its everyday horror and tragic banality, but a ritualized, stylized, and aestheticized death."[115] The Nazi themselves used the term "cult of death." In 1936, for example, architect Wilhelm Kreis presented Hitler with his first sketches for setting "the heroic cult of death" into stone.[116] Friedlander also holds that "[t]he yearning for destruction and death" underpinned the Germans' attitude toward Hitler.[117] "To love death" was one of the mottos of the SS, while one of the Hitler Youth's more notorious slogans was "We were born to die for Germany." The aim of dying a violent death was further emblematically embodied in the Nazi cult of Horst Wessel.[118] Death was considered an act that united individuals, weaving them into the nation's destiny,[119] and the iconic double-edged blade signified the glory of death in battle and the duty to punish the enemies of the German state:[120] "Death, destruction and heroic self-sacrifice, the willingness to commit suicide for Germany, were key Nazi concepts especially during the Second World War."[121]

The occult also played an extremely important role in Nazi ideology and was critical to the development of the Nazi cult of death. As Nicholas Goodrick-Clarke points out in his book *The Occult Roots of Nazism*, the ideas of the ariosophists of Vienna were directly incorporated into Nazi doctrine, the Nuremberg racial laws of the 1930s, and the Nazi vision of a future of "racial purity."[122] The ariosophists had proclaimed the imminence of German world rule.[123] Believing that "inferior races" were conspiring against Germans and the German state, they established various secret orders dedicated to the revival of what they considered the "vanished esoteric knowledge." Unlike the Russian symbolists and decadents, who had never felt any affinity with uneducated Russians and had no interest in what they thought or felt, the ariosophists tried to merge occultism both with the volkish German nationalism and with long-standing and still current racial theories.[124] Central to those occult practices was the cult of Wotan, the principal god of the pagan Germanic pantheon, which contained some clearly sadistic and necromantic elements:

> In the Edda, Wotan was worshipped as the god of war and the lord of dead heroes in Valhalla. He was also identified as a magician and a necromancer in the poems. The 'Havamal' and 'Voluspa' described how Wotan performed ritual acts of self-torture in order to win the magical gnosis of natural mysteries.[125]

Notwithstanding the Nazis' heavy involvement with the occult, their endorsement of death-centered cults and rituals, and their veneration of Gothic and medieval symbolism, the appeal of death did not usher representations of death into all spheres of everyday life. The clothing or food carried no death symbols. Even the Totenkopf—a symbol featuring the skull and crossbones—appeared only on the uniform of the Stabswache (later the Schutzstaffel). Perhaps this was not coincidental, since the Totenkopf was not a Nazi invention. It dated back to a Hussar regiment formed in Prussia under Frederick the Great and had remained in use in the German army until 1918 before re-emerging under the Nazis.[126]

The Soviets, unlike the Nazis, could never permit the use the of word "cult," which had inappropriately religious connotations. Soviet society was officially atheist: religion was all but prohibited; many churches were demolished, closed or repurposed; and recalcitrant priests were imprisoned and executed.[127] But while the occult was never directly present in the Soviet discourse, Soviet propaganda was very much fixated on death and the dead. Bolsheviks adapted the figures of the nationalist rhetoric that had emerged in nineteenth-century Europe to serve its "internationalist" ideology. Death was understood as the noble and ultimate sacrifice for the cause of the working class, the Communist Party, the Soviet people, and so on.

Very soon after the Revolution of 1917, the funerals of Bolshevik leaders were already being exploited as an extremely powerful tool of ideological mobilization. The Bolsheviks had actually used funerals to promote their cause even before the Revolution, but only after the Bolshevik takeover did state-sponsored funerals reveal their true potential as a tool of ideological indoctrination. The first state funerals of soldiers who had died for the cause took place in 1918, at which time a "Revolutionary necropolis" was established on Moscow's Red Square.[128] The funeral of Yakov Sverdlov, a prominent party leader, in 1919 served to establish the key elements of the new "rites of the rulers."[129] Among these rituals, the embalming of Lenin's corpse and its public display in the Lenin Mausoleum is unique. The cult of Lenin, which revolved around his dead body, played an important role in the development of Soviet rites, mythology, and propaganda, as Nina Tumarkin has amply demonstrated.[130] The deaths and funerals of Bolshevik leaders were also used as pivotal points in Communist Party politics. Stalin perpetuated the tradition of staging grandiose funerals for political rivals that he had dispatched at the peak of their popularity and renown. Such was the case with Mikhail Frunze, Felix Dzerzhinsky, Sergo Ordzhonikidze, Sergei Kirov, and many others. Each funeral was followed by the creation of a posthumous cult, in which the dead leader was declared a symbol of "our common struggle" and had cities, streets, and ships named after him. Violently radical rhetoric directed against "the enemies of the proletariat" and the fomenting of a dark, shared hatred and "class anger" against the "socially alien" were enlisted to generate a sense of unity through the performance of histrionic acts of mourning.[131] The cults of dead leaders proved to be a highly effective tool of Soviet propaganda and contributed to the creation of a Soviet pantheon.[132] Loyalty to dead Soviet demigods who had sacrificed their lives "to the cause of working class," "to the happiness of all the peoples," etc. was so strongly inculcated into the minds of the Soviet masses as to prove an important resource in the rehabilitation of the Soviet regime under Vladimir Putin.[133] Yet the occult and death-related cults could never have been integrated into official Soviet doctrine. Stalinism claimed to be, in Romain Rolland's infamous words, "the last hope of humanity," the very image of a victory of science and reason.

We may conclude from our brief historical overview that despite certain superficial parallels, none of these episodes could be considered commensurate in scale or significance to the phenomenal contemporary fascination with death. The 1970s saw the beginning of a new phase in representations of death that gradually acquired a very specific meaning in contemporary culture and ultimately led to the emergence of the cult of death.

Death: A New Phenomenon?

As we have seen in this chapter, the beginning of the new millennium has witnessed the expansion of death into almost all spheres of social and cultural life. If in the post-Fordist period entertainment "has become one of the dominant sectors of the economy," today death occupies a central place in it.[134] Is it possible to demonstrate that the changes in social practices that we have observed are indeed manifestations of the cult of death as a new and distinct movement in popular culture?

The analysis of the reasons for the unexpected popularity of Halloween in the late 1980s may help shed light on the new meaning of the cult of death in contemporary culture and provide some preliminary explanations for the exponential growth in the commodification of violent death and the demand for it as a form of entertainment. One trend in Halloween studies holds that Halloween has grown into a favorite mass festival due to a "love of the macabre." The "powerful emotions" associated with death, such as fear and fantasy, and "the aura of mystery"[135] are often held responsible for the rising popularity of Halloween. Since "fear and fantasy are the strongest human emotions" and Halloween invokes both, that holiday is described as the motive force behind the growing interest in everything mystical over the past decade. Halloween is said to have created a demand for the mysterious and the supernatural, expressed in the popularity of Gothic music, the zombie craze, etc.[136] But, as discussed in the introduction, the psychological explanations are insufficient to fully account for the infatuation with death in today's culture. The opposite view reverses these causal relations and suggests that, on the contrary, vampire and zombie movies have been instrumental to the allure of Halloween. The choice of costumes influenced by currently popular films featuring zombies, vampires, or other representatives of the living dead seems to support this observation. Russia could be taken as a test case, since there the success of vampire movies and of the Harry Potter series in translation are clearly identifiable as primary sources of information on the holiday and the consequent adoption of Halloween into Russian culture. But this does not explain why there is such a compelling interest in zombies and vampires to begin with. The commercialization that drives Halloween has been offered as yet another explanation. Halloween is a relatively inexpensive holiday compared to Christmas or Thanksgiving; in fact, its affordability has most likely contributed to its popularity.[137] But there is also an opposing view that holds that financial considerations are basically irrelevant to the enthusiasm for Halloween.[138] The rise of neo-paganism and Wicca in the United States as well as in Russia has been also regarded as an important root of Halloween's popularity.[139] But the appeal of Halloween is clearly not restricted to adepts of witchcraft and pagan practices. Some scholars advance an argument that Halloween developed from a "marginal survivor of a dying tradition" into a "postmodern festival" due to its symbolism, which is rooted in pre-Christian paganism, combined with its ability to embrace elements of the popular culture, which makes this festival attractive to people of various ages, interests, and backgrounds.

But why did it lie dormant for so long before resurfacing now? And what are the symbols that feed the fascination it has for millions? Could the profound changes in the celebration of Halloween that occurred in the mid-1990s, as documented in a study of Halloween's expansion across America published in 2002, be responsible for its huge success?[140] Researchers left personal testimonials of the vast difference between the Halloween of the 1990s and their childhood memories of it:

> In addition to the public processions [parades that began in the late 1980s in New York and San Francisco—D.K.], I also noticed a rise in the number of homes that were decorated, often elaborately, for Halloween, to an extent that rivaled even Christmas. Whole families were now involving themselves in this late-year festival. (. . .) Unlike when I was a child, many parents today don costumes them-

selves to accompany their children on their rounds; many people handing out the treats also wear costumes.[141]

Back in the early 1990s, researchers were drawing attention to the murky side of the Halloween celebration by comparing it with more traditional holidays such as Christmas:

> Halloween is a little studied consumption holiday that is in several significant respects a mirror image of the other major American consumption holiday: Christmas. In the contemporary American Christmas celebration adults wear costumes (of Santa Claus) and extort good behavior from children with threats that rewards of durable goods will be withheld [. . .]. In contemporary Halloween celebrations, American children wear costumes (often of "evil" beings) and extort treats of nondurable goods from adults with threats of property destruction. (. . .) In Christmas rituals gifts are exchanged within the family and each is personally and lovingly acknowledged. In Halloween rituals non-family members provide gifts to masked and anonymous children who pose a vague menace.[142]

Readers of those early studies of Halloween were reminded of the festival's original meaning in Irish culture: "These associations with spirits, the dead, debauchery, and evil remain attached to contemporary Halloween celebrations."[143] In 1990, Belk relates the popularity of Halloween to a major refocusing of that holiday from children to adults, a change linked to those rumors about Halloween that were rife in the mid-1970s and early 1980s. The mid-1970s witnessed an upwelling of urban folklore concerning razor-spiked candy apples, poisoned "treats" given to children by strangers, and the abduction and murder of young children in some sinister Halloween ritual: "In the past two decades such fears have caused parents to prohibit or limit their children's trick-or-treating, have led hospitals to offer free X-rays of Halloween goodies."[144] By 1987 and 1988, these myths had reached so broad an audience as to cause "a nationwide panic."[145] And although the razor blades, poison, broken glass, and pins appear to have no basis in fact, the tales were widely disseminated, both orally and in the media, and commanded implicit belief. In parallel with those urban legends, a new trend begun by John Carpenter's *Halloween* in 1978 has produced several dozen Halloween-related horror movies that hit screens toward the end of October every year and play to packed houses.[146]

Belk interprets these cruel constructions on Halloween as an expression of social and political anxiety. He ties Halloween's popularity to a socio-political conjuncture, presenting Halloween as a way to exorcise anxiety stemming from society's reaction to a perceived loss of control. Follow-ing Wood, who described the resurgence of horror films in the 1970s and 1980s as a response to the rise of conservatism, religious fundamentalism, and AIDS, and the increased political, religious, and sexual repression that ensued, Belk believed that these factors could serve to explain Halloween's popularity.[147] Attempts to attribute its success to the angst caused by the Vietnam War or, later, to the misgivings engendered by the "divisive poli-tics and (. . .) uncertain economy" of the George W. Bush administration were once common, and their successors continue to proliferate to this day.[148] But why should social and political anxiety be mitigated through sadistic hoaxes or the observance of a pagan celebration of death rather than, say, through a stronger engagement with any of the existing holidays? And why should the macabre be necessary to the venting and remedying of political and social unease?

Bill Ellis also examined those urban legends and their influence on Hal-loween practices. Ellis confirms that none of the stories of tainted treats has ever been proven. He believes that the myths were a tool to restrict chil-dren's activities and bring the holiday under adult control, "claiming that those who rebel against adult-enforced Halloween 'rules' now risk death."[149] Ellis further suggests that the macabre legends allowed adults to take over the holiday by threatening children with the horrors of an adult world and that the scare tactics and the irrational fears they evoked constituted the core meaning of Halloween.[150] Passionately interested as he is in the child/adult dynamic, Ellis does not consider that the spread of those cruel hoaxes might signify more than an age-role reversal. The legends could have been invented because both adults and children wanted new myths and new sto-ries to express newly emerging attitudes.[151] However sanitized, safe, and respectable Halloween may appear in a well-to-do community, this does not change the nature of the cultural dynamic that drives it.

By the 1990s, thanks in part to those urban legends, the meaning of Halloween was readjusted to accommodate new realities and new longings. The ancient roots of the holiday, with its passion for sacrifice and yearning toward the dead, were revitalized and reinvigorated, spurring the holiday on to even greater success. The sadistic legends were critical for initiat-ing its popularity. This aspect of the festival cannot be overlooked simply because it is its supreme selling point, which is aggressively highlighted in promotional texts:

Everything a boy needs to make his Halloween the scariest ever is compiled right here. Blood, torn flesh, masks, slime, and more! Readers will unleash their inner mad scientist as they master their comprehension of procedural language. Photographs accompany step-by-step instructions that will guide even the most reluctant readers into creating their own Halloween horrors.[152]

Children being invited to liberate their "inner mad scientist" in preparation for Halloween, macabre Halloween legends, and Halloween-related horror movies, all of which emerged in the late 1970s and became popular in the 1980s, unequivocally relate the popularity of Halloween to the antihumanist and antimodern origins of that festival. Halloween's persistent association with violent death and human sacrifice—which may or may not be historically viable—accounts for its stunning success in the new cultural atmosphere of the 1990s. The exponentially growing renown of a festival that had been expected to "fade away" in the intellectual climate of the 1950s and 1960s is attributable to the new meaning that our contemporary culture has invested in it.[153] And further proof of this tendency is that other holidays are coopting Halloween to boost their own popularity, as Morton concludes in her recent study:

Halloween is becoming both more openly horrific, with increasingly violent and realistic haunted attractions, and extending its influence, both around the globe and throughout the year. In 2011, there were haunted attractions opened on other festivals—Sinister Pointe in Brea, California, for example, now offers themed hauntings at Christmas and Valentine's Day—and there is a trend toward year-round haunted attractions.[154]

Halloween's "success story" clearly indicates a growing demand for entertainment focused on violent death. It is driven by a denial of the exceptional value of human life that has become fashionable in contemporary culture.

Can we use these observations to throw light on the reasons behind the proliferation of other death-related beliefs and practices? Are there grounds to believe that the same emphasis on the idea of human sacrifice, the premodern attitudes to people, and the violence that inspired the Halloween revival was the driving force behind the spreading popularity of Santa Muerte worship in the early 2000s? Dark tourism is undoubtedly inhabited by a powerfully morbid curiosity in that it uses real settings to offer visitors a simulated involvement, in the role of "included observer," of heinous crimes of the past. Recent studies of dark tourism reveal that the owners of these sites and those who guide thanatotourists around them are not solely responsible for the gruesome excesses of the dark tourism fad. They are, in fact, responding to a mounting public demand for the images of violent death on which death-oriented fashion, entertainment, and other commercial ventures thrive.[155] It is not Halloween or death-centered entertainment per se that has nurtured this demand but the new attitude toward human beings that they express. Could the fixation on violent death and the rapid diversification of death-related practices, rooted as they are in a culture of resolute death denial, be regarded as an element in the commodification of death in contemporary culture?

The unprecedented upheaval in funeral rites that we have observed is part of a pattern of wider transformations. Anthropologists have identified a "surge of interest in ritual" and "anxiety over passages" in general, not only with respect to death.[156] From the 1980s on, the approach to ritual has become more innovative than ever before, to the point of making sense only to the individuals performing them, since "otherwise they are meaningless."[157] In other words, rituals are losing their collective meaning. The plethora of innovations in death-related social and cultural practices may be interpreted as one of the manifestations of postmodernity, which holds individualization and the rejection of tradition in high regard.[158] It may also be regarded, however, as an indication of confusion as to the very meaning of death and, therefore, as an important indicator of a changing system of values and beliefs relative to death.

Or when we consider what has rendered established rites redundant, why they have so often proven unsatisfying, and what has so profoundly disturbed the underpinnings of these social practices, one reason that comes compellingly to mind is a denial of previously traditional forms of human collectivity.[159] Given that all these innovations and activities are happening in the culture of radical death denial, dissociating oneself from the rest of "mortal humans" may have played some role in these reconsiderations. But to verify this hypothesis we will need to look more closely at the fiction and movies of popular culture to see how violent death is represented there and the new role that humans are accorded in these narratives. Let us turn now to popular fiction and movies featuring violent death. Their analysis will help us understand the intrinsic meaning of these cultural and social changes that we have discussed so far.

THREE

The Monsters and the Humans

We will focus now on the new cultural role of the monster. We will analyze how the adoration of undead monsters has affected our understanding of humanity, placed our most important food taboo in question, and promoted the cult of death. Using vampires as a case study but also with an eye to zombies, cannibals, serial killers, and ghosts, we will compare contemporary monsters with their nineteenth-century predecessors to evaluate the novelty of present-day thinking about monsters and humans. We will examine representations of nonhumans and violent death through the lens of human exceptionalism.

The Hobbit, the Monster's Godfather

Among the several contributions to the evolution of monsters to the lofty status of a new ideal, John Ronald Ruel Tolkien's works are in a class of their own. In a profound sense, Tolkien's writings did more to change globally the attitudes toward monsters and our understanding of their cultural role than Bram Stoker's prototypical Dracula had done for the image of the vampire. Tolkien was preparing his antihuman revolution and laying the foundations of Gothic Aesthetic in the 1930s, while still a professor at Oxford and not yet famous as the author of *The Lord of the Rings*.

The first impression from a tour of Tolkien's creative laboratory is that his writings are perplexing, with oddly dismissive and even offensive remarks regarding fellow scholars in the field of medieval English literature. Tolkien seemed skeptical about science in general and had deep reservations about current literary scholarship in particular. He was eager to point out that the understanding of *Beowulf*, a medieval English epic that he studied and greatly admired, had been "killed by Latin learning"[1] and that the banality was "so often the last revelation of analytical study."[2]

Tolkien's discontent with his fellow academics is clearly explained in his writings, where he reproaches his peers, among all else, for not giving the dragon the respect it was due. That viewpoint, he held, rendered them unable to penetrate into the world of the epic poem and hence incapable to interpret *Beowulf* in any meaningful way. Arguing the importance of the dragon, he compared his fellow academics' inability to comprehend the intent of *Beowulf*'s poet to the approach of a zoologist: "He [the author of *Beowulf*—D.K.] esteemed dragons, as rare as they are dire, as some do still. He liked them—as a poet, not as a sober zoologist; and he had good reason."[3]

Certainly, Tolkien was fundamentally correct in criticizing his fellow academics in medieval studies for their lack of appreciation for dragons. He could actually have said the same of art historians. Even Erwin Panofsky, in his *Gothic Architecture and Scholasticism*, pays so little attention to chimeras that he might as well have been studying not Gothic cathedrals but edifices designed by Le Corbusier.[4]

Why is the dragon so important to Tolkien? He responds clearly and thoughtfully to that question in his scholarly works: the dragon is needed to communicate a universal, transcendent meaning to the narrative. But more than that, as he states in his "Beowulf: The Monsters and the Critics":

> It is just because the main foes in Beowulf are inhuman that the story is larger and more significant than this imaginary poem of a great king's fall (. . .) [I]t stands amid but above the petty wars of princes, and surpasses the dates and limits of historical periods, however important.[5]

How should we interpret this statement? Is Tolkien claiming that the human res gestae and human history acquire their true significance from nonhuman feelings or forces? Is he arguing against anthropocentrism? In any event, a serious attitude toward the dragon as the nonhuman monster par excellence was actually made a foundational principle of the new aesthetic canon that Tolkien laid out in his academic writings.

According to Tolkien, the dragon animates in the reader a distinct spectrum of emotions, its presence producing what might be called "the pleasure of reading." "There could be no good poem without a dragon," he concludes. And:

> As for the poem, one dragon, however hot, does not make a summer, or a host; and a man might well exchange for one good dragon what he would not sell for a wilderness. And dragons, real dragons, essential both to the machinery and the ideas of a poem or tale, are actually rare.[6]

Leaving aside other possible interpretations of Tolkien's attitude toward dragons, let us focus on the one that is most germane to our purposes. He happens to have been the first to recognize the newly emerging demand for monsters in Western culture and the desire to have them as subjects of literature and the arts. "There are in any case many heroes but very few good dragons," Tolkien observes, in yet another broadside against human-centered fiction. It should be mentioned that the literature of modernity almost totally deprived readers of the pleasure of meeting monsters on its pages. Monsters were limited to the "low genres," such as the fairy tale or the Gothic novel. The rational aesthetics of the Enlightenment and modernity had created a firewall to protect serious literature and art from them.

Tolkien's ardent criticism of scientism in studies of medieval literature, as well as his fledgling career as a writer of fiction, could suggest that he already decided to pen an epic that would showcase a truly spectacular dragon and render all the rules of scientific rationality redundant.

The Dragon's Gift

Tolkien lays the foundations of Gothic Aesthetic in his "Beowulf" article, in which he maintains that the "illusion of historical truth" could be produced in literature and the other arts, even if their heroes are hobbits and dragons:

> The illusion of historical truth and perspective, that has made Beowulf seem such an attractive quarry, is largely a product of art. The author has used an instinctive historical sense—a part indeed of the ancient English temper (and not unconnected with its reputed melancholy), of which *Beowulf* is a supreme expression; but he has used it with a poetical and not an historical object.[7]

The elements of Gothic Aesthetic that he discovered stem from a deep disenchantment with humanity and human civilization, which he traces back to the medieval epic he so admired. Analyzing *Beowulf,* Tolkien shows that the central element of its poetics is based on the idea of defeat: downfall is the destiny of kings, heroes, and simple mortals: "The monsters had been the foes of the gods, the captains of men, and within Time the monsters would win."[8]

People have no chance of controlling their destiny, while the only reward for heroic resistance is death, Tolkien pessimistically concludes: "Disaster is foreboded. Defeat is the theme. Triumph over the foes of man's precarious fortress is over, and we approach slowly and reluctantly the inevitable victory of death."[9]

Tolkien's main aesthetic principle is a disregard for human beings, who are, according to him, no longer the measure of all things. By the 1990s, this new aesthetic would inject new life into vampires, zombies, werewolves, and witches, the true masters of contemporary culture.

There are obvious reasons why the medieval English epic was such an important source of inspiration for Tolkien. He had been deeply affected by his service in World War I. He wrote his articles between two wars, in the bleak atmosphere portrayed by Erich Maria Remarque and Evelyn Waugh. And for this reason alone, the profound cultural pessimism of the medieval epic may have sat well with him. Deeply disappointed with humans for their inability to meet his high moral standards, Tolkien decided to replace them with hobbits, elves, and so forth, thus creating a universe that readily accommodated dragons. For the first time since the dawn of modernity, an epic appeared whose principal protagonists and positive heroes were non-humans. Monsters became the focal point of interest and attraction that had earlier been reserved for people. In Tolkien's writings, hobbits further his advocacy of the dragon in literature because, no less than the dragon, the hobbit too negates human subjectivity and the significance of people as ideal of art.

Tolkien summarized this idea as follows: "He is a man, and that for him and many is sufficient tragedy."[10] But he is not referring here to the vicissitudes of human existence in the sense of ancient Greek tragedy or Shakespearean drama. He is, rather, implying that humans are inferior and imperfect creatures. Contrary to the admiration for the perfection of human nature inspired by the Enlightenment and the core belief of the aesthetics of modernity—which consistently presented people as the victors, even if only spiritually—Tolkien radically challenges that aesthetic canon. A determined denial of anthropocentrism, which had been modernity's uncontested ideal, becomes a necessary part of his aesthetic system. Hobbits and dragons take over from people in Tolkien's writings and inhabit a new universe in which humans, their history, and their culture have no role to play. Hobbits, a nonhuman species and therefore categorizable as monsters (although they have high morals and do not drink human blood), oust people from the focus of the writer's and the reader's attention and sympathies. Curiously enough, aside from their shared symbolic role, Dracula and hobbits have one morphological feature in common: Dracula has hairy palms, while hobbits have hairy feet.

Yet critics have consistently overlooked this antihumanist aspect of Tolkien's work; on the contrary, they stress the anthropomorphism and humanism of his protagonists. A common reading of Tolkien's prose is that of a coming-of-age novel that offers sublime moral lessons to children and even teaches them Christian morality.[11] When speaking of "nonhumans," critics generally mean elves, dragons, and so forth, but not hobbits, whom they consider human by default.[12] Clearly, the critics are still underestimating the dragon and his kin!

Another important secret that the dragon offers Tolkien in exchange for his future popularity is that the dragon, an incarnation of evil, is a concrete and personified horror. But the source and origins of this evil remain as mysterious and enigmatic in Tolkien's epic as they were in *Beowulf*.

Certainly, Tolkien, a devout Roman Catholic, endows hobbits with the strong moral compass that humans clearly lack in his eyes. Yet he obviously misjudged the dragon's influence on morality, and it is interesting to watch him negotiating the differences between his own morality and the moral maxims that prevail in *Beowulf*.[13] Sometimes he feels uncomfortable about the moral norms of medieval England that he observes there and even criticizes them eventually. Yet he still strives to reconcile his beloved protagonists' moral judgments with his own. For example, he is initially repulsed by the treatment of vassals in *Beowulf*, which is characterized by utter ignorance and irresponsibility that the vassals are required to repay with undivided loyalty. Later in his discussion of *Beowulf*, however, this principle is translated into a romantic ideal of "heroic love and obedience." In other words, the aesthetic system Tolkien created in consequence of his admiration of the medieval epic has a strong potential to impact moral judgments. The nonhuman universe of Middle-earth, with its nonhuman population, is hardly an ideal environment for the preservation of a human morality. Can moral judgments even exist in a world where people, and their lives and dignity, are disregarded and humanity is not the highest value?

Since John Ruskin's *The King of the Golden River* (1841) and George MacDonald's *The Princess and the Goblin* (1871), magic and supernatural phenomena have been crucial to fantasy plots. Medieval, mythical, legendary and folkloric characters are expected to provide moral examples for children to follow. Alice of Lewis Carroll's *Alice in Wonderland*, Wendy of J. M. Barrie's *Peter Pan*, and Dorothy of L. Frank Baum's *The Wonderful Wizard of Oz* conditioned the reception of fantasy as juvenile literature, which was clearly articulated by C. S. Lewis in his "On Juvenile Tastes." Fantasy's close relationship with fairy tales has preconditioned the anthropocentric, humanistic interpretation of Tolkien's works, even though his epic universe does not require the existence of humans in order to function perfectly well. This feature has also concealed Tolkien's significance as the first writer to position nonhuman creatures—hobbits and dragons—as protagonists of literature not for children now but for adults.

The Bloodsucker: A New Aesthetic Ideal

The Vampire, a Hero of Our Time?

"Where are the Bibles in your bookstore?" "Look in the bestseller section. They're right next to *Twilight*." But while there is indeed a true word spoken in jest, Stephenie Meyer's novel *Twilight* (2005), which has been translated into thirty-seven languages, has not conquered the globe singlehandedly. Other vampire sagas—for example, *The Vampire Diaries* (novel series by L. J. Smith; TV series written and produced by Kevin Williamson and Julie Plec, 2009) and the TV series *True Blood* (Alan Ball, 2008)—are successfully competing with it in the international market for vampire films and fiction.[14] As David Punter and Glennis Byron put it, "no other monster has endured, and proliferated, in quite the same way—or been made to bear such a weight of metaphor" as the vampire.[15] To appreciate the scale of the international vampire boom, one need only consider the rapidly growing subculture that involves vampire role playing and the enormous popularity of vampire fan sites.[16] The intense emotions expressed by both American and Russian teenagers on the vampire forums—"I would give up everything to become a vampire!"[17]—have even prompted some observers to believe that horror may be well-positioned to become a new form of religion.[18] Indeed, Russian audiences that read fiction and watch North American films more often than domestically produced offerings are equally enthralled by those vampire sagas. The Russian vampire subculture that has grown up around the vampire boom in Anglo-American fiction and movies is similar to its counterpart in the United States, and there is little to distinguish Russian vampire fan sites from those hosted in America. That said, post-Soviet vampires appear only occasionally on the international vampire market. Among Russian vampire novels, *Night Watch* (1999) by Sergei Lukyanenko (now available in English due to its remarkable success in Russia) is a rare case. But this international underrepresentation of Russian vampire texts is not particularly surprising.

Vampires are in no way a post-Soviet, Soviet, or even Russian invention. The cultural origins of vampires in the Western European literature is so exhaustively researched that there is probably no need to reiterate it here. As for Russia, *The Vampire* (1841), a novella written by Count Alexei Tolstoy, is the first piece of Russian prose dedicated to vampires, but it can hardly be argued that even this story sprang from an authentic folk tradition. On the contrary, it is clear that Tolstoy's tale echoes the vogue for vampires in Western Europe, especially in England and France. His first vampire story, *La Famille du Vourdalak* (1839), was actually written and first published in French; its Russian translation followed much later. Early literary portrayals of vampires—Lord Byron's "The Giaour" (1813), "Christabel" (1816) by Samuel Taylor Coleridge, "The Vampyre" (1819) by John Polidori, and "La Morte amoureuse" (1836) by Théophile Gautier—were well-known and had been enthusiastically received by the Russian reading public, which usually did not have long to wait before works originally written in English, such as the first three in our list, appeared in French translation.[19] Since the literacy of the time primarily involved a good knowledge of French, the translations into Russian would come later, if at all.

Vampires, however, remained peripheral to Russian art and literature during the nineteenth and twentieth centuries, meriting only a passing mention in the poetry and prose of the time. In that respect, Alexander Pushkin's short verse *Vourdalak* (1835) is highly representative: it is a comical piece that mocks Vanya, a poor, scared boy who mistakes a dog for a vourdalak in a cemetery at night. Beginning in the late 1830s, under the commanding leadership of literary critic Vissarion Belinsky (1811–1848), Russian opinion makers considered social criticism and the struggle for a better future to be the main purpose of literature, and for that reason, nineteenth-century Russian prose was dominated by the Natural School (a Russian version of Realism), which wanted no truck with vampires.

The early-twentieth-century vampire craze in Western Europe sparked by Bram Stoker's *Dracula* (1897) made little impact on either Russian literature or art. In fact, it took fifteen years for the Russian translation of

Dracula to appear. Even under the influence of the Fin-de-siècle movement, Russian literature was not all that receptive to nonhuman monsters. And the brief Gothic revival that affected mainly the penny press at the turn of the twentieth century made little impression on literature on the eve of the Bolshevik takeover.

Under the Soviet regime, vampires were given short shrift, since "socialist realism," the only aesthetic trend officially permitted by the Communist Party from the 1930s on, frowned on the supernatural.[20] Every phenomenon had to be explained in material and realistic terms in accordance with Marxist ideas of history, culture, and society. The few works in this genre by the classical writers of the nineteenth century were tolerated, but in Soviet times it would have been absolutely impossible to publish a new nonsatirical novel featuring, for example, vampires. It was not until the mid-1990s, after the collapse of the USSR, that nonhuman monsters—primarily vampires—began to enjoy unprecedented popularity in Russia in the wake of the international vampire boom.[21]

The Beauty of the Dead

A comparison of contemporary vampire bestsellers with the classics of vampire fiction and film allow us to address three central questions. First, who are the protagonists of contemporary vampire texts (films or novels)? Second, how do vampires relate to humans? And, finally, how culturally particular are the contemporary vampires as compared to their literary and cinematographic predecessors?

The response to the first question reveals an important aspect of present-day vampire films and fiction: the modern vampire is the protagonist and often the narrator, and his or her feelings and emotions are central to the story. To give just a couple of examples: in the film *Interview with the Vampire* (Neil Jordan, 1994), vampire Louis, who has been "turned" by the powerful and enigmatic vampire Lestat, is the one who tells the tale. In the television series *Kindred: The Embraced* (John Leekley, 1996), Julian Luna, the protagonist, is a vampire "prince," while in the hit movie *Only Lovers Left Alive* (Jim Jarmusch, 2013), the two principal protagonists, Adam and Eve, are vampires.

But this is by no means an American peculiarity; vampires hold the same strategically important position in Russian vampire blockbusters. The vampire Anton, protagonist and narrator of Sergei Lukyanenko's cult novel *Night Watch*, recounts a story whose main characters are all vampires, werewolves, witches, or shape-shifters.[22] In another famous post-Soviet vampire novel, *Empire V: The Story of a True Superman* (2006) by Victor Pelevin, the narrator is the neophyte vampire Roma.[23]

The term I will use for movies and novels whose primary protagonist and/or narrator is not a human but a vampire, through whose eyes we see the story, is the strong model of vampire texts. The privilege of being the first-person narrator is not, of course, restricted to vampires: werewolves and zombies are equally likely to assume that role. For example, in the movies *Wasting Away* (Matthew Kohnen, 2007) and *Warm Bodies* (Jonathan Levine, 2013) and Hugh Howey's novel *I, Zombie* (2012) the events are narrated from the zombie's point of view. And Jacob, a werewolf, is the narrator in *Breaking Dawn*, the concluding book in the *Twilight* saga. Pelevin has also published two books other than *Empire V* that feature nonhumans as their primary protagonists and first-person narrators, *The Sacred Book of the Werewolf* (2004), which is the diary of a were-fox, and *Batman Apollo* (2013), narrated by a vampire. In one of Pelevin's early stories, the main protagonist, Sasha, is a young scientist who turns into a werewolf.[24]

The weak model includes those vampire sagas that feature people among the central protagonists. As examples of the weak model, one could cite the first three books of the *Twilight* series (*Twilight*, *New Moon*, and *Eclipse*), in which Bella Swan, a schoolgirl, begins dating Edward Cullen, a vampire, and wants to become a vampire like him. A love triangle develops involving Bella, Edward, and a werewolf, Jacob Black. Bella marries Edward, and when she dies giving birth to their child, her husband finally "turns" her. A similar love triangle between a girl and two vampires is presented in *The Vampire Diaries*. Here, Elena Gilbert, the young protagonist who is in love with a vampire, also becomes a vampire herself. *True Blood*, another American television drama series, features a love story between a girl and a vampire. Van Helsing in the movie *Van Helsing* (Stephen Sommers, 2004) offers another example: at the end of the movie, Van Helsing kills Dracula but is himself transformed into a werewolf.

In this respect there is a remarkable difference between contemporary vampire stories and the classics of the vampire genre. Vampires first appeared in poetry, in Heinrich Augustus Ossenfelder's "Der Vampir" (1748), followed by Samuel Taylor Coleridge's long narrative poem *Christabel* (First part, 1797), and Robert Southey's *Thalaba the Destroyer* (1801). But vampires had to wait almost two decades after *Christabel* before making their debut in literary prose. The first published vampire tale was *The Vampyre* (1819), written by John William Polidori, who had been motivated by the same contest that inspired Mary Shelley to produce her *Frankenstein*.

The vampire of his tale—one Lord Ruthven—bears some of the traits of Lord Byron, to whom Polidori was a personal physician and to whom his story was initially attributed. Ruthven is, however, not the protagonist here but an unpleasant and undeniably dangerous antagonist. In Alexei Tolstoy's *La Famille du Vourdalak*, the first-person narrator of the tale within a tale is the young and handsome Marquis d'Urfé, who tells the story of his encounters with vampires in Serbia to amuse a society gathering. The narrator of Joseph Sheridan Le Fanu's *Carmilla* (1872) is a girl named Laura, who tells how she befriended Carmilla, a beautiful young woman later discovered to be Countess Mircalla Karnstein, a vampire. Here, as in numerous less distinguished nineteenth- and twentieth-century vampire narratives (both fiction and films), the characters who convey the story to us, whose emotions the audience shares and whose sufferings it sympathizes with, are not vampires but human beings. Likewise, Bram Stoker's paradigmatic *Dracula* (1897) is an assemblage of several accounts written by human protagonists, not a tale told by a vampire.

This is also true of the early vampire movies. In *Le Manoir du diable* (Georges Méliès, 1896), which pioneered this genre on film, Mephistopheles appears as a bat and eventually vanishes at the sight of a crucifix wielded by a noble chevalier. In *Nosferatu, A Symphony of Horror* (F. W. Murnau, 1922) the vampire is a repulsive antagonist. In *Dracula* (Tod Browning and Karl Freund, 1931), the vampire, despite Bela Lugosi's eerie charm, is still an evil antagonist. The role of monsters in these vampire tales as well as in other stories was therefore limited and secondary, as a source of horrors or marvels, a symbol of seductive evil or a backhanded tribute to the triumph of good. Human sentiments, rather than those of nonhuman monsters, were the prime focus here. This pattern persisted in vampire narratives from the mid-eighteenth century until the late 1970s to mid-1980s, at which point people were replaced by monsters as protagonists and narrators. Consequently, the target of the audience's identification underwent a seismic displacement.

It is this shift in cultural dominance—from anthropocentric to a nonhuman focus—that makes the figure of the monster so crucial to our understanding of contemporary culture. It might be best illustrated by Stuart Beattie's movie *I, Frankenstein* (2014), which is told from the viewpoint of the monster (now named Adam). The reader need hardly be reminded that the protagonist of Mary Shelley's novel, through whose eyes we observe the events, is the scientist Victor Frankenstein, not the monster he created.[25]

Contemporary vampires have not only taken the structural place of humans in the narratives: compared to people, they are also omnipotent and invincible. Classical vampire texts offer several ways to kill a vampire, with a silver bullet, for example, or a wooden stake.[26] Until recently, those methods were sufficient to secure a human victory over the vampire and were powerful enough to destroy even Dracula. But now the old remedies are less effective. In fact, according to Stephenie Meyer, humans are altogether incapable of killing a vampire. In Lukyanenko's *Night Watch*, people are completely helpless against vampires; only a werewolf or a superior vampire can end the life of an inferior one. In other novels and movies, vampires can be killed by sunshine, fire, or the bite of a werewolf. Barring that, however, vampires are immortal and superior to humans in every possible respect: they can fly; they possess magical powers; they can read the thoughts of mortals and set objects ablaze by the sheer force of their will. They are able to pass through walls and foresee the future. These fantastic qualities of contemporary vampires match their traditional qualities well, with one important exception: at some point in the traditional Gothic tale, vampires invariably show themselves as the hideous creatures; like Dracula, whom the narrator, Jonathan Harker, observes with great disgust:

> There lay the Count, but looking as if his youth had been half restored. (. . .) The mouth was redder than ever, for on the lips were gouts of fresh blood, which trickled from the corners of the mouth and ran down over the chin and neck. Even the deep, burning eyes seemed set amongst swollen flesh, for the lids and pouches underneath were bloated. It seemed as if the whole awful creature were simply gorged with blood. He lay like a filthy leech, exhausted with his repletion. I shuddered as I bent over to touch him, and every sense in me revolted at the contact. (. . .) A terrible desire came upon me to rid the world of such a monster.[27]

Poor Harker had been physically repelled by the creature's proximity at their first encounter, before he had even had time to learn what exactly he was dealing with:

> As the Count leaned over me and his hands touched me, I could not repress a shudder. It may have been that his breath was rank, but a horrible feeling of nausea came over me, which, do what I would, I could not conceal.[28]

In Le Fanu's *Carmilla*, the memories of Countess Mircalla, despite her beauty, fill the young narrator's heart with horror as Laura recollects her girlfriend as a monstrous vampire:

It was long before the terror of recent events subsided; and to this hour the image of Carmilla returns to memory with ambiguous alternations—sometimes the playful, languid, beautiful girl; sometimes the writhing fiend I saw in the ruined church.[29]

And Snedka, the beautiful Serbian peasant girl from *La Famille du Vourdalak*, turns into a hideous skeleton right in front of the bewitched marquis.[30]

Vampires in contemporary texts can be frightening, but they are never intended to be repulsive. If they ever turn into animals—as, for example, in *Kindred: The Embraced* and *The Vampire Diaries*—these transformations only make them more appealing and intriguing. Even a metamorphosis into a bat is described in such an outstandingly artistic way by Victor Pelevin in *Empire V* that the reader is completely won over by the bizarre hermeneutics of the vampire's inner experience.[31] None of this has anything in common with Harker's squeamish description of Dracula crawling "in a sidelong way" down the castle wall like a monstrous lizard.[32] Animalistic features were widely used in the classical stories only to emphasize the vampire's monstrosity. Carol Senf, for example, points out that Dracula and the other vampires in Stoker's iconic book are represented as an entirely different species, closer to animals than to humans.[33] The fact that Dracula himself moves like an animal—or even a reptile—is designed to disgust the reader as "something so unhuman that it seemed to sober us all from the shock of his coming."[34]

In a striking contrast, every contemporary vampire saga shows vampires as supernaturally beautiful. This is the impression that they make on a schoolgirl in *Twilight*:

The tall one was statuesque. She had a beautiful figure, the kind you saw on the cover of the Sports Illustrated swimsuit issue, the kind that made every girl around her take a hit on her self-esteem just by being in the same room. Her hair was golden, gently waving to the middle of her back. (. . .)

I stared because their faces, so different, so similar, were all devastatingly, inhumanly beautiful. They were faces you never expected to see except perhaps on the airbrushed pages of a fashion magazine. Or painted by an old master as the face of an angel.[35]

And the vampire Edward Cullen is described in even more glowing terms:

I couldn't imagine how an angel could be any more glorious. There was nothing about him that could be improved upon. (. . .) Edward in the sunlight was shocking. I couldn't get used to it, though I'd been staring at him all afternoon. His skin, white despite the faint flush from yesterday's hunting trip, literally sparkled, like thousands of tiny diamonds were embedded in the surface. He lay perfectly still in the grass, his shirt open over his sculpted, incandescent chest, his scintillating arms bare. His glistening, pale lavender lids were shut, though of course he didn't sleep. A perfect statue, carved in some unknown stone, smooth like marble, glittering like crystal.[36]

Vampires are also elegant and have undeniable good taste. But beyond their physical perfections, they are also artistically gifted, and their intelligence and social skills match their other abilities, surpassing those of humans in every way. Vampires are, in addition, denizens of high culture. In *Kiss of the Damned* by Xan Cassavetes (2013), vampires represent a refined artistic elite. But perhaps the most telling recent example of this trend is the film *Only Lovers Left Alive*, in which all the achievements of human culture are ascribed to vampires, who over time have composed the world's greatest music and written most of Shakespeare's plays.

Ever since the Renaissance, people—their nature, body, and mind—have been considered the epitome of aesthetic perfection. In contemporary vampire sagas, however, people are not even worthy to consort with such perfect creatures as vampires. In fact, the human protagonists are there mainly to share with the readers the humiliation of comparison, as Bella does in this fragment: "He was too perfect, I realized with a piercing stab of despair. There was no way this godlike creature could be meant for me."[37] Yet this is relatively low-key in comparison with the allure of the vampires portrayed in Hollywood movies by the likes of Brad Pitt and Kate Beckinsale.

Importantly, the authors of vampire sagas explicitly compare people to vampires, stressing the bungling unattractiveness of the human protagonist. For example, Bella Swan in *Twilight* is described as at best a maladroit girl with few, if any, redeeming qualities. Even on her wedding day, standing alongside the female vampires, she looks unattractive and gauche. One of vampires has to use all her skills to bring her physical appearance up to par. *Night Watch* is also rife with descriptions of human mediocrity:

I ran past the bright shop windows with their displays of fake Gzhel ceramics and stage-set heaps of food. There were cars rushing past me along the avenue, a few pedestrians. That was all fake too, an illusion, just one facet of the world, the only one accessible to human beings. I was glad I wasn't one of them.[38]

The people in Pelevin's novel are so socially inept and intellectually underdeveloped that neophytes vampires have to be put through a training program that focuses on "discourse and glamour" designed to bring them to the requisite level of social aplomb and philosophical sophistication. Pelevin's protagonist Roma, recently "turned" and now sporting his vampire name, Rama, conceptualizes the human adoration of vampires in this way:

> For some strange reason people tend to idealize vampires. We are portrayed as refined stylists, solemn romantics, pensive dreamers— and always with a great deal of sympathy. Vampires are played by attractive actors; in video clips, pop stars are delighted to impersonate them. In the West and in the East, no celebrity finds it shameful to play a vampire. It really is peculiar—child molesters and violators of tombs are much closer to the average man than we vampires are. Yet there is no sympathy for them in human art. But vampires are indulged with compassion, understanding and love.[39]

This adoration is not limited to the fictional world. The fact that *Forbes* magazine accepts articles that exploit vampire themes provides another indication of the vampire's all-embracing popularity in contemporary culture.[40] The various lists of "vampire baby names" available on the Internet is yet another expression of this odd infatuation with the undead.[41] Siblings of the dragon that once caught Tolkien's fancy, vampires represent Gothic Aesthetic better than any other monster because they incarnate the nonhuman ideal of our times.

Coming-of-Death Novel

Contemporary vampire stories—both novelistic and cinematographic— feature another important similarity. Many of them happen to be Bildungsroman or coming-of-age novels. Since the inception of the genre in the late eighteenth century, the main purpose of such narratives has been to help adolescents become adults according to the cultural norms of their society and their time. As critics have repeatedly emphasized, such tales as *Twilight, The Vampire Diaries, Interview with the Vampire*, and *Empire V* revolve around an adolescent on the brink of adulthood experiencing a first love or a first mature relationship. The point that critics have missed, however, is the impact on human protagonists of having the living dead as a role model. There can be no misunderstanding about the nature of this particular variety of the coming-of-age novel. The role model that young readers are being offered here is not that of a human being but of an undead monster. As Damon Salvatore, a vampire protagonist in *The Vampire Diaries*, eloquently states, "I like being a living dead person."[42]

All vampire stories—the old and new—treat vampires as the undead. In the vampire classics, vampires literally slept the days away in their coffins. Readers of *Dracula* will certainly remember Jonathan Harker's diary entry for June 30, which describes Count Dracula lying in his coffin. Dracula was even obliged to travel with that coffin and some soil from his gravesite. While this venerable custom has remained intact in some contemporary stories such as *Interview with the Vampire* and *Van Helsing*, most modern vampires would not dream of behaving in such an outmoded way. All that remains of it is the vampire's fear of sunlight, as it is the case in *The Vampire Diaries*, in *Kindred: The Embraced*, and *The Queen of the Damned* (Michael Rymer, 2002). In *Twilight*, the vampire's skin only glistens in the sun. In *Empire V*, meanwhile, Pelevin has proposed what may be the most original substitute for the coffin: a vampire spends his time off in a kind of closet known in the vampire vernacular as a "hamlet," hanging head-down like a bat.

Expectedly, in contemporary vampire sagas—for example *Empire V*, *The Twilight Saga*, and *The Vampire Diaries* (2009–)—the human protagonist (a girl or, less frequently, a boy) is always in serious trouble.[43] The opening scene of *Empire V* describes the murder of the young male protagonist by a vampire. We see Bella Swan and Elena Gilbert wounded and covered in blood; as the target of a vampire hunt; being kidnapped as a prelude to being killed; or barely surviving a car accident. The first words of *Twilight* describe a teenager having a nightmare about her murder totally in agreement with nightmare hypnotics of Gothic Aesthetic: "I'd never given much thought to how I would die—though I'd had reason enough in the last few months—but even if I had, I would not have imagined it like this."[44] These stories center on a lonely teenager who is not particularly smart and (certainly in the case of Bella Swan as conceived by Stephenie Meyer) not beautiful, who puts himself or herself into a variety of perilous situations, often taking suicidal risks. And the descriptions of these episodes are nothing if not graphic:

I was definitely sick now. There was pain coming, I could see it in his eyes. It wouldn't be enough for him to win, to feed and go. There would be no quick end like I'd been counting on. My knees began to shake, and I was afraid I was going to fall. (. . .) Then he slumped forward, into a crouch I recognized, and his pleasant smile slowly widened, grew, till it wasn't a smile at all but a contortion of teeth, exposed and glistening.[45]

The vampire saga trivializes acts of violence against people and assigns to humans a victim status that reinforces the internal plausibility and coherence of this variety of the "coming-of-death novel." Even the most "romantic" vampire sagas, such as *Twilight*, leave us in no doubt that the vampire is not just a lover. Vampires kill people, and generally do so with great gusto:

She smiled a wide, ominous smile. "We have another fairly superfluous weapon. We're also venomous," she said, her teeth glistening. "The venom doesn't kill—it's merely incapacitating. It works slowly, spreading through the bloodstream, so that, once bitten, our prey is in too much physical pain to escape us. Mostly superfluous, as I said. If we're that close, the prey doesn't escape."[46]

Torture and violent death are what await human protagonists under the guidance of the dead in these coming-of-death novels. For example, in *Twilight* Bella tries to commit suicide by jumping off a cliff so that she can be "turned" into a vampire. The description of her wedding night, when she is described as destroyed by coitus with her undead groom, is rife with sexual violence, as graphic as is the account of her death, which comes as she gives birth to Edward's child. It is perhaps no coincidence that the novel *Fifty Shades of Grey*, which features scenes of extreme sexual violence, was originally a fanfic piece written by a *Twilight* aficionado.[47]

Literary scholars have argued that the vampire narratives are escapist literature that especially appeals to young adults on the verge of adulthood.[48] And the psychologists have shown that readers have a propensity to identify with the nonhuman protagonists: "Both implicit and explicit measures revealed that participants who read about wizards psychologically became wizards, whereas those who read about vampires psychologically became vampires."[49] This is not all that surprising when one considers the strikingly high number of people who believe that vampires, witches, zombies, etc. are real. According to a Gallup study, three in four Americans believe in various paranormal entities, including ghosts, the living dead, and witches.[50]

The Monster's Food

We are ready now to take a closer look at human-vampire relationships. One of the most frequent arguments put forward to explain the popularity of vampire novels is the focus of their narratives on romantic love. Yet the question why our culture needs a man-eating monster to communicate this feeling—central to the novel since Longus—remains unanswered. All the twisted romances between humans and contemporary vampires notwithstanding, the bottom line is that humans are the vampire's natural prey and favorite food. We will begin by discussing the works of two popular post-Soviet writers, Victor Pelevin and Sergei Lukyanenko.

Pelevin's *Empire V* is a story told by a recently "turned" vampire who begins by recollecting a black bat that hung on the wall by his bedside in his childhood.[51] The nightmare in Pelevin's novel *Empire V* is launched by the murder of a boy, Roma, by Brahma, a vampire. Brahma bites Roma, kills him, and transplants into his dead body the vampire's tongue that is the essence of vampire:

> Maybe my whole vampire career is just that—death—and I am trying to hide it from myself? (. . .) I tried to suppress the thought but could not. On the contrary, I kept finding new proofs of that horrible idea. I remembered that vampires had forever been considered the living dead. By day, blue and cold, they lie in their coffins, rising only by night to warm themselves with hot blood. (. . .) Maybe to completely turn into a vampire one must simply die?[52]

This new creature, a vampire now called Rama II, is the novel's first-person narrator; through his eyes we see the story unfold. Rama is trained by vampires in their habits and rituals and, most importantly, in their philosophy and mythology. Older vampires explain their origins to Rama. They are all descendants of a primordial bat that was the beginning of everything. He also learns that since the dawn of time, vampires have bred humans like cattle to feed on their blood and mental energy. The cultivation of humans involves complex undertakings such as the invention of culture and civilization (and, more importantly, of money and philosophy), which are necessary to keep people in the dark about their purpose and help the vampires effortlessly govern them. Here is how Emil Maratovitch, a mentor-vampire, explains the issue to his protégés:

> [V]ampires consider humans as cattle, bred like livestock (. . .) vampires decided to switch from beef cattle to dairy farming. They decided to create cattle that they could milk. This is the origin of humans.

And when the narrator-vampire asks, "And how did the vampires create humans?" the mentor explains, "The correct way of putting it is to say 'breed,' not 'create.' It happened in the same way as dogs and sheep were bred by humans."[53]

Although Rama is taught that modern vampires do not consume human blood on a daily basis, which would be uncouth, humans still have no purpose other than to nourish their overlords. Emil Maratovitch continues to lecture Rama:

> Humans are part of our food chain. Like a Frenchman and a frog, or like a Frenchman and a tomb-worm. Humans think they are the height of creation because they can eat everything they please, any time they please, how and as much as they please. Human self-respect is based on this notion. But in fact, there is a higher stage of the food chain of which most of them are simply unaware. That is we vampires. We are the highest link of the food chain on Earth. (. . .) Vampires are not only the highest link in the food chain but also the most human link. The most highly moral link.[54]

The human body can also be made to carry the "tongue" that transforms it into a vampire. And when that body grows old, the tongue simply finds a new one to inhabit.

In Lukyanenko's *Night Watch*, the two clans of Dark and Light vampires who govern all other monsters are engaged in a global struggle for dominance. People have no role to play in that war nor can they influence its results. The vampires decide their destinies. The following describes the repercussions of the decisive clash between the Dark and the Light:

> How are those moments perceived by humans? (. . .) They might develop feelings of despair and unprovoked aggression, or bursts of unexplainable happiness, heart attacks, unmotivated actions, quar-

rels among best friends and infidelity of the most faithful lovers.
(. . .) Humans are incapable of seeing and understanding what is
going on in our world but our fight determines their souls and their
destinies.[55]

People are deprived of all initiative and denied any political life. They
are regarded as an inferior species whose dignity, morality, and freedom are
at best a joke. Vampires express those attitudes in various ways, including
the following:

> I'd stopped giving a damn about the human world a long time ago.
> It's our basis. Our cradle. But we are Others. We walk through closed
> doors and we maintain the balance of Good and Evil. (. . .)
>   We're not obliged to like the ordinary, everyday world.
>   We only guard it because we're its parasites.[56]

People can never become vampires, or werewolves or magicians (other
important protagonists in the novel). Those monsters' abilities are innate,
making them a whole different species. Even the choice of name for the
vampires in *Night Watch* is telling: they are called Others, to emphasize
the ontological gap that separates them from humans. At the beginning
of the novel, the Dark vampires are portrayed as more human-friendly
than the Light vampires, but the reader soon recognizes that the behavior
of both Light and Dark toward humans is essentially the same: cynical
and cruel.[57] Unlike the Light vampires, the Dark vampires avoid forcibly
drinking human blood, using instead willingly donated or animal blood.
But both clans eagerly suck up the mental energy, both positive and negative, that humans produce. All vampires respect the treaty that governs the
rules for hunting humans, but humans can still be killed for food, so long
as it is all done by the book. "Can vampires hunt people?" a boy asks. And
a vampire responds:

> "Yes, they go hunting," I said. (. . .) "If they have a license. Some-
> times . . . sometimes they need living blood." (. . .)
>   "Then they could have attacked me (. . .) under that treaty of
> yours? With a license?"
>   "Yes," I said.
>   "They could have drunk my blood? And you would have just
> walked by and looked the other way?" (. . .)
>   "Yes."[58]

In the *Night Watch* universe, people who are assigned as food have only one purpose and one destiny: to be eaten. Treating them in any other way would be a violation of the Treaty:[59]

> I walked to the end of the narrow brick alley and scuffed a sheet of newsprint with my foot. This was where the unfortunate vampire had been reduced to ashes. He really had been unfortunate; the only thing he'd done wrong was to fall in love. Not with a girl-vampire, not with a human being, but with his victim, his food.[60]

Later in *Night Watch*, a vampire instructs another vampire as follows: "Kostya, in order to live, you need blood. And, sometimes at least, human blood."[61]

It should be stated clearly that considering people as food is not at all unique to post-Soviet vampires; the same is true of their Western counterparts.[62] Even if vampires are sometimes forced by their creators onto the relatively PC path of vampire "vegetarianism," drinking animal blood or donated blood (or the artificial substitute Tru Blood, in the appropriately named *True Blood*), that basic rule remains the same. A vampire with what passes for a conscience (Stefan in *The Vampire Diaries*, for instance) refuses to drink human blood but is mocked for this by his vampire brother, Damon, who points out that animal blood may not be available forever.[63] In the weak model of vampire texts too, vampire "vegetarians" coexist with less fastidious vampires who eagerly hunt people. The human-vampire relationship is most cogently presented by Stephenie Meyer, who is no less candid than her post-Soviet counterparts in defining it. For her protagonists, the vampire is a predator, pure and simple; this is an attitude concisely articulated by Edward, who tells Bella, "I'm the world's best predator, aren't I? Everything about me invites you in—my voice, my face, even my smell."[64]

Although Edward emphasizes that he does not want to frighten Bella, the food analogy for his feeling toward his "girlfood" is just too perfect to pass up:

> "You know how everyone enjoys different flavors?" he began. "Some people love chocolate ice cream, others prefer strawberry?"
> I nodded.
> "Sorry about the food analogy—I couldn't think of another way to explain."
> I smiled. He smiled ruefully back.[65]

Werewolf James is more straightforward about it; sniffing out Bella's presence, he exclaims, "Oh, you brought a snack." In *True Blood*, people are called a "meat snack."[66] And *Twilight* routinely presents vampire predation as a remarkable skill and a feature to be admired:

> As predators, we have a glut of weapons in our physical arsenal—much, much more than really necessary. The strength, the speed, the acute senses, not to mention those of us like Edward, Jasper, and I, who have extra senses as well. And then, like a carnivorous flower, we are physically attractive to our prey.[67]

Twilight also popularized a euphemism that has been widely accepted by English-speaking vampire fans. Vampires, we are told, do not kill or murder or slaughter people; they just "feed" on them. Let us not forget that Bella's odor, the smell of her blood, is really the only source of her irresistible appeal to Edward (in the novel she is, after all, so pale and unprepossessing that she even jokes about being albino on her mother's side). Elena Gilbert (in *The Vampire Diaries*) also occasionally "feeds" Stefan, her vampire boyfriend, with her blood. A vampire may even claim that killing people is the key to his identity, as Damon does in the following dialogue from *The Vampire Diaries*:

> ANDIE: But why do you kill people?
> DAMON: Because I like it. It's in my nature, it's who I am (. . .) [A]nd she wants me to be the better man, which means I can't be who I am. Do you see the problem I'm having, Andie?[68]

Audiences must still find it hard not to empathize with Damon, the handsome bloodsucker portrayed by Ian Somerhalder, even when he says: "Vampires eat people. It is part of the natural food pyramid."[69]

The question "To bite or not to bite?" plagues the vampire texts. But "vegetarian" or not, vampires consider people their natural food, even if they choose to abstain from it. It is especially important for my analysis that the success of this kind of fiction is determined, according to critics, by this very capacity of monsters—vampires or werewolves—to devour humans: "Rice seems to have forgotten that readers don't want werewolves with good taste; they want werewolves who think humans taste good,"[70] one *Washington Post* reviewer says of Anne Rice's 2012 novel *The Wolf Gift*.

This image of vampires has changed radically from that found in the classic tales. Until the end of the twentieth century, in the canonical vampire narratives vampire attacks on people—be that in Stoker's *Dracula* or Tolstoy's *La Famille du Vourdalak* or other novellas, novels, and movies—were seen as an anomaly, a violation of the natural and moral order, and in no way were people ever categorized as the vampire's natural prey and food.[71] People, not vampires, were the true heroes of these stories. Vampires and werewolves, witches, warlocks, and shape shifters elicited horror and disgust and were the very embodiment of mortal danger.

In contemporary popular fiction and film, nonhuman monsters incarnate the aesthetic ideal and structure the narrative, and it is their feelings and desires with which the audience is expected to identify. The scale of this challenge is difficult to overestimate: For the first time in the history of Western civilization, people are routinely thought of and represented in fiction simply as food for other species, imaginary though they may be. Ravening beasts, the criminally insane or bug-eyed aliens—whatever form the man-eater du jour happened to take—were never previously portrayed as an ultimate aesthetic ideal, as perfect creatures of a higher order who therefore had every right to claim people as food. Today, by contrast, the monsters that "feed" on humans incur no disgust or moral reproach. As inferior allies, cherished pets, or barely tolerated mistresses, humans quite simply belong to an inferior species, and there is nothing questionable about putting that species on the menu.

Unlike their literary predecessors in previous epochs, contemporary monsters express a deep disenchantment with people or even an outright loathing for the human race. Damon articulates this issue in two episodes of *The Vampire Diaries*. In the first, he explains to Elena why the idea of becoming human is so repugnant to him:

ELENA: You would rather die than be human, and you expect me to be okay with that?
DAMON: (. . .) Yes, I would rather have died than be human. (. . .) I'd rather die right now than spend my last final years remembering how good I had it and how happy I was, because that's who I am, Elena, and I'm not gonna change.[72]

In the second episode, he tries to indoctrinate Rebekah, a vampire who wants to "revert," by explaining exactly how degrading it is to be human:

DAMON: Do you really want the cure? I mean, really. Look, let me give you a little bit of advice. See these girls, they look happy. Now, in five years they're gonna settle for a mediocre starter husband

and a mind-numbing career. And about that time they're gonna realize something you're never gonna have to learn.

REBEKAH: And what would that be?

DAMON: Life sucks when you're ordinary. And what makes you exactly not like them? You're a vampire. You take that cure and become human, well, you're no one, nothing. Trust me, losing this cure was the best damn thing that ever happened to you.[73]

A dialogue between the two vampire brothers Stefan and Damon about the human-vampire relation is equally revealing:

STEFAN: They are people, Damon. She's not a puppet, she doesn't exist for your amusement, for you to feed on whenever you want to.

DAMON: Sure she does. They all do. They're whatever I want them to be.[74]

This deep disdain for people is at the heart of contemporary vampire texts. In another episode, Damon goes a step further speaking about a vampire:

She's given up her humanity. (. . .) You can turn it off, like a button you can press. (. . .) The problem is, as a vampire, your instinct is not to feel. (. . .) [N]o guilt, no shame, no regret. I mean, come on, if you could turn it off, wouldn't you? (. . .) Of course I have [turned it off—D.K.], Rick, that's why I'm so fun to be around.[75]

This message is common to the majority of contemporary vampire tales. In *Only Lovers Left Alive*, the pair of vampire protagonists believes that the human race is doomed. They even label humans with the scornful sobriquet "zombies." Symbolically, the film closes with this vampire couple, Adam and Eve, who initially resisted drinking human blood, targeting a human couple as their prey. And a protagonist in *Night Watch*—a vampire initially introduced as human-friendly—asks humankind ironically if he is supposed to "waste my life for your cause?"[76]

The revised status of nonhuman monsters in contemporary fiction and film raises yet another question: What does this aesthetic idealization of nonhumans signify for the concept of humanity and for our perception of the human being? This question has been largely overlooked by critics, despite the enormous abundance and variety of interpretations of vampires in the humanities. If people can be thought of as food for a superior species—a species that is not only more powerful but also more aesthetically pleasing—this signals a radical reconsideration of their status. The vampire narratives can then be seen as part of a larger questioning, if not a wholesale rejection, of the idea of human exceptionalism.

In this respect, it is hard to avoid drawing parallels between the contemporary intellectual climate and that of the eighteenth century, which witnessed the birth of the Gothic novel. The Gothic authors (Mary Shelley, for example) were cognizant of the ongoing debates among Britain's philosophers and natural scientists about the particularity of humans relative to other living organisms.[77] At that time, however, scientific progress constituted a powerful ideology, harboring as it did the optimistic promise of the imminent perfecting of human society and human nature. For these reasons, any controversy over the status of humans was routinely resolved in favor of human exceptionalism.

Today, given the prevailing disappointment in the theory of progress and rationality, we are witnessing a very different trend, which seems to be pushing that venerable debate in the opposite direction. The social sciences—to say nothing of philosophy—now provide ample examples of the blurred boundaries between humans and nonhumans. Anthropologists deny human exceptionalism arguing that there is no major difference between humans and the bald mole rat, and they promote network analysis, in which humans and objects, books, and laboratory rats are given equivalent status and are considered equal partners in social interactions.[78] In other words, even the human sciences are actively involved in a process of renegotiating the status of people in a way that does not favor human exceptionalism.

It is important to stress that in the contemporary vampire texts, vampires (like all other nonhuman monsters) do not stand for anything but themselves. Unlike the animals in the fables of Aesop or La Fontaine, the nonhuman beings in fairy tales or the protagonists of medieval Menippean satire, they are never presented as allegories of human vices or virtues. Contemporary monsters have only one function, which is to deny the worth of human life and the value of humanity as a subject of art. Today's monsters are not to be mistaken for reincarnations of the Nietzschean Übermensch, although Pelevin ironically subtitled his *Empire V* "The Story of a True Superman." Nonhumans incarnate the rejection of the idea of human exceptionalism. That, in fact, may be one of the reasons why a novel titled *No Humans Involved* (2007) did so well in its day on the *New York Times* bestseller list.[79]

Ghosts, Zombies, and Ancient Gods: Verifying a Hypothesis

Ghost, zombies, and Greek gods help verify the hypothesis that the extraordinary admiration for vampires and other man-eating monsters is rooted in their promotion of antihumanistic attitudes. A comparison of the Soviet and post-Soviet literature and movies featuring ghosts is especially telling with respect to the dynamics of the monsters' presence in contemporary culture.

Although the Soviets strongly opposed everything mystical and irrational, even the school curriculum could not hold ghosts entirely at bay. Specters were omnipresent in Russian classical literature, which had been strongly influenced by the English Gothic novel and European Romanticism. And since the Soviets had coopted the heritage of the Russian classics, ghosts were there to stay; Soviet propaganda was ultimately powerless to purge them from classical Russian literature.[80]

Popular specters haunting the Soviet classroom were the ghost of the Commander in Alexander Pushkin's play *The Stone Guest* (1830); the ghost of Akaky Akakievich, a poor clerk, in Nikolai Gogol's short story "The Overcoat" (1842); and of course the ghost of Hamlet's father. Last but not least there was "the specter of communism" in the opening sentence of *The Communist Manifesto*. Yet a child's first encounter with ghosts could have come far earlier: Oscar Wilde's "Canterville Ghost" was featured in a popular cartoon that entertained generations of Soviet children.[81]

Remarkably, after perestroika and the abolition of censorship, the ghosts that had survived the onslaught of Soviet materialism did not gain in fame as might have been expected, but gradually began to cede their popularity to vampires, werewolves, zombies, and other of the nonspectral undead. The ghosts that still hang around are often perceived ironically, their appearances in second-rate Russian thrillers but mainly in musicals and comedies doing nothing to boost their cultural significance.

One exception is Aleksandr Veledinsky's film *Alive* (2005).[82] Produced during the crisis years of the Chechen war, this film tells the story of Kir, a soldier who returns from Chechnya after enlisting to earn money for his wedding. Trying to get a ride home, he suddenly hears the screeching of brakes and the shouts of the fellow soldiers who had sacrificed themselves in Chechnya to save his life. He accepts the company of their ghosts even though he knows perfectly well that they are dead. And, unable to adjust to the corrupt and humiliating realities of post-Soviet society, Kir finally joins his ghostly comrades. This reunion happens at the end of the film, which concludes by rerunning the opening scene: an empty highway, the squeal of brakes, and ghostly screams. The entire storyline undoubtedly represents the near-death nightmare that Kir experiences after being hit by an oncoming vehicle. The film connected well with Russian audiences, but not because it was a ghost story. Produced by an outstandingly talented director, it raises an acute political problem while also successfully imitating the powerful trope of nightmare.

The declining popularity of ghosts becomes even more intriguing in light of the omnipresence of other mystical and surreal monsters in post-Soviet culture. Vampires, zombies, werewolves, and other varieties of the undead handily dominate popular cultural production in today's Russia. Ghosts seem to command much less attention than vampires from the English-speaking audience as well. If one considers numbers of Twitter followers as an indication of popularity, the distinction is striking: the most popular ghost shows and movies do not come even close to the popularity of their vampiric counterparts. In fact, there is at least a two- to threefold difference.[83]

This leads us to wonder: What do ghosts lack that limits their charm and prevents them from winning over the general public as other non-human monsters, especially vampires, have done? That question may be answered by an exploration of the ways in which ghosts differ from vampires and other popular monsters in their interactions with people. The ghost of the Commander appears in Pushkin's *The Stone Guest* to punish the main protagonist—Don Juan, a notorious womanizer—for having seduced the Commander's widow, Donna Anna. The Commander's statue turns into a ghost, grabs Don Juan and drags him down to the netherworld. The ghost therefore performs a moral function by punishing Don Juan for his vices, albeit at the cost of his life. In Gogol's "The Overcoat," the main character is a poor clerk, Akaky Akakievich, whose only purpose in life is to save what he can from his paltry salary to purchase a warm new overcoat. The overcoat, however, is stolen from him the first day he wears it. After a general to whom he has turned for help berates and humiliates him, he dies in misery, only to return as a ghost that haunts St. Petersburg at night and terrifies high-ranking clerks while stripping them of their overcoats. One of his victims is the very general who refused to help him. Once again, this ghost, while unnerving, is actually a force for justice. In a similar vein, the ghosts of Kir's dead friends in Veledinsky's film cause him to re-examine his own moral code and that of the post-Soviet society in which he feels so ill at ease. The very presence of the ghosts of those dead soldiers (who are portrayed as undistinguishable from the living, making jokes and talking back to Kir) in an everyday setting brings up a disturbing contrast between their choice to die on the battlefield while rescuing their injured friend and the absurdity of their mission in the shameful Chechen war. It highlights the unbridgeable gap that separates the corruption and petty values of a provincial Russian town from the ideals of friendship and compassion, and the poverty and destitution in post-Soviet society from Russia's ridiculous imperial ambitions. Kir and his dead friends come together to hold up a horrifying mirror to a post-Soviet society that makes no allowance for human dignity and morality and feels no remorse for wasting young lives.

All these ghosts follow in the footsteps of the ghost of Hamlet's father. Since Shakespeare laid down the ground rules, ghosts have traditionally haunted and frightened human villains and guided human avengers, as in Sir Walter Scott's *The Tapestried Chamber* or Charles Dickens' *A Christmas Carol*. They extract what they deem a just revenge, even when that involves killing their victims. The ghost's role in these narratives is to articulate moral judgments and/or punish those who, in their estimation, deserve it. Usually their acts are morally grounded and driven by the urge to repair some injustice done in the past. Like Marx's "specter of communism," which was invoked to terrorize capitalists, foretelling their imminent destruction for their brutal exploitation of the workers, the purpose of ghosts is to right wrongs. They are the incarnation of conscience.[84] On the contrary, the idea of moral retribution is never associated with vampires in contemporary texts as well as in the classical ones.

The moral and spiritual mission of ghosts goes hand in hand with the etymology of the word. The Latin *spectrum*, which means "appearance" or "apparition," finds parallels in many modern languages: English, for example has "specter," which relates to the Latin verb *spectare* ("to look at, see, watch"). In English and French, the word "spirit" or "esprit" can mean either "soul" or "ghost." In Russian, the word *dukh* ("ghost" and "spirit") and the word *dusha* ("soul") differ only in gender and in one phoneme. The visual and immaterial nature of specters is also manifested in other Russian words such as *privideniya* ("apparitions," derived from a verb meaning "to see" or "to dream") and *prizraki* (from the obsolete verb *zrit'*, which means "to see" and also "to predict").

This aspect of the ghost's image is reflected in the way it is conceptualized: unlike vampires, werewolves, or zombies, a ghost is an incorporeal spirit. Fluid and transparent, ghosts take various shapes but remain deeply associated with the human psyche. The incarnations of souls, ghosts are projections of the human spirituality. In fiction and legends, ghosts are often explained in terms of stranded or wandering souls unable to find eternal peace.[85] When a human character dies and becomes a ghost, therefore, it is never by choice; a character cannot become a ghost by explicitly denying his or her human nature. By contrast, to be "turned" and become a vampire in a contemporary vampire saga, one must choose to reject one's human nature, to die and be "reborn." In the vampire universe, being "turned" is considered a social advancement and aesthetic achievement. Death offers the opportunity to become a vampire. Bella Swan is finally "turned" after dying in childbirth and is thrilled to have accomplished her dream at long last: "I've never felt normal, because I am not normal, and I don't wanna be. (. . .) I have also never felt stronger, like more real, more myself, because it's my world too. It's where I belong."[86] Jessica, the heroine of *True Blood*, is also excited about shedding her humanity and becoming a vampire. Elena Gilbert initially fears vampirism but later accepts it as her destiny. Unlike the good old days of Dracula, when transforming into a vampire meant becoming a repulsive creature, a monster and a threat to one's near and dear, joining the living dead today means achieving eternal life and beauty.[87] Ghosts, by contrast, have no fans whose dearest desire is to become one.

Another feature that fundamentally distinguishes ghosts from vampires (and from zombies too) is diet. Ghosts do not regard people as natural food. They do not sink their teeth into people, do not drink human blood, do not eat human flesh, have no taste for brains, and do not treat people as prey. They may kill people, but never in order to nibble on them. In other words, spirits do not challenge the concept of humanity; rather, they reinforce morality as one of the prime foundations of human exceptionalism. Clearly, ghosts are no part of Gothic Aesthetic because they are products of a system of values that is actually based on the idea of human exceptionalism that considers humanity the ultimate value. And this is also why they are important to the Gothic novel. And, I would argue, it is precisely this quality that makes ghosts less apt to engage contemporary audiences than the man-eating monsters of the new canon. Vampires differ profoundly from ghosts because they reflect a strikingly new stage in the reimagining and reconsideration of the place of human beings in what Arthur Lovejoy has memorably analyzed in his *The Great Chain of Being*.

Indirect confirmation of this hypothesis can be found in the rising popularity of zombies. While George Romero's famous *Night of The Living Dead* (1968) kick-started their popularity, the upsurge of their attraction is more likely due to Dan O'Bannon's *The Return of the Living Dead* (1985). Unlike Romero's zombies, which fed indiscriminately on human flesh, O'Bannon's zombies are ground-breakers in that they eat human brains. And once zombies were portrayed as an archetype of the disregard for human exceptionalism, their celebrity was assured. Among the many types of monsters that represent the uncanny in the history of the Western culture, the image of the brain-eating undead epitomizes a new perception of human beings. What stronger metaphor for the rejection of human personality and spirituality could there be than the consumption of human brains? And yet this propensity and their messy appearance notwithstanding, a zombie can actually be—for some—a "likable and believable" character.[88] The fact that zombies feature as first-person narrators in such movies as *Warm Bodies* (Jonathan Levine, 2013) proves this point. As discussed in chapter 1, this element of zombie symbolism seems much more important and on-point than their supposed role of critics of "capitalist society."[89]

Death is the default message of the vampire saga. This is not a coming-of-age but a coming-of-death novel, in which physical demise becomes a rite of passage, a transition from an undistinguished humanity to the perfection of a man-eating monster. The contemporary living dead, whose cultural mission is to deny human exceptionalism and reject the notion of the human being as an aesthetic ideal, embody and promote the rising cult of death. The cult of death is therefore the ultimate expression of the currently fashionable disgust with people, their values, and their civilization. Ghosts, on the other hand, have a far more modest role to play in the rising cult of death because they have contributed little if anything to the dehumanization of the human race.

Another thought experiment supports the hypothesis that the popularity of vampires is tied to their ability and willingness to feed on human beings, thus reducing them to a foodstuff. If we compare the gods and goddesses of ancient Greece and Rome to contemporary vampires, we will see that they share much in common, both being inhumanly beautiful, able to flout the laws of physical reality and read minds, not limited by the constraints of space, and immortal. And the divinities of classical antiquity bear no resemblance to the tediously impeccable Christian saints because they also enjoy all the human imperfections, being lavishly promiscuous, wildly jealous, and unashamedly greedy. One would expect all of this to sit well with the consumption culture of today, but then why do the Greek gods not exert the same appeal as vampires? What qualities do contemporary vampires have that set them apart from the Olympians? One possible answer could be that the Greek gods did not feed on people or treat people as cattle. On the contrary, their cultural role in Western civilization was to showcase the beauty of the human body and demonstrate the ways human nature could be godlike. Their ultimate role was to inspire epoch-making innovations of science, philosophy, and democracy; they stood at the wellsprings of Western civilization. None of this would go any way toward ushering them into the canon of Gothic Aesthetic or the cult of death.

The Monster's Evolution: The Vampire, the Serial Killer, and the Cannibal

Vampire and Serial Killer

Alongside zombies and vampires stands another protagonist, one that has actually been called "the exemplary modern celebrity." This is the serial killer, a target of intense public interest, as amply attested by the launch of a new special-interest magazine *Serial Killer Quarterly*, of which its founder said, "We're focusing exclusively on serial murder cases due to the immense and enduring public interest in the topic."[90] The sale of "murderabilia" (objects associated with serial killers) and the market of serial killers' art is another important hallmark of this zeitgeist. David Schmid, the author of *Natural Born Celebrities: Serial Murder in American Popular Culture*, speaks of the development of a "huge serial killer industry" that has become "a defining feature of American popular culture since the 1970s. A constant stream of movies, magazines, T-shirts, trading cards, videos, DVDs, books, websites, television shows, and a tsunami of ephemera have given the figure of the serial murderer an unparalleled degree of visibility in the contemporary American public sphere."[91]

Serial killers themselves are well aware of their ability to attract the public's attention. Discussing the serial murder boom in the early 1990s in *Using Murder: The Social Construction of Serial Homicide*, Philip Jenkins cites cases that demonstrate unambiguously how some serial killers were influenced by the public fascination with them.[92] Most importantly, according to Schmid, "action and identity are fused" in the serial killer, which tends to combine that person's selfhood with his or her murders and inducts them into the celebrity culture.[93] As Schmid also shows, a slew of serial killer movies were made in reaction to the growing serial killer celebrity culture in the 1990s and early 2000s.

The serial killer was, in fact, riding a general wave of interest in monsters, which connects the immense popularity of vampires and zombies to the relatively recent surge in movies and TV series featuring a serial killer and/or cannibal as their main protagonist. For example, Melissa Rosenberg, writer and executive producer of the Showtime series *Dexter* (2006–

2013), whose protagonist is a forensic scientist and unrepentant serial killer, says that the *Dexter* character has "something in common with 'Twilight' because it's about a 'good' serial killer with 'internal demons he's trying to control.'"[94] This particular multiple murderer is presented as a moral avenger who hunts down and kills criminals who have escaped justice.

Several researchers, including Philip Simpson, have noted the link between the serial killer and the vampire and have demonstrated the ways in which these images merge.[95] Jenkins observes that this association may be traced to the late 1980s, when journalists began occasionally referring to real murders as "vampire killings," and one of them, Richard Trenton Chase, was even termed "the Dracula Killer." Jenkins also makes the important point that the serial killer can be coopted as a substitute for all the fears that are associated with the supernatural: "If serial killers were not literary monsters, they were as close to the reality as could be conceived within the intellectual framework of a scientific age. The cultural imagery applied to serial killers from the late 1970s has decisively shifted toward portrayals of monsters, savage animalistic beings at war with the society."[96] He therefore believes that the "serial killer nowadays replaces what in other eras might well be fastened onto supernatural or imaginary folk-devils—vampires, werewolves, witches, evil sorcerers, conspiratorial Jews."[97] The coupling of serial killer and supernatural monster hit a peak in 1992, "when PBS's quality documentary series Frontline gave the title 'Monsters among Us' to a study of sexually violent offenders like Westley Dodd."[98] Jenkins explains that the image of the serial killer has been structured as that of a dangerous outsider, a monster "to be dealt with only by means of social warfare."[99]

While vampires have abandoned their habit of transforming into bats and sleeping in their coffins, the serial killer has taken on the contemporary vampire's superior demeanor, supernatural intelligence, and elegance. Cecil Greek and Caroline Joan Picart analyze how *Henry*, the fact-based story of a serial killer, is reduced to Gothic tropes in the eponymous movie.[100] They also show that several films portraying serial killers "exploit the contemporary seductive glamour of the vampire myth to render the serial killer a charismatic and elegant Übermensch, transcending bourgeois distinctions of good and evil."[101] But they do not develop this argument and do not consider how this image challenges our understanding of human beings. They also do not relate the evolution of these monsters to the concept of human exceptionalism or to the social and cultural changes in death-related practices over past decades.

David Schmid considers the serial killer a "quintessentially American" phenomenon and "contemporary American culture's ultimate deviant."[102] The serial killer has also been ironically described as an "American Original, a romantic icon, like the cowboy."[103] This is rather too parochial, though; the serial killer's popularity has, in fact, become a global trend.

In Russia, the serial killer captured the public imagination in the 1990s and also demonstrated a comparable tendency to merge with the image of the vampire. In *Night Watch*, Lukyanenko portrays one of his vampires, Maxim, as a serial murderer whose discourse seems to have been lifted almost wholesale from psychological descriptions of this pathology. Yet he is presented as a positive hero. Maxim's feelings about his victims play an important role in the story and are evidently intended to make readers empathize with him, not with his victims. Unaware as yet that he is a vampire, Maxim believes that his mission is to distinguish the good people from the bad and to execute the latter. That said, though, his "calling" soon gives way to his instincts when he kills first a young woman, then a father of a little boy, and then attempts to take the life of a twelve-year-old child. And every one of these murders is recounted with naturalistic precision.[104] Nevertheless, neither these grisly scenes nor the fact that the victims are not guilty, not even according to the vampire's own criteria, is expected to cast any shade over Maxim. Lukyanenko instead works the reader's emotions in his favor, calling him an "absolutely lonely Light magician."[105] In the novel, this serial killer ends as a supreme judge, an arbiter between the Light and Dark vampires. The author makes this monster to decide the fate of his imaginary universe. This fits the trope perfectly: *Night Watch*'s protagonists, like those in so many other post-Soviet texts, are committed to displaying their superiority to any run-of-the-mill morality.

Several attempts were undertaken to explain public fascination with the serial killer. The premise of the scholars referenced above is that the serial killer–vampire discourse originated in a striving to preserve conservative ideas about morality and create grounds to justify conservative political action.[106] Indeed both Jenkins and Schmid have emphasized the FBI's important role in constructing the phenomenon. But although the FBI may have contributed to the initial fascination with serial killers, this alone cannot explain the steady ascendancy of this new star in the constellation of popular culture.

Jenkins also points to the rise of conservative Protestantism in the 1980s and 1990s, which added to the gothization of the image of the serial killer and served to transform him from someone who is simply criminally insane into a full-fledged monster. But while it may well be that the Protestant revival has made its own contribution to the monster boom, the flourishing popularity of monsters of all kinds (and especially their idealization) cannot be wholly attributed to changes in the religious mindset. Nor it is limited to the devotees of Protestantism. Jenkins himself, however, has opened the way to another solution, with reference to the declining interest in the serial killer's psychological background.[107] This sits well with my argument about the slackening concern for humans and the human psyche and the obsession for nonhumans whose actions lie outside the scope of human psychology and morality. This process actually reveals changing attitudes toward humanity that cannot legitimately be associated with any point on the political or religious spectrum.

The serial killer, real and fictional, therefore stands on a par with the other monsters described in these pages that have seized the popular imagination. Like them, he (or, in far rarer cases, she) exerts a powerful attraction because his crimes set him above conventional morality (which is in fact not even part of his ethical compass). The serial killer symbolizes a rejection of humanism and of the sacredness of human life. And that is perhaps a key feature that makes monstrous protagonists so popular nowadays.

Vampire and Cannibal

The images of cannibal, vampire, and serial killer first began to merge in the early 1990s. Today it is clear that the nature of the crimes committed by protagonists such as serial killers/vampires/cannibals and the attitudes toward people that their actions exemplify have contributed to the evolution their images have undergone. Two movies—*The Silence of the Lambs* (1991) and *Hannibal* (2001)—played an especially important role in this:[108]

> So identified has Anthony Hopkins become with the role of Hannibal Lecter that the fulsome praise that has greeted Hopkins's performances in the role can reasonably be taken as relatively unguarded expressions of fascination with and admiration of Lecter himself.[109]

The "cult" of Hannibal Lecter, which launched in 1992 after *The Silence of the Lambs* won Oscars in five major categories, may therefore be attributed not only to the film's artistic qualities, which are undeniable, but also to public fascination with its monstrous protagonist.

Prior to the late 1980s and the 1990s, serial murder and cannibalism had been categorized as a prehistoric atavism and animal savagery; serial killers were compared to beasts of prey, such as tigers.[110] But since mass murderer James Huberty first used the expression "hunting humans" in 1992, both it and the idea of the serial killer as a predator that feeds on people have become firmly embedded in the popular culture. In the 1990s, the intense interest in the idea of people as an object of predation became an overarching cultural theme, which elevated the denial of human exceptionalism to the status of a cultural watchword.

That shift is remarkably evident when we consider the differences between the two hypostases of Hannibal: the character in Thomas Harris' novels and as embodied in the movies by Hopkins, the quintessential Lecter, on the one hand, and by Mads Mikkelsen in the television series *Hannibal* (Bryon Fuller, 2013–2015) almost twenty years later, on the other. In both the novels and the 1991 movie, Lecter displays several vampiric traits. Craig McKay, the movie's editor, even described him as "leaning back, drinking it all in, vampirically." In the script, one of the guards asks positive protagonist Clarice Starling if Lecter is "some kind of vampire."[111] Lecter also possesses an outstanding intellect. This ambiguity is clearly drawn from the novels, where his name appears as a kind of rebus, the duality of Hannibal/Cannibal Lecter/Lector underscoring the intellectual nature of this man eater. This "aestheticization" of the serial killer and cannibal could not have happened had the public perception of monsters, people, and the value of human life not already been undergoing a profound change. Yet at least some degree of moral justification was required back in 1991 to enable audiences to validate their attraction to Hopkins' Hannibal, and it was provided in the following terms:

> Perhaps it is Lecter's absolute amorality conjoined with an ethics of personal behavior and pretentious dedication to the good life. Lecter is a good old-fashioned snob. He has exquisite taste and impeccable style, and, whenever possible, prefers to "only kill rude people." We all gripe about the "idiots" at work and the "rude" people we run into every day, so maybe on some level Lecter's selective killings appeal to our own fantasies of creating our particular vision of a better world, at that same time that his character and lifestyle appeal to our own champagne wishes and caviar dreams. Whatever the reasons, Hannibal is clearly in awe of its title character, and repeatedly suggests that, like Clarice Starling and Mason Verger, we are all, or would like to be, Hannibal Lecter.[112]

For all his elegance and seductive charm, though, Hopkins' Lecter is undeniably and unmistakably a criminal. However "attractive and fascinating" a monster Lecter was, he was still a monster crafted in line with "traditional concepts of monstrosity."[113] It was precisely the stark contrast between his great sophistication and his penchant for cannibalism (that in this age was still considered the utmost denial of civilization) that made him a protagonist of a new type.

In the television version of 2013, that contrast is no longer valid. Here, Lecter is portrayed not by an older actor but by the handsome Mads Mikkelsen as the very embodiment of good taste, elegance, and high culture. Like his predecessor, he too hates "rude people" and eventually punishes them by killing them and dining on their remains, but this is not his predominant motivation.[114] In an interview, Mikkelsen explains his character in highly positive terms, stressing that Hannibal has "certain standards of morals," because he does not eat "just anyone!"[115] He added, "There is a lot of humor in the script." Most importantly, the TV series puts considerable effort into showcasing Lecter's skills in the kitchen and invites viewers to appreciate his finesse in the cooking of human flesh and his ability to pair those dishes with the perfect wine. There are a lot of tight close-ups of "meat" being sliced and diced in preparation for a meal. This is nothing short of an entertaining master class in the serving and consumption of human flesh. The names of the episodes further highlight this theme: all the titles in the first series are taken from French haute cuisine and in the second from its Japanese counterpart. The two main protagonists, whose complicated psychological life we are invited to share and whose prowess in the kitchen we are encouraged to admire, are seen sharing their cannibalistic repasts with each other.[116] The objectification of people reaches its apogee in the Hannibal TV series, where people are not only processed as food but may also be used as soil fertilizer, since there are similarities between the structures of fungi and the human brain, as the serial killer in the *Hannibal* episode "Amuse-Bouche" carefully explains.[117] Among myriad bodies mutilated in all imaginable ways, we are presented an interconnected collage of naked bodies, a dead body posed like Shiva, another victim's body turned into a picture . . .[118] So what distinguishes the Hannibal of 2013 from its predecessors is that Mikkelsen's man-eater is presented as an indubitable aesthetic model, and cannibalism is shown not in contrast to but as an integral part of Lecter's urbane attraction, not incompatible with human civilization but the most sophisticated part of it.

The message of the critically acclaimed movie *We Are What We Are* (Jim Mickle, 2013) continues the theme of Hannibal in an even more frank way: here, man-eating is simply a family tradition that must not be abandoned. As the title points out, with a sham naivety, people are different and there is nothing wrong with that. This story is told by two young sisters, both man-eaters, who, after some hesitation, finally agree to continue their family's long-standing custom of cannibalism, in an understanding that the viewer is apparently expected to sympathize with.[119]

Critics and the industry in general fell all over themselves to praise these offerings.[120] For example, Hannibal was lauded by *Metacritic*, the *New York Post*, and *HitFix* as the best of the current season's serial killer shows.[121] *Entertainment Weekly* characterized it as "deliciously subversive" and *Variety* called it "the tastiest drama the network has introduced in a while."[122] A critic from *Review* added, "A prequel TV series about Hannibal Lecter has to overcome a lot of preconceptions. (. . .) But guess what? None of that matters when you actually watch the show, because Hannibal is terrific."[123] And the *Chicago Sun-Times* reportedly told its readers that Hannibal was "deliciously disturbing" and would leave viewers "hungry for more."[124]

So the critics were impressed, but what about audiences? Statistics permits us to answer that question with ease. The first episode of *Hannibal*'s first season was watched by 4.36 million viewers in the United States alone.[125] Against this background, the fact that as of August 2015, a surprisingly well-documented YouTube clip on cannibalism titled "What does human taste like?" had racked up 115,604 likes and only 4,744 dislikes, from a total of 7,590,323 views, comes as no surprise at all.[126]

Nowadays, the vampire and the cannibal are packaged together, for example in novels such as *The Vampire & The Man-Eater* or in games like *Monsters Revolution*, which is promoted in these terms: "You will have to eat enough humans and you will be able to turn into a new and more powerful monster."[127]

Critics and Monsters

Looking at the vast literature on vampires, we see that some critics seem to have joined forces with monsters' fans in their admiration of the vampire's virtues and sympathy for the zombie's loneliness and isolation. Since René Girard first pioneered this concept, the interpretation of the monster as scapegoat has been extended to the interpretation of the monster as various marginalized groups.[128] The idea that the scapegoated victim does not need to perform the evil for which it suffers is fundamental to Girard's construction. An understanding of the monster as a symbol of all that is sidelined, dominated, or oppressed was developed in the works of Jacques Derrida, Gilles Deleuze, and Pierre-Félix Guattari, with special reference to vampires and ghosts. Interestingly enough, the vampire had initially been treated as a metaphor for evil in left criticism. Marx, whose every allusion to vampires has been carefully itemized, employed the notion to denote the evils of capitalism. Marxist tradition uses the image of the vampire as an ideological device to whip up hatred for the bourgeoisie, which figuratively drinks the blood of the working people.[129] Paradoxically, Marx's use of the vampire metaphor has, furthermore, tended to legitimize them as a subject of critical reflection. Deleuze and Guattari contributed to this transformation by considering the vampire as a "hybrid" that "infects" and therefore ushers in difference and the anomalous.[130] In deconstruction discourse, the vampire plays the role of destroyer of bourgeois society, of a marginalized Other who establishes important symbolic boundaries for a given community, a view of the vampire as a symbol of rebel and outcast that has been fully embraced in cultural studies.[131] These works set the stage for a paradigmatic shift in the understanding of monsters, making them a focus of attention in the humanities. In this spirit, scenes such as the one in George Romero's *Day of the Dead* (1985), in which zombies "tear apart and eat the flesh of American soldiers" have been explained away as "an explicit commentary on the dead ends of the American family, post-Fordist consumerism, and the barbarism of the military-scientific complex."[132] Besides, vampires have been interpreted as symbolizing the victims of political oppression and as embodying the radical criticism of capitalism. Readings of vampires as images of gender intolerance remain popular, as do interpretations of vampires as symbols of racial or ethnic discrimination or economic inequality.[133] Vampires have also been considered as contemporary "middle level Greek or Roman deities (. . .) minor gods of lifecycle and death" and vampire texts are also read as a manifestation of the "domestication" of vampires, of their "humanization": "Meyer is showing us the—forgive the term—humanity in the vampires."[134] These studies are inspired by the idea that the monster symbolizes and stands for the Other and should therefore be treated with sympathy, dignity, and respect. Monsters and monstrous behavior are to be accepted and understood on their own terms. Nina Auerbach's *Our Vampires, Ourselves* (1999) is a down-to-earth formula that has proven extremely prolific.[135] "Our Monsters, Ourselves" became a slogan of the time, and in the two decades following Auerbach's publication, titles such as *Our Cannibals, Ourselves*, "Our Serial Killers, Our Superheroes, and Ourselves," "Our Zombies, Ourselves," and "Our Animals, Ourselves"[136] flooded the press and the bookstores.

The inflation of the concept of the Other, originally an expression of cultural and political tolerance, has been instrumental in normalizing murderous monsters and no longer only as an incarnation of and metaphor for the victimized and marginalized.[137] The monster becomes the Other and "our deepest self."[138] Readers and viewers are expected to see the fictional world through the eyes of a vampire, a zombie, a cannibal, a serial killer, and to empathize with that Other rather than with their victims. A tendency to "redefine the victimizer as himself a victim—of a broken home or abusive parents" is clearly distinguishable in the studies of monsters.[139] These interpretations blind critics to the antihumanistic significance of monsters as cultural representations, in that audiences identify with them not only against unjust institutions and political or economic oppression but also against humanity and humanistic ideals in general.[140]

Some critics came to consider monsters from the perspective of the social construction of reality, blaming the conservative discourse for having "invented" monsters to validate censorship. Jenkins suggested, for example, that the image of the serial killer had been socially constructed to justify "campaigns of control."[141] The changes in the attitudes to monsters and their crimes—including cannibalism—are reflected in the way researchers position cannibalism in relation to the concepts of culture and civilization. In 1994, Jenkins, in his analysis of *The Silence of The Lambs*, equates cannibals with "threatening outsiders" and argued that cannibalism is a major symbol that represents "the threat of a reversion to primitive savagery."[142] Jenkins agrees with anthropologist William Arens that there "could be no better way of distancing oneself from other people than to call them cannibals."[143] Picart in 2014, however, seemingly stressed the opposite by emphasizing the attractiveness of the cannibal's image: "Cannibalism, conjoined with vampirism's ability to hypnotize and seduce, became a feature of the powerfully heterosexual, upper-class and brilliant Dr. Lecter."[144] There is apparently no contradiction between Jenkins' and Greek and Picart's statements, just evidence of the passage of time. Back in the 1990s, cannibalism was still seen as a dire threat to civilization. By the 2000s, the "monster turn" had made it seductive and appealing. We may, I believe, assume that the questioning of the food taboo forbidding the consumption of people as an expression of the ultimate rejection of human exceptionalism—is precisely what has rendered the image of the vampire/serial killer/cannibal so attractive to the mass audience over the past decade that separates these two studies.

Yet the idealization of monster and the importance of this paradigmatic shift in the understanding of the new role that contemporary monsters play in the aesthetic system are routinely overlooked by critics and scholars. They rarely compare contemporary monsters with those of previous epochs and do not consider the difference between them as an important hallmark of a change in cultural history.

Humans as Food?

In 1999, the Russian postmodernist artist and writer Vladimir Sorokin published a novel titled *Blue Lard*.[145] Blue lard is a product that the clones of writers and poets—iconic Russian cultural figures such as Fyodor Dostoevsky, Leo Tolstoy, and Anna Akhmatova—generate in their bodies when they write their simulations of those writers' works. The blue lard is stored at a classified plant, but its purpose is unclear even to the military men who guard it. In fact, Stalin and Hitler—close personal friends in this scenario—are planning to use it to achieve immortality. One way of interpreting this image is to say that Russia's great culture had been appropriated by the totalitarian (not to say cannibalistic) Soviet regime. Another way is to view it as a reaction against historical amnesia in a country that has chosen to ignore its "Unmasterable past" and to continue living with the illusion of a glorious, heroic, and entirely unproblematic history.[146] More relevant to our analysis, however, is that the *Blue Lard* metaphor, by directly equating a product of the intellect and a physical emanation, presupposes a consummately utilitarian approach to people and signifies the end of culture and civilization in a dystopian future (the story begins in January 2048). A central episode in the novel portrays Stalin and Khrushchev cooking and eating the liver of one of their guards, who had been casually summoned and murdered for the sole purpose of being consumed. *Blue Lard* proffers cannibalism as the extreme expression of barbarization. A cultural critic, Sorokin makes his reader concerned about the imminent questioning of the fundamental food taboo and the contemporary inversion of the meaning of cannibalism, which has transformed it into something that almost qualifies as chic.

Today the obsession with food as a subject of both scientific research and intellectual discussion and the debate about what can and cannot be eaten is growing on an international scale, while in the academic discourse the representation of people as food in popular culture is regarded as par for the course: "As in the case of cannibals and vampires, the possibility that humanity itself is transformed into food constitutes the underlying theme of many narratives."[147] This trivializing denial of human exceptionalism opens the door to statements about "death for food." Val Plumwood's "food approach to death" and assertions that "we are all food, and through death nourish others," and that "mortuary practices might affirm death as an opportunity of life for others in the ecological community"[148] epitomizes the cult of death.

The shift from the view of monsters as criminals to an engaged and

Fig. 4. Popular Halloween cookies. *(Copyright GreenArtPhotography, from iStock.)*

sympathetic attitude toward monsters as the victims of social oppression, both in academic writings and in popular culture in general, has repackaged monsters as an object of compassion and idealization. The aestheticization of violence certainly played an important role in the commodification of the concept of Other. It has given rise to a subculture that sympathizes with zombies and idolizes vampires, and to a serial killers celebrity culture.[149] The idealization of monsters does not promote tolerance for Otherness; on the contrary, it reifies a scenario in which the human species turns against itself. Rather than creating a more harmonious world that readily embraces all living organisms, the rejection of humanism and human exceptionalism articulated in the texts we have analyzed in this chapter instead affirms a radical dehumanization of humanity. These new attitudes to monsters and their revised cultural role have stimulated the rise of "fear entertainment"[150] and fueled the cult of death, the quintessential expression of those ideas.

The Monsters of Post-Soviet Russia

Throughout this chapter we have focused our attention on both the common features that unite post-Soviet and English/American monsters and the distinctions between them. It is now time to examine what makes them culturally specific. The most important difference consists in the contrasting social roles that Russian- and English-speaking vampires play in their imaginary societies.

Vampires are marginal in fictional American society. They fear exposure by humans and thus keep their existence strictly secret. In the television series *Kindred: The Embraced*, a vampire prince rules a vampire clan whose existence is hidden from human society by means of a "masquerade," a complex set of rules the vampires follow to the letter. Those who break the rules are severely punished. Even those vampires who function in a public role do not rule any part of human society and in general prefer not to engage with it any more than they have to. In *The Vampire Diaries*, the humans fight against the vampires; the Founders' Council, which runs local politics, works to expose the vampires in order to protect the town. However powerful vampires might be compared to humans, they in no way determine the laws of human existence in anglophone vampire offerings.

It is especially telling that some vampire writers and filmmakers explain this vampire marginality historically. According to *Underworld* and *Twilight*, during the Middle Ages human society was under vampire domination. In time, however, humans took over, resulting in a contemporary society that is free from vampire rule. Modern-day vampires have come to accept their marginality. American vampires do socialize somewhat with humans, have adapted to human society, and, to some extent, adhere to its norms. In *Twilight*, for example, the vampires go to school and must be constantly on the move to hide the fact that they never age. This "social marginality" of the English-speaking vampire is probably one of the features that has elicited sympathy from the general public, academia, and critics and has prevented scholars from fully appreciating monster's broader cultural role from standpoints comparable to those in this book.

The role that post-Soviet vampires play in their imaginary society is dramatically different from that of their English-speaking counterparts. They also form secret societies, but these are by no means marginal in relation to the world of humans. Their position of power closely resembles that of an invincible secret police in a totalitarian state modeled after the Federal Security Service of the Russian Federation (the KGB's successor, the FSB), supplemented by a Mafia-like order. Vampires govern human society; they establish the rules and reign supreme over humans. Medieval allusions are omnipresent in the fiction of post-Soviet society as well as in its political discourse. But unlike offerings from the United States or United Kingdom, Gothic allusions in Russia are far from implying that the totalitarian rule of the vampires harks back to the remote historical past. On the contrary, these allusions relate to the restitution of quasi-medieval social norms in contemporary society. Post-Soviet monsters embody currently ongoing social transformations effected by the Putin regime.

In my book *Gothic Society: A Morphology of a Nightmare* (2007), I argued that post-Soviet fictional and cinematographic monsters acting in nightmare scenarios are expressions of the unprocessed memory of Stalinism. I emphasized there that post-Soviet fantasy can prove productive in exploring the hidden mechanisms of the unprocessed and uncondemned memory of the terror that corrupts and corrodes post-Soviet society.[151] In these vampire sagas, humans are treated by vampires much as concentration camp prisoners must have been, which communicates in a most disturbing way a perverted post-Soviet historical memory of the Stalinist terror. Post-Soviet fiction and film, which appear to have no traces of realism, nevertheless function as a valuable tool in understanding Russian realities because they reflect the changing social norms. In that book I also analyzed the historical amnesia that has been instrumental to Putin's memory politics, which are focused on the rehabilitation of Stalinism.[152]

Post-Soviet cultural production differs from its Western counterpart in that it reveals the emergence of new moral relations and a new social order in post-Soviet society. The fictional Gothic monsters serve as a perfect metaphor for the neo-medieval Gothic society that is taking shape in contemporary Russia; the way in which those monsters relate to humans is redolent of premodern laws, customs, and ideas of the state. Today we are witnessing in Russia the emergence of a quasi-feudal social dependence as the basis for interpersonal relations, paralleled by the rapid dehumanization of the "lower orders" (who appear destined for eventual enserfment), a passive acceptance of the conditional nature of property, and the total absence of an independent legal system. Gothic Aesthetic provides the imagery and vocabulary to conceptualize those changes, which are rooted in the Soviet Gulag, Russia's Unmasterable Past. Putin's regime indulges in the victorious memory of the perpetrators.[153] Even though the cult of death has no political bearings at the moment and Gothic Aesthetic manifests itself uniquely as a cultural and attitudinal trend in the United States and Europe, the Russian experience suggests that this antihumanistic aesthetic may have social and political potential.

FOUR

Harry Potter, Tanya Grotter, and Death in the Coming-of-Age Novel

The Riddle of Potter's Success[1]

Why have the Harry Potter books "outsold everything under the sun?"[2] This question haunts the abundant corpus of literature about the boy wizard, which now totals more than seven thousand titles. Reviewers contemplate the million-copy print runs and the sales records and even try to calculate the number of trucks that would be needed to deliver the latest installment to its eager audience. They marvel at the flourishing global entertainment franchise that has sprouted on this fertile soil. There is no question that the reach of Pottermania expands way beyond popular culture: top universities—Durham and Yale, to mention just two—have recently introduced the Harry Potter books into their curriculum, with the declared aim, in the case of Yale, of exploring "Christian themes such as sin, evil and resurrection."[3] Less ambitious campuses are offering "the Harry Potter experience" as an extracurricular activity.[4] Elsewhere, "Wizardry from Elementary School to College" is invoked to encourage students to study well and acquire leadership skills.[5] And education is not the only area where Pottermania is thriving. Psychologists are even using the series' nonhumans and werewolves to analyze human behavior, in the conviction that their studies can help "young people overcome moderate levels of worry, anxiety or depressive feelings."[6] One can only guess how many psychoanalysts actually bring Harry Potter into their counseling sessions.

The orthodox reading of the Harry Potter plot is that it revolves around the "fight of good against evil," because Harry, the good young wizard, finds himself under constant attack from Voldemort, a horrible old wizard and the utmost evil. The plot of all seven books is driven by Voldemort's desire to lay his hands on "the last of the Potters."[7] And until the very end, Harry miraculously escapes all possible dangers. But even with all the witchcraft added, does this impress the reader as an original, fresh, or one-of-a-kind plot? With that in mind, the question of how this unsophisticated framework has been able to enthrall a vast audience of children and adults alike and has had such a powerful impact on contemporary mass culture merits serious consideration. What ingredients went to make this unassuming—and totally predictable—storyline such an unprecedented sensation? Because Harry, part of a tradition that harks back to (and even beyond) Peter Pan, is far from the first literary protagonist in possession of supernatural powers, the magic alone cannot explain his stunning success.

The lack of originality and the conformity of the fantasy world the series has constructed are sometimes viewed as a major secret of its success.[8] Rowling's works are described as a "secondary secondary world, made up of intelligently patchworked derivative motifs from all sorts of children's literature (. . .) written for people whose imaginative lives are confined to TV cartoons, and the exaggerated (more exciting, not threatening) mirror-worlds of soaps, reality TV and celebrity gossip."[9]

The artistic quality of J. K. Rowling's creation is at best in serious dispute. The sporadic attempts to compare Rowling's prose with Lewis Carroll, Jane Austen, and Dickens cannot sustain any serious literary analysis.[10] On the contrary, the Harry Potter stories belong to the old genre of boarding-school novel: their characters do not develop, their plots and puzzles are predictable, and they lack any original authorial philosophy. Written in a "pedestrian, ungrammatical prose style," they represent a "bad case of cultural infantilism."[11] In his famous review "Can 35 Million Book Buyers Be Wrong? Yes," Harold Bloom sees its style as rife with "clichés, all of the 'stretch his legs' variety."[12]

Sometimes the success of the Harry Potter books is attributed to their ability to engage "the social, cultural, and psychological preoccupations of our times," to represent "anxieties and fixations about individuality," and to help overcome them.[13] But since this implicitly assumes that literature has a therapeutic role, the same could be said of any novel. Besides, expressing her protagonists' passions, torments, or joys is not the author's forte. The reader can hardly enjoy the books for their depictions of the finer movements of Harry's soul. In fact, we mostly learn about Harry's emotions and feelings on what is literally a gut level: at the most dramatic turns of the narrative, we hear—time and again—about Harry's stomach "lurching," "writhing," and "turning over."[14] "Soaring sensations in his stomach" communicate his anxiety, happiness and he even feels shame "in his stomach."[15] And when the stomach is not directly involved in the description of how Harry feels, his emotions still do not escape the alimentary canal: for example, he might feel that his heart has just "shot upward into his throat."[16]

Much has been written on the connection between the spread of occult practices in the United States and the United Kingdom and Harry Potter's success. Although it remains debatable whether the Harry Potter's books helped promote Wicca, paganism, and witchcraft, or if they simply capitalized on the growing popularity of those beliefs, the series is much more popular than any books on Wicca itself.[17] Harry Potter's success is certainly symptomatic of a "vast hunger for unreality," as Harold Bloom puts it, but this begs the question of why that hunger is so prominent in the culture today.[18]

Economic factors dominate the explanations for the series' enthusiastic reception in every corner of the globe.[19] The commercialization and commodification of children's literature, the success of the Harry Potter marketing campaign, and Rowling's techniques for building anticipation and demand are justifiably listed among Pottermania's major triggers.[20] Commercialization and a strong market orientation, however, cannot explain why, among the plethora of for-profit books aimed at the young audience, the offering titled "Harry Potter" is way out ahead of the field.

However significant all these factors may be, I will not consider them further in the analysis that follows. Instead, using the concept of Gothic Aesthetic, I will explore in this chapter the essential components of the Harry Potter series. I will demonstrate that its success has much more to do with the specific nature of contemporary cultural conditions than with any other element. We will learn that Pottermania has grown out of the current celebration of death, and its relationship with that important cultural movement will be examined in all its complexity. And I will end by showing that the Harry Potter phenomenon is, in fact, nothing less than a manual on the art of death and dying, couched as a coming-of-age novel.[21] As Rowling puts it, "My books are largely about death."[22]

No Humanism for Muggles

Let us now take a closer look at why the invention of Muggles (as ordinary people are called in the series) has played such a vital role in the story's popularity.[23] Harry's friend Ron explains the implication of the word "Muggle" early in the tale: it is the supreme insult to call a wizard or witch a Muggle,[24] a disgrace to have a Muggle in one's family, and any witch or wizard who does would rather not talk about it.[25] From the wizard's point of view, living with Muggles is the worst misfortune imaginable.[26] The etymology of the word "Muggle" seems to relate to "mud," with the "d" replaced by a "g." On a number of occasions we see the word "Mudblood" used as a synonym for Muggle or to insult "human-born" wizards or witches, as the portrait of Walburga Black implies when it starts screaming "MUDBLOODS! SCUM! CREATURES OF DIRT!"[27] In the series' hierarchy of beings, Muggles are on a par with other inferior creatures such as the elves that are employed as house serfs. The books are saturated with a scornful disdain for the human race and humanity:

> Harry looked more closely and realized that what he had thought were decoratively carved thrones were actually mounds of carved humans: hundreds and hundreds of naked bodies, men, women, and children, all with rather stupid, ugly faces, twisted and pressed together to support the weight of the handsomely robed wizards. "Muggles," whispered Hermione. "In their rightful place. Come on, let's get going."[28]

The author exerts considerable effort in persuading her reader to despise Muggles. The first Muggles we meet in the story are Harry's foster family, the Dursleys, who have raised him since he was a baby. They are described as the most contemptible, obnoxious people; Harry views them with revulsion. His aunt Petunia is horse-faced and bony, her voice shrill and unpleasant.[29] Uncle Vernon is extremely rude and constantly shouts at everyone; he has "sausage-like fingers" and is compared to "a winded rhinoceros" with "small, sharp eyes" or to "a mouse being trodden on."[30] Harry thinks his cousin Dudley looks like a gorilla but more often sees him as a pig.[31] Dudley is "so large his bottom drooped over either side of the kitchen chair"; we see his "piggy little eyes fixed on the screen and his five chins wobbling as he ate continually."[32] Those portrayals walk a fine line between something that a school bully might say and the kind of hate speech in which people are compared to "filthy animals." These revolting Muggles are described as treating Harry, a male Cinderella, very badly, in way intended to rouse the reader's sympathies with the poor little orphan.[33] And the Dursleys are hardly the exception that proves the rule, because humans in general are represented here as disgusting, nasty, inferior creatures.

The series goes a step further than the writings of Tolkien (Tolkien is one of Rowling's favorite writers), who disdained humans for their inability to maintain high moral standards and was thus moved to invent hobbits and place them on a superior moral plane. The attitudes toward Muggles in the Harry Potter books involve no moral judgments about them: there are no universal values and no abstract good in Harry Potter's world.[34] Good is utterly subjective; it cannot be defined without reference to Harry himself.

The main reason for detesting humans is their innate incompetence in magic.[35] Humans belong to a different—an inferior—species.[36] Although the young witch Hermione campaigns out of the goodness of her heart for better conditions for house-elves, and Mr. Weasley, a pure-blood wizard, fights for Muggles' rights, this only highlights the hierarchical gap that separates wizards from humans and other nonwizards. And even though we belatedly learn that Dumbledore had "gained (. . .) many enemies" due to his "determined support for Muggle rights," this does not alter the overall perception of Muggles as by definition an inferior race.[37]

Unlike the witches or wizards of fairy tale, who are related—for better or worse—to the world of humans, wizards in the series are preoccupied with concealing the existence of the wizarding world from humans by modifying their memories, which is not presented as an ethically dubious act but as merely a matter of bureaucratic routine.[38] It has nothing to do with protecting humans from the shock of discovering a wizard's powers. Its goal, rather, is to prevent humans from getting in the wizards' way. This makes the wizards' attitudes similar to those of contemporary vampires. Another important similarity with the contemporary vampire saga consists in the fact that humans have nothing to contribute to the novels' internecine struggle between wizardly clans. Humans are passive bystanders, incapable of even grasping what is going on in those battles. They are so irrelevant that the potential effect of Voldemort's victory on the human world does not even warrant a mention. The notion of helping humans or doing anything simply because it would be good for them is totally alien to the wizards' reasoning. As Hagrid explains to Harry at the very beginning of the story, it would be too much trouble for wizards to provide humans with magic solutions to their difficulties.[39] On the contrary, levitating Muggles into the sky or making a Muggle child suffer may be fun for a wizard.[40]

The series present human beings as powerless and helpless creatures, inferior both mentally and aesthetically to the nonhuman protagonists who capture the full attention of the writer and her reader. The distinction between humans and nonhumans has nothing to do with morality or any other spiritual quality. It is purely biological or, one might even say, racial.

Superior in all respects to humans to the same extent as vampires, wizards, and witches can be seen as belonging to a different race, with innate powers that cannot be acquired through training or by force of will.

From this standpoint alone, the story meets some of the important requirements of Gothic Aesthetic that we discussed in earlier chapters. The Potter series' enormous success may indeed rest, at least in part, on its articulation of a deep scorn for humanity, but the Harry Potter phenomenon could not have triumphed as it did on the strength of that alone. Various other strategies operated in these books to achieve their commercial goals. The ambiguity of her boy wizard allowed Rowling to combine the features of various popular protagonists into one character, whose peculiar relationship with his antagonist will be seen as key to the series' success. We will now go on to consider who (or what) Harry Potter is and to explore the secrets of his irresistible appeal.

Harry's Nightmares

Nightmares occupy a significant place in the Harry Potter plot, and that is among the reasons for the Potter saga's success. Harry is dogged by nightmares, which persist in coming true, thus throwing light on some of the story's key events and unriddling some of its key puzzles.[41] Rowling follows a general trend in pop culture by employing several of the clichés of hypnotics (discussed in the introduction) to imitate a state of nightmare in her books.[42]

Harry's story actually begins when his Aunt Petunia comes to wake him up, and, like many of his literary predecessors in the preceding two centuries, he is trying to remember the dream he was having.[43] Also like them, he is inclined to interpret the extraordinary events that have happened to him as a dream.[44] Readers can, in fact, never be sure if Harry really did wake up at the very beginning of the story or if that was only a "false awakening," which would mean that the whole story is the recounting of his nightmare, which has no protagonist other than him. This impression is reinforced by the elegiac end to his adventures when he is "thinking now only of the four-poster bed lying waiting for him in Gryffindor Tower."[45] As in a true nightmare state, anxiety and uncertainty stalk the reader from beginning to end.[46] Like many other literary protagonists (victims of manmade nightmares) before him, Harry often wakes up with his heart beating wildly, "drenched in cold sweat."[47] As Harry's nightmares become more frequent from book to book, they also grow more terrifying.[48] Most are focused on the pursuit that corresponds to the structural framework of the plot: his attempts to escape a mortal danger.[49] Often his nightmares predict events that eventually happen in literary reality of the story.[50] By "literary reality" I mean what we, the readers, deem credible in a work of fiction, what we readily accept as a trustworthy account of life as depicted in the literary text. Prophecies as well as nightmares confuse the readers' sense of time and send the narration in reverse, thus helping to reproduce the temporality of nightmare.[51]

Another cliché of hypnotics that Rowling employs is that Harry's sight is often obstructed: He peers around corners, through cracks, or down into a bathroom sink.[52] Or he blinks or only opens "his eyes wide enough to squint"[53] at critical points in the narrative. In *The Chamber of Secrets*, for instance, he hears a hissing voice commanding the basilisk to kill him and keeps his eyes tight shut so that the creature will not stare into them and kill him.[54] Actions often take place in darkness, and objects are blurred.[55] Is this yet another dimension of Harry's shortsightedness, which has afflicted many other nightmare-prone protagonists before him? His vision is frequently "foggy," or he feels that everything is "dissolving in a whirl of dull color."[56] The text persistently focuses on dizziness and vertigo, on a rapidity of movement that blurs everything into a "swirl of colors." Nightmare, flight, and pursuit are rarely described without mentioning that Harry is feeling "dizzy" or "drowsy," with everything around him "spinning," reeling, and eddying.[57] Or he falls "through something icy-cold and black; it was like being sucked into a dark whirlpool."[58] The point of these descriptions is to disorient the reader, to wrest away the habitual perception of reality, and to build an association with the sounds and visual effects of cinematographic nightmares.

The repetitions—of words, phrases, and entire passages—that also inhabit Rowling's prose have been assessed as improving the attraction of Rowling's descriptions for her readers.[59] In fact, repeating phrases help to bemuse and bewilder the reader. Along with eerie spinning motions and vertigo, they draw the reader deeper into the nightmare's narcotic trance. Essentially meaningless words and phrases such as *Expecto patronum!* or *Expelliamus!* trigger Harry's nightmares and alert perceptive young readers to prepare to enter a trance-like state.

The point in a void, another device of literary hypnotics, which prompts nightmare trance in the protagonist—and in the reader—also has a role to play here. To give just one example, in *The Goblet of Fire*, Harry falls asleep during a lesson and dreams of flying. This happy dream turns nightmarish when his gaze is fixated on a point, which first materializes as a house and then as a dark window.[60] Harry hears that Voldemort is planning to kill him, he sees a horrible, hissing snake, and he watches Wormtail being tortured. After Voldemort utters one of those magic words, Harry loses control over his body and his emotions and starts screaming in pain. He comes to his senses to see his entire class standing around him. As he stands up, his classmates back away, looking "unnerved."[61] Professor Trelawney tells Harry that he had been "rolling on the floor, clutching his scar."[62]

As in so many literary (and real-life) nightmares, Harry also sees his doubles. In the nineteenth-century classics, doppelgangers obscured the boundaries between literary reality and nightmare and shook the reader's sense of normalcy. Dostoevsky in *The Double* and Jerome K. Jerome in his unfinished novel, for example, used doubles to communicate a disturbed sense of nightmare temporality.[63] This device of literary hypnotics has been widely adopted in horror movies and especially in the vampire sagas. But there is a great deal of difference between those contemporary cinemato-graphic doppelgangers—and Harry's doubles too—and those described by the classical works. In contrast to the nightmare of Dostoevsky's poor clerk Golyadkin or the nightmare portrayed by Jerome, Rowling's doubles are droll and lifeless dolls. In *The Deathly Hallows*, Harry watches no less than six of his doppelgangers in action, and the only feeling this produces in him is a mild sense of outrage at this violation of his privacy.[64]

Nightmares are every bit as important to the Harry Potter plot as they are to the vampire sagas. The nightmarish agenda that serves to dimin-ish the readers' critical abilities and render them more compliant with the author's intentions is the perfect setup for the Harry Potter plot. But unlike the great writers who explored and scrutinized human emotions and the human psyche to understand what distinguishes nightmares from literary reality[65] and literary reality from reality itself (as well as from madness), Rowling does not distinguish between her protagonist's nightmares and his other states of mind. She has no interest in investigating this psychological experience through the optics of literature.

The Skeletons in Harry's Closet

Vampires and Harry

The Harry Potter books were written at the end of the 1990s, when the popularity of vampires, in both fiction and movies, was growing. Did Row-ling, for all her sense of the market, miss the opportunity to include those trendsetting characters in her books? Or is the Harry Potter series yet another playground for vampires? Here we will explore the various profiles of pop-culture icons that Rowling accumulates in her protagonist and see exactly what image emerges from all those "shades of grey."

At a first glance, vampires seem to be marginal here, even though they are mentioned quite early on.[66] There is talk of a textbook, *Voyages with Vampires*, of the "trouble" that Professor Quirrell had with vampires in southern Europe, and also rumors that the next defense against the dark arts teacher might be a vampire, a speculation that pleasantly surprises the students who hear it.[67] Dementors are often interpreted as vampires because they possess several vampiric qualities. Like the vampires in Sergei Lukyanenko's *Night Watch*, they suck the happiness out of their victims, and they are described much as the walking dead might be, with empty eye sockets and gaping holes instead of mouths.[68]

Is Voldemort, the sinister wizard, a vampire too? His name has frequently been described as suggestive of a vampiric nature: "Vol-de-mort" translates from French as "flight-of-death," which is reminiscent of the traditional depiction of a vampire swooping in on the wings of a bat.[69] Voldemort is also half-dead, he "has no body."[70] He has "a half-life, a cursed life," which sounds eminently vampiric. He describes himself as having been "less than spirit, less than the meanest ghost," and Dumbledore tells Harry "not being truly alive, he cannot be killed."[71] We also learn that he needs Harry's blood to repossess his body. Readers are exposed to scenes of blood drinking as graphic in their brutal naturalism as anything the contemporary vampire sagas might have to offer:

> Squinting down, struggling hopelessly at the ropes binding him, he [Harry] saw the shining silver dagger shaking in Wormtail's remaining hand. He felt its point penetrate the crook of his right arm and blood seeping down the sleeve of his torn robes. Wormtail, still panting with pain, fumbled in his pocket for a glass vial and held it to Harry's cut, so that a dribble of blood fell into it.
>
> He staggered back to the cauldron with Harry's blood. He poured it inside.[72]

The overwhelming majority of critics who agree that Voldemort is "the classical archetypal figures of horror fiction: the vampire,"[73] consider him Harry's total opposite and his committed antagonist.[74] For example, Annette Klemp claims that one of Rowling's greatest accomplishments is that she has made "good a great deal more interesting and attractive than evil."[75] But is this indeed the case or is there an alternative interpretation of Harry's persona?

Since Harry watched Voldemort drinking a unicorn's blood in *The Sorcerer's Stone*, he has been suffering from persistent headaches and begins having recurrent nightmares about a blood-drinking vampire.[76] On one occasion, Hermione asserts that he ought not to try a blood-flavored lollipop, as it is probably more to the taste of vampires[77] (a remark that seems totally unrelated to anything else in this episode). Later, though, we learn that Harry actually manages to do a good job compounding a Draught of Living Death (another name for a vampire?). It is, in fact, the only potion that he ever manages to make perfectly, to the major astonishment of his friends and teacher.[78] We also know that Voldemort plans to achieve immortality by killing Harry and he also wants Harry's blood.[79] As we have just seen, the author shows him consuming Harry's blood in *The Goblet of Fire*.[80] She stresses that Harry's blood now runs in Voldemort's veins: "He took your blood and rebuilt his living body with it!"[81]

Immortality—one of the reasons frequently evoked for the recently burgeoning popularity of vampires—is an issue of considerable concern in the Harry Potter saga.[82] All the most powerful characters, including Dumbledore and Voldemort, strive toward it.[83] The author is quite straightforward (not to say repetitive) in using the phoenix as a symbol of immortality and of the return to life after dying: the secret society formed to fight Voldemort is called the Order of Phoenix; a phoenix saves Harry's life on a number of occasions; and Voldemort's and Harry's wands contain a feather from the same phoenix.[84] Once having achieved immortality, Harry is hailed as "the worthy possessor of the Hallows" and a "true master of death."[85] And he comes back to life, as the undead should.[86] (Rowling even has him accepting the accolades of the portraits of the dead headmasters and headmistresses of Hogwarts.[87]) As discussed in the previous chapter, immortality is the most common characteristic of the vampire in the contemporary vampire sagas; one must submit to the vampire's bite in order to be "turned" and live forever. The plot-arc of all seven books culminates in Harry's murder: "'I let him kill me,' said Harry. 'Didn't I?' 'You did,' said Dumbledore, nodding."[88] Has Harry too been turned?

There are other parallels between the Harry Potter story and the vampire sagas that support this interpretation. Like those sagas' protagonists—Bella Swan in *Twilight* or Elena Gilbert in *The Vampire Diaries*—Harry is constantly seen bleeding, wounded, suffering intense pain, tortured, hiding, and fleeing. The whole story of this sad little orphan boy revolves around his attempts to escape a violent death, and his death is the true culmination of the plot. It plays an extremely important role in the narrative because (among other reasons we will discuss later) all riddles are solved and seemingly all keys are given to the reader when the dead Harry is in the netherworld. In the final chapter he is called "the would-be victim who had survived," which offers an interpretation of his persona as one hunted and hounded by Voldemort the vampire.[89] In other words, Harry Potter's story follows all the major tropes of a vampiric coming-of-death novel. If we accept the series plot at face value, in terms of a distinct protagonist and an equally distinct antagonist (Harry and Voldemort), Harry will learn in the course of the countless flights and pursuits in this seven-volume-long nightmare how victimhood feels and will realize that he cannot escape a violent and horrific death, even though this ultimately brings him immortality.

The reason Harry bears so many vampiric traits without actually being called a vampire is clear. When the Potter saga began, vampires were not yet the well-established protagonists in fiction and films that they are today. It was at the time by no means a given that parents would willingly present their children with a boarding-school novel featuring a vampire as the main positive hero. Disguising a vampire as a skinny, bespectacled little boy allowed the series to profit from the vampire's incipient popularity without alarming parents unnecessarily. But do other pop culture icons go to make up this boy wizard? That is what we will explore next.

Harry's Medical History

Harry's resemblance to a vampire may have contributed to his success, but it is still insufficient as an explanation of his enormous popularity; many other vampires, all more impressive than he, were available to audiences when he was being invented. Then what is it about him? Since the plot culminates in Harry's death, another plausible interpretation of the story is that it is a tale of horror, of a boy fleeing from a maniac, a murderer who wants to kill him for no particular reason at all other than to fulfill some obscure "prophecy" (Professor Trelawney's prophecy in Harry's case[90]). What, then, are the other qualities that have made this protagonist so universally appealing?

Harry is, as we have seen, neither an outstanding student nor a morally superior individual. In addition, he is not portrayed as handsome (in fact his appearance is barely described at all), and he is not even particularly healthy. When we meet Harry at the age of ten, he is described as a skinny, black-haired, bespectacled boy.[91] His look is "unhealthy," and he is constantly described as looking "terrible," "pale," and sometimes "pale and scared-looking."[92] "Harry, are you all right?" is a question frequently asked by his friends.[93] He is quite sickly, to the point of being mocked for spending so much time in the hospital wing (Draco Malfoy teases him, saying that being out of the hospital wing for "a whole week" must be Harry's record[94]). He is portrayed as frequently feeling feverish or "sweating and shaking."[95] His hands are often seen "trembling."[96] He has problems sleeping, wakes up "drenched in cold sweat," and he sleeps less and less well as the plot progresses.[97] We see him in "shock" or filled with "lethargy," and at other times he shows signs of hyperactivity, when he is described as "shaking" and incapable of sitting down.[98] Although, as we will see later, it would be too much to say that Rowling is portraying symptoms that fit any particular diagnosis, is it mere chance that what Harry is experiencing so closely resembles the typical side effects of, and symptoms of withdrawal from, antidepressants such as Prozac, Sarafem, or Fontex? Those drugs were commonly prescribed in the UK in the 1990s, when Rowling was struggling with her own depression.[99] (An upset stomach—a constant issue for Harry—is another common side effect.) But even apart from these symptoms, Harry's psychological state is far from normal. Often he feels "familiar flutterings of panic."[100] He is spoken of as "violent" and "unbalanced."[101] But we do not need to rely on third-party accounts to realize that the boy has serious problems with anger management. He shouts to adults and yells at his closest and most loyal friends, to whom he is repeatedly rude and intolerant.[102] He is notoriously prone to fits of anger that sometimes last "for days."[103]

Is Harry just an unbalanced teenager who finds it hard to control himself? No, there is definitely more to it than that: when he is in a rage, he actually becomes dangerous. For example, when filled with a "white-hot anger" against Dumbledore, his role model and mentor, he ends up destroying furniture in his headmaster's office.[104] And the furniture is not the only potential target; sometimes Harry is even murderously angry: "A boiling hate erupted in Harry's chest, leaving no place for fear. For the first time in his life, he wanted his wand back in his hand, not to defend himself, but to attack . . . to kill."[105] Harry is often described as feeling "exhausted," "drained and strangely empty," and in a state of "shock and exhaustion," especially after these fits of violence.[106] But was our author aware that violence followed by fatigue is a cause for serious concern? From the very first book we know that Harry often feels "strange."[107] Early in the narrative, he starts hearing menacing yet enticing voices: "Come . . . come to me. . . . Let me rip you. . . . Let me tear you. . . . Let me kill you . . ."[108] and "'. . .

kill . . . time to kill . . .' Harry strained his ears. Distantly, from the floor above, and growing fainter still, he heard the voice: '. . . I smell blood . . . I SMELL BLOOD!'"[109]

We are told that Harry had his first auditory delusion at the age of eleven, which is typically when certain mental illnesses tend to emerge.[110] And as he grows older, those hallucinations become part of his daily experience. Apart from the ominous voices, those of his dead parents also "intrude" into his mind, making it hard for him to concentrate in class.[111] An empty picture on the wall tells him that the "first sign of madness" is "talking to your own head."[112] The author does seem to be well aware of the medical side of this problem: she has Ron tell Harry that hearing voices is not a good thing, "even in the wizarding world."[113] Harry's fits of anger and the voices he hears affect him physically, leaving him "sweating and shaking," another symptom of a serious mental health issue; and he also faints.[114] Since no one else hears the voices, Harry alone knows what they are telling him, so he tells what he hears to Ron and Hermione, in reports that become an essential part of their interaction. On occasion, Ron and Hermione follow Harry's instructions with little idea of what is going on.[115]

Constant fear for his life paralyzes Harry and interferes with his daily activities and his studies; he expects Voldemort "to come bursting through the door at any moment," plotting Harry's murder.[116] He relates the surges of fear to his episodes of headaches.[117] The reader does not need to be reminded that Harry is chronically prone to headaches, which are often described as causing him terrible pain.[118] As the plot moves forward, his famous scar hurts more and more often, until he develops persistent migraines. While he interprets his headaches as a sign of approaching danger[119] and refuses to acknowledge that he might simply be sick, the author alerts the readers to his misjudgment by having his friends advise him to get medical help.[120] The narration shows how his angst produces physical symptoms apart from the headaches: his scar "aches," he feels "almost feverish" and "shivery."[121] And the reader may well begin to suspect that Harry is not experiencing all this just because he is upset. In addition, Harry sees danger everywhere and is frightened by the most ordinary events.[122] One might at first think that Voldemort, the incarnation of evil, is the only one he fears. But that is not the case at all. For example, he reacts badly to the cool welcome he gets from one of his teachers. At first he thinks it is just a matter of simple dislike, but before long he becomes certain that Snape wants to see him dead. At one point, he even believes that Snape is about to poison him, which sits well with his general belief that his potions teacher is plotting against him, to "finish [him] off," as he "feverishly" explains to

Ron.[123] Another of his near-paranoid convictions is striking: he sees a black dog on the street and decides that this must be a dark wizard coming to get him.[124] Later, he learns that this shape shifter is his godfather, who appears variously as a black dog and a burning log in the fireplace, strange feats of magic that are hard to distinguish from hallucinations. And as the plot progresses, those hallucinations become increasingly intense and frequent. Especially telling is the scene in which Harry confuses himself with his dead father toward the end of *The Prisoner of Azkaban*.[125]

Harry's Delusions

Harry Potter's story really begins when he suddenly learns that he is rich and famous and that his survival is critical to the salvation of a clandestine universe, the wizarding world.[126] When he finds out about his new situation, he does not believe it at first, feeling that this unexpected fame is completely undeserved.[127] Not long after, though, he gains some assurance of his extraordinary magical powers and abilities. He discovers, to his delight, that he can fly (on a broomstick, at least) and cast magical spells. Soon he also learns that his unique position in this newly discovered world full of magic also entails a threat to his life, from Voldemort, the Dark Lord. He assumes that this ultimate Evil has just one goal—to kill him in order to regain its power and reassert its dominance. As the plot advances, Harry loses his earlier doubts about his unique powers and his mission, and becomes supremely self-assured.

From the very beginning, Harry denies his human identity. He does not want to be an ordinary boy.[128] But even his new wizardly persona does not fully satisfy him. He still wants to be "somebody—anybody—else" but himself.[129] He is only too aware that his friends think he loves "playing the hero."[130] He becomes persuaded that the very fact of his existence is a miracle and that the world is divided between those who want to protect him (and join the Order of Phoenix, a secret society whose current purpose is to shield him from Voldemort and his Death Eaters) and those who will ally with Voldemort to ultimately kill him. These unfolding discoveries may well raise concerns about Harry's mental health: they resemble the first symptoms of schizophrenia.

Soon we learn that Harry believes he is several different persons at once, and a snake. Are Voldemort and Harry two separate characters? The author insists that Harry himself is not sure about it: "He was Harry . . . Harry, not Voldemort . . . ," and Harry also knows that he and Voldemort are one and that Voldemort—and he himself—are the world's most powerful magicians.[131] Harry is designed to share Voldemort's soul from his earliest days, when part of that soul lodged within him.[132] In the "King's Cross" chapter of *The Deathly Hallows*, the reader is offered confirmation that Harry and Voldemort are one, that their destinies are bound together closer than "two wizards have ever been," and that "their lives are inseparable."[133] We are told on a number of occasions that Harry feels Voldemort inside him and that Voldemort speaks through Harry's mouth and shares his "thoughts and emotions."[134] Voldemort's voice is the one Harry hears most often in his hallucinations, the one that merges with his own inner voice. In addition, Voldemort is called "a man who was both kin and mortal enemy" to him.[135]

The author goes so far as to describe Harry feeling his body becoming intertwined with Voldemort's until he can no longer distinguish them. He sees through "the creature's red eyes" and the "creature" (Voldemort) speaks through his mouth:

> He was gone from the hall, he was locked in the coils of a creature with red eyes, so tightly bound that Harry did not know where his body ended and the creature's began. They were fused together, bound by pain, and there was no escape—
>
> And when the creature spoke, it used Harry's mouth, so that in his agony he felt his jaw move. . . .
>
> "Kill me now, Dumbledore . . ." (. . .)
>
> And as Harry's heart filled with emotion, the creature's coils loosened, the pain was gone; Harry was lying facedown on the floor, his glasses gone, shivering as though he lay upon ice, not wood.[136]

As often happens in this narrative, the scene has ended with Harry lying on the ground shivering and wondering where his glasses are.

Amanda Cockrell has noted that Voldemort is "Harry's shadow side," his "dark twin," who is as important to the plot development as Harry himself, to the point that that they could even be considered doppelgangers.[137] But there is certainly much more to be said about their relationship, since the text actually allows us to trace the construction of Voldemort's image as a figment of Harry's imagination. That image emerges as a visualization of the "spasm of horror" that grips Harry as he tries to make sense of the nightmare from which he has just awoken. At first, however hard he tries, Harry cannot picture Voldemort's horrible face but gradually it resolves into a vaguely snake-like image.[138]

Harry is also made to look oddly similar to the young Tom Marvolo

Riddle (Voldemort's original name).[139] There are "strange likenesses" between them, both being thin, black-haired boys, and they even tilt their heads in the same way.[140] Harry is said to carry "the mark of a Dark Wizard," another similarity to Voldemort.[141] Voldemort, like Harry, was an orphan and his schoolmates thought him mad. In sum, "Voldemort" sounds like nothing so much as the imaginings of a naïve young megalomaniac who has invented this fearsome identity in order to be unique and great and to escape the dismal mundanity of his life. Riddle tells Harry a very personal story about an unhappy childhood, which may make the reader wonder if what we are hearing here is not Harry's own inner voice.[142] Finally, Harry simply feels sorry for both of them.[143] This has even prompted a suggestion that Harry Potter's whole story could be read as a wish-fulfillment fantasy fashioned to compensate for an unpleasant childhood.[144]

Yet the times when Harry takes on Voldemort's personality are not portrayed as harmless flights of the boy's imagination. He is described as suffering serious physical symptoms: when he visualizes Riddle, his brain "seemed to have jammed,"[145] he experiences "strange flashes of Voldemort's thoughts or mood" that cause his scar to "prickle."[146] As we know from *The Sorcerer's Stone*, Harry converses freely with snakes, a fact that alone might have given readers cause to worry about his well-being. But Harry's symptoms are not confined to a fictional universe and the wizarding world. Let us consider this description:

> During a visit to my office, a young man hesitantly reveals his belief that snakes are living behind the mirror in his college dormitory room and that they are forcing their thoughts into his head.[147]

Is this "young man" Harry Potter, who talks to a boa constrictor in the zoo at the very beginning of his story? No, this subject's name is Paul, and he is a real patient described by a real psychiatrist. In his monograph, Dr. Robert Freedman uses Paul's case to explain that delusions such as this are characteristic of schizophrenia. These symptoms sound alarmingly similar to those we encounter in Harry Potter, who imagines himself not only as the horrific Lord Voldemort but also on occasion as the Dark Lord's gigantic snake, the symbol of his power and a terrifying weapon. He identifies with the snake to the point of calling its fangs "my fangs": "I was inside that snake. (. . .) I was the snake."[148] And he is portrayed thoroughly enjoying the experience:

The dream changed . . .

His body felt smooth, powerful and flexible. He was gliding between shining metal bars, across dark, cold stone. . . . He was flat against the floor, sliding along on his belly. . . . It was dark, yet he could see objects around him shimmering in strange, vibrant colors. . . . He was turning his head. . . . At first glance the corridor was empty . . . but no . . . a man was sitting on the floor ahead, his chin drooping on to his chest, his outline gleaming in the dark . . .

Harry put out his tongue. . . . He tasted the man's scent on the air. . . . He was alive but drowsing . . . sitting in front of a door at the end of the corridor . . .

Harry longed to bite the man . . . but he must master the impulse . . . he had more important work to do . . .

But the man was stirring . . . a silvery cloak fell from his legs as he jumped to his feet; and Harry saw his vibrant, blurred outline towering above him, saw a wand withdrawn from a belt. . . . He had no choice. . . . He reared high from the floor and struck once, twice, three times, plunging his fangs deeply into the man's flesh, feeling his ribs splinter beneath his jaws, feeling the warm gush of blood . . .

The man was yelling in pain . . . then he fell silent. . . . He slumped backward against the wall. . . . Blood was splattering onto the floor . . .

His forehead hurt terribly. . . . It was aching fit to burst.[149]

Harry later tells Professor McGonagall that he was the snake that had attacked Mr. Weasley, his friend's father. He reports to Dumbledore that he saw the whole thing "from the snake's point of view" and, looking back on that discussion, acknowledges to himself that "I felt like I wanted to attack Dumbledore, too . . ."[150]

In this altered state, when he becomes both Voldemort and his snake, the only thing he desires is to sink his fangs into human flesh.[151] The author makes it clear that Harry regularly conflates himself with Voldemort or a snake and can easily become lost in those various identities:

He felt dirty, contaminated. (. . .) He had not merely seen the snake, he had been the snake, he knew it now . . .

And then a truly terrible thought occurred to him, a memory bobbing to the surface of his mind, one that made his insides writhe and squirm like serpents. . . . (. . .)

I did attack Mr. Weasley last night, it was me, Voldemort made me do it and he could be inside me, listening to my thoughts right now. . . .

Yes, thought Harry, that would fit, he would turn into a snake of course . . . and when he's possessing me, then we both transform.[152]

Harry wonders if the uncontrollable craving to attack people he supposedly loves (which he confesses to his godfather Sirius) means that he is going mad.[153] He is obsessed with images of his dead parents and friends and is seeing them everywhere. He is described as regularly experiencing episodes that greatly resemble psychotic breaks: he faints, falls to the floor, and has visions and hallucinations.[154] Sometimes they are triggered by a sudden surge of anger. As occasionally happens to patients in the throes of psychosis, when angry enough Harry is seized by an irrational desire to kill. He usually comes to his senses lying on the floor, sometimes even vomiting or trying hard not to. For example, when he dreams that he sees himself reflected in a mirror as Voldemort, he falls out of bed.[155] Once realizing that the "wild laughter" of the murderous Voldemort was "coming out of his own mouth," he falls "panting on the floor," "shaking," and willing himself not to "vomit all over Ron."[156]

These episodes happen throughout the narrative, in bed, in his teacher's office, in class, during exams.[157] At such times, Harry is unable to distinguish himself from Voldemort, even when he is told to "stop acting like a maniac": "'I was You-Know-Who,' said Harry, and he stretched out his hands in the darkness and held them up to his face to check that they were no longer deathly white and long-fingered."[158] He is also "terrified that he might become the serpent again in his sleep and awake to find out that he attacked Ron."[159]

It has been noted that Rowling may have drawn on popular medical literature in depicting Harry's symptoms of psychological illness.[160] The fact that she never lets her imagination lead her too far from the clinical descriptions of mental illness was observed, for example, in a study comparing the real symptoms of headaches and migraines to descriptions in the Harry Potter series.[161] Readers versed in psychology have speculated that Harry suffers from multiple personality disorder or displays symptoms of schizophrenia.[162] As anyone who has ever consulted the *Encyclopedia Britannica* (the most commonly used encyclopedia in pre-Internet Britain) on schizophrenia would immediately recognize, Harry's symptoms make him almost a textbook case. The *Britannica* describes the primary manifestations of schizophrenia as "the presence of hallucinations and delusions, disorganized speech and behavior" and states that the first signs of schizophrenia typically manifest themselves during the teen years or in early adulthood. Another typically schizophrenic syndrome is the delusion of grandeur, which is described as the "fixed, false belief that one possesses superior qualities such as genius, fame, omnipotence, or wealth." Individuals suffering from that delusion may believe that they can fly and that if they are not famous themselves, they at least have a close relationship with a famous person. And being kept for long periods in a closet, as Harry was, creates prime environmental conditions for schizophrenia.[163] In addition, he exhibits all the commonly recognized features of the psychotic break such as "auditory hallucinations (hearing voices), paranoid delusions (believing everyone is out to cause you harm), anxiety, anger, emotional distance, violence, and suicidal thoughts and behavior."[164] Indeed, the descriptions of Harry's "transformations" into Voldemort or a snake parallel the nonspecialist medical literature on psychotic breaks with surprising accuracy.

Some of Harry's symptoms may also be identified in descriptions of paranoia for the layperson. As the *Britannica* tells us:

> A person suffering from paranoia thinks or believes that other people are plotting against or trying to harm, harass, or persecute him in some way. The paranoiac exaggerates trivial incidents in everyday life into menacing or threatening situations and cannot rid himself of suspicions and apprehensions.

To this impressive list of mental disorders, the Harry Potter author adds seizures (or "fits" as his friend calls them: "I thought you were having a fit or something"[165]). Beginning in *The Chamber of Secrets*, Harry starts having episodes that closely resemble attacks of hallucinatory epilepsy.[166] The *Britannica* tells us that epileptic seizures begin as "visual or auditory hallucinations that last from a fraction of a second to a few seconds. The individual may also experience intense fear, abdominal pain or discomfort, or an awareness of increased respiration rate or heartbeat. (. . .) A person undergoing a convulsion loses consciousness and falls to the ground. (. . .) Immediately afterward, the individual is usually confused and sleepy and may have a headache but will not remember the seizure."[167]

This description recapitulates countless scenes in the Harry Potter series. After Harry has heard his dead parents' voices or visualized Voldemort or imagined being a snake, he is found lying on the ground (or in his bed or in the hospital wing), his glasses knocked off, exhausted, in a cold sweat, vomiting and shivering.[168] As Amy Billone has pointed out, the descriptions of Harry's headaches and the sound of spells such as "Expecto patronum!" resemble the "aura" that precedes an epileptic seizure.[169] He feels a "horribly familiar wave of cold sweat" immediately before a seizure; it is "as though freezing water were rising in his chest, cutting at his insides."[170] When the seizure comes on, the room starts "blurring" and he feels his insides "turning" and his scar "burning" and "aching." In the course of the seizure, which is often triggered by extreme fear, he may imagine his parents' murder or hear his mother's voice "inside his head." He blacks out and comes to lying "in the hospital wing" or, on one occasion, on the classroom floor with Professor Lupin tapping him "hard on the face."[171] These blackouts frighten his friends.[172] As the series progresses, Harry feels steadily worse and by *The Deathly Hallows* the clinical details are being conveyed with what seems to be increasing gusto.[173]

Voldemort is a madman too. The author directly calls him mad on a number of occasions; his teachers and schoolmates thought he was out of his mind.[174] In an interview, Rowling pulled no punches in describing Voldemort as a murderous psychopath: "[I]f you are writing about evil, which I am, and if you are writing about someone who's essentially a psychopath—you have a duty to show the real evil of taking human life."[175] (In other words, Voldemort is to be blamed for the atrocities showcased by the author.)

Rather than the eternal battle between good and evil,[176] what has made this boarding-school novel so exceptional is its main protagonist. He is a schizophrenic who believes he is the evil and simultaneously the world's savior from that evil (not to mention a snake), and he also suffers from epileptic fits. Yet there is still another dimension to Harry Potter's personality.

Harry Potter and His Games

Critics have considered Rowling an unreliable narrator, an author who is "fond of hiding things in plain sight and then leading us in the completely wrong direction in the narrative."[177] John Pennington points up the inconsistency of Harry Potter's world, and John Granger has suggested that "narrative misdirection" may be Rowling's conscious writing strategy.[178]

With this in mind, let us perform a little experiment with the Harry Potter story. Let us dispense with all the magic elements of the plot (as John Pennington does, for example, to expose the banality of Rowling's fantasy world) and collect together everything we know about Harry besides magic, which we will draw from the literary reality.[179] It should not be too difficult: the stripped-down narrative will fall well within the bounds of "consensus reality," firmly embedded as it is in the actualities of British society.[180] The reason we are doing this is to examine the rationale, concealed behind the "wizarding world," that drives the Potter plot. What is the structural skeleton that holds its ostensible magic together?

Harry's neighbors in Privet Drive, where he lives with his nonmagical foster family, talk about his "'delinquent' appearance."[181] They are terrified of "that Potter boy," whom they believe to be "a hardened hooligan" appropriately consigned to St. Brutus's Secure Center for Incurably Criminal Boys.[182] We know that his uncle, aunt, and other relatives do not think much of his dead parents, especially his father, whom Aunt Marge calls a "wastrel" and "a no-account, good for nothing, lazy scrounger," believing that he probably drank too much.[183] (We later learn that Harry's father was not a very nice person and bullied other students at school.) The Dursleys have always told Harry that his parents died in a car accident. So could the gist of the plot revolve around a double road fatality; did James Potter kill himself and his wife while driving drunk? And could that be why Harry's aunt and uncle are concerned that the orphaned boy grows up as normally as possible?

Harry is spoken of as "mentally subnormal."[184] There are rumors at Hogwarts that he is out of his mind: "half of the people inside Hogwarts thought him strange, even mad."[185] Even his friends sometimes think that he looks "funny," and Hermione is already worried about his sanity in *The Prisoner of Azkaban*.[186] The question "Are you all right, Harry?" often refers not only to his general health but to his mental condition.[187] And as we have concluded, there are plenty of reasons to be concerned about Harry's sanity. He is known for seeing things that no one else can see, and is mocked—for instance by Peeves—for hearing voices, seeing visions, and speaking Parseltongue, the language of snakes.[188] Maybe one reason why Harry's character and personality do not grow and change (as critics have acknowledged on a number of occasions) is that this story is not about the development of the boy's personality but about the development of his mental disorder. At one point it is even suggested that Harry tell Professor Umbridge that Voldemort is "a figment" of his imagination, and, as discussed earlier, the text actually allows us to trace how such an image could have formed in his mind.[189] In the series' seminal scene, the author suggests that everything in the story, including Harry's death and his after-death experience, has been a product of his fancy: "Of course, it is happening inside your head, Harry," says Dumbledore, "but why on earth should that mean that it is not real?"[190]

Harry's mental disorder is therefore a cornerstone of his story, and his symptoms of severe mental illness are absolutely indispensable to the plot. Harry's identity, in fact, is wholly dependent on his hallucinations of Voldemort, the omnipotent evil: without Voldemort and his strange connection to Harry, the story would have been indistinguishable from thousands of others. And the inclusion of the snake adds an extra layer of intrigue, a triple identity for Harry that nurtures the plot's internal logic. What would Harry be without his self-identification with Voldemort and Voldemort's snake? Just an unfortunate boy, a latter-day Oliver Twist. That sad story could certainly have served as the foundation for a heart-rending human interest plot. But would it have been a comparable commercial success?

As readers well know, Harry's hallucinations constitute the major events of the Harry Potter series. He interprets his headaches, delusions, and seizures as a symbolic means of communicating with the ultimate evil, with Voldemort. They are key to the plot because they demonstrate his "magical unity" with Voldemort. But Vol-de-mort—this Flight-of-Death—is just another name for Harry's mental disorder. That is why Harry is never supposed to break the connection he feels between himself and Voldemort, the connection that becomes so explicit during their duel after Cedric's death.[191]

Harry's story has been compared on several occasions to a game, and it is how Rowling wants her text to be perceived:

> I met a really nice boy yesterday, here in Washington. He said to me, "when I'm reading, its like a video playing inside my head." And I said—I said to him, "that's one of the best things you could say to me, because obviously you can visualize it really really clearly."[192]

Indeed, the tale has transitioned smoothly into any number of commercially successful computer games.[193] The ambiguity of Harry's personality has certainly helped to make those games more interesting and flexible, but what are they really about? The books' readers are involved in imitating mental disorders: Harry's schizophrenia, his psychotic breaks, and his hallucinatory epileptic seizures.

Harry is the only reliable source of information on Voldemort's whereabouts, which places him in a unique position relative to both his friends and the plot.[194] He cannot stand the idea that everyone may eventually lose interest in the special qualities of his scar and is horrified by the thought that his scar hurting may no longer be considered an important warning of Voldemort's presence, which reflects his state of mind as *The Order of the*

Phoenix begins.[195] We also know that Harry has been given the reputation of a fabricator of stories: his enemies describe him as "an attention-seeking person," who "loves being famous and wants to keep it going."[196] He is accused of spreading "fibs about reborn Dark wizards" and other "evil, nasty, attention-seeking stories."[197] Harry knows that many people at his school, both students and teachers, share this view about him and want him to learn "the difference between life and dream."[198] Occasionally, he feels "as though he were trapped in a nightmare,"[199] and sometimes even he sees the absurdity of his hallucinations and experiences a "sense of complete unreality," but these moments do not last for long.[200] We cannot be sure if Harry is a deliberate "fibber" or if he believes that his hallucinations are true.[201] And we will never know for sure. In any event, Ron and Hermione learn how Voldemort feels and what he does through Harry's accounts of what he believes he has witnessed.[202] Ron usually cannot see what Harry is seeing and does not understand what is scaring him, but he assumes that it is all true merely on the strength of Harry's conviction. Hermione and Ron re-enact Harry's hallucinations.[203] Their involvement in Harry's delusions shows how excited and entertained they are by his mental disorder, and in similar fashion, Harry's hallucinations and other symptoms have delivered endless hours of amusement to gamers all over the world.[204] Taken all together, this seven-book series offers a perfect setting in which to observe and enact mental disorders as a game.

Harry the Killer?

We have seen, then, that Harry has the reputation of being "disturbed and possibly dangerous."[205] He knows that his fellow students think he has committed a murder and avoids them for this reason.[206] As the series progresses, Harry is growing and—need we add?—becoming physically more capable of murder. Most critics tend to ignore these clues, preferring instead to follow the mainstream interpretation that Harry and Voldemort are two different characters, protagonist and antagonist, and that it is the villain Voldemort who kills Cedric, Sirius, and so many others.

Readers will certainly remember that whenever Harry hallucinates being a snake—or Voldemort—he wants to kill. He imagines killing his godfather and helping to torture him; in his mind he threatens the life of Dumbledore, his mentor and role model. Even though we are told that he is doing this on Dumbledore's command, we see him forcing his headmaster to drink a potion that almost kills him.[207] This scene is written in such a way that even a sympathetic critic acknowledges that "Harry forces Dumbledore to drink Tom's poison; in doing so Harry experiences the pleasure of dominance that Dumbledore's intimate lessons have modeled."[208] Dumbledore is aware of Harry's dark intent: he tells the boy "I thought I saw a shadow of him [Voldemort—D.K.] stir behind your eyes."[209]

We know that Harry enjoys being the great, powerful, and hateful Lord Voldemort. He is excited by that power, and he takes pleasure in torturing his victims: he is described laughing at the agonies of his godfather Sirius, whom (we are told) he loves dearly.

> Harry's stomach contracted with fear . . . with excitement . . .
>
> A voice issued from his own mouth, a high, cold voice empty of any human kindness.
>
> (. . .) Harry saw a long-fingered white hand clutching a wand rise at the end of his own arm . . . heard the high, cold voice say "Crucio!"
>
> The man on the floor let out a scream of pain, attempted to stand but fell back, writhing. Harry was laughing. He raised his wand, the curse lifted and the figure groaned and became motionless.
>
> "Lord Voldemort is waiting."[210]

On another occasion when Harry transforms into Voldemort, he is elated by the thought of the murder he is planning:

> Aware that Hermione was watching him suspiciously, Harry hurried up the stairs to the hall and then to the first landing, where he dashed into the bathroom and bolted the door again. Grunting with pain, he slumped over the black basin with its taps in the form of open-mouthed serpents and closed his eyes . . .
>
> He was gliding along a twilit street. The buildings on either side of him had high, timbered gables; they looked like gingerbread houses.
>
> He approached one of them, then saw the whiteness of his own long-fingered hand against the door. He knocked. He felt a mounting excitement.[211]

How could we doubt, after this and many similar descriptions, that Harry is a murderer, a Lord Voldemort himself? The author consistently stresses that Harry feels "excitement" from murdering and torturing people, which is surely a key feature of how serial killers are portrayed. Some readers have suspected him of at least killing Cedric, his competitor in the Triwizard tournament and his rival for the affections of Cho Chang.[212] We are, in fact, never told who murdered Cedric. We only know that while the murder was being committed, Harry heard the voices of Voldemort and Wormtail, which may well have been voices in his own head.[213] The following passage could, in fact, be interpreted as Harry's confession and/or expression of remorse for killing Cedric: "He didn't want to think about anything that had happened since he had first touched the Triwizard Cup. He didn't want to have to examine the memories, fresh and sharp as photographs, which kept flashing across his mind (. . .) Cedric . . . dead. . . . Cedric asking to be returned to his parents."[214] Later he has nightmares about this episode.[215] Is it by chance that far too often Harry turns out to be the one who last sees the victim alive?[216]

Depicting Harry's engagement in various atrocities, the author intends to leave the reader in no doubt that that Harry is "possessed" by Voldemort at those times and that the possessed Harry is not himself and therefore not responsible for his actions.[217] He is evidently not in control of himself during the psychotic breaks that begin with a pain in his head, which he cannot resist any more than he could resist "the urge to be sick."[218] It has to be said that none of the physical symptoms exhibited by the "possessed" Harry—the trembling hands, the collapsing, the excruciating pain in his scar, the vomiting—are necessary accompaniments to psychotic breaks. Most likely, these physical manifestations of epileptic seizures were added to the mix to make Harry's sickness more vivid to readers and prove to them that whatever happens, he simply cannot help it.[219] Harry's friends (or are they just voices in his mind?) also speculate that his self-identification with Voldemort—the "connection," as it is called—is an illness. When his friends ask him why he is not trying harder to break his link with Voldemort and to avoid even witnessing the Dark Lord's acts of brutality, he claims that he is not capable of freeing himself from that evil.[220] The author makes Harry confess that he cannot separate himself from Voldemort because Voldemort "is inside" him.[221] When Hermione tells him that he has never put in enough effort to break free from Voldemort, they come to a hostile impasse.[222]

Hermione has every reason to suspect that Harry is capable of murder, because she knows how cruel he can be (as, for example, when he wishes death on a teacher[223]). On another occasion, he casually orders the house-elf Kreacher to torture Mundungus Fletcher, whom he suspects of treason. And as he watches the torture, he gives clear instructions that the victim must not be allowed to pass out: "'We need him conscious, Kreacher, but if he needs persuading, you can do the honors,' said Harry."[224] In any event, Harry—in his own identity or as his alter ego, Voldemort—is not responsible for his actions because he is "possessed," mentally disturbed and unable to choose not to commit his crimes.[225] Thus, one possible interpretation of Harry is that he is a deranged maniac.

While using the narrative misdirection to counter readers' immediate understanding of the plot, as authors of detective stories often do, Rowling cannot hide completely the skeleton of her story. The Harry Potter series became a young adult literature pioneer when it hit this mother lode of mental disorder. As we have seen in the previous chapter, maniacal serial killers were first featured as the "good guy" and first-person protagonist in Hollywood movies of the late 1980s and early 1990s. The serial-killer celebrity culture, then in its infancy, was destined for resounding success. Rowling followed this Hollywood trend as she had with the vampire motif. And later on, the series inspired this kind of Hollywood movies. There are several parallels between the Harry Potter plot and the iconic tale of perhaps the world's most famous fictional serial killer as presented in the television series *Hannibal* (2013–15). Like Harry, Graham has nightmares and dreams about a stag (the stag, Harry's patronus, appears in his daydreams as well as his nightmares).[226] There is also Randall Tier (another serial killer), who had come as a youngster to Dr. Lecter for treatment to deal with his conviction that he is an animal in a human body (not a snake though!).[227]

Apart from the rising glory of the serial killer, there may be other reasons why Rowling would find a mentally unbalanced character so appealing. For example, she makes no secret of the fact that she herself has experienced depression. A resultant empathy for the mentally ill may have morphed into a plot line whose main protagonist is a mentally disturbed boy. In one interview, she described using her experience of depression in her writings, not with direct reference to Harry but in the form of an acknowledgment that the dementors were based on her own painful sensations. As a suicide-related website reports, she wanted people with mental conditions "to fight the stigma associated with mental illness. (. . .) 'I have never been remotely ashamed of having been depressed. Never. What's there to be ashamed of? I went through a really tough time and I am quite proud that I got out of that,' she said."[228]

This is also why any assertion that since "madness is culturally determined," Harry Potter "is not sick by wizard's standards" completely misses the point.[229] Even less could these books be considered, as some psychoanalysts have suggested, a "therapeutic tool."[230] Indeed, the admiration for the series from members of the medical profession raises a real concern.

(Some go as far as to claim that the Harry Potter series helps in "injury prevention"![231]) This is not to say that literary descriptions of mental diseases cannot be conducive to an understanding of the pathologies involved. But the driving motivator behind fiction of that kind should be anything but commercial success.

When Telling Names Tell Too Much

The series contains additional proof that the ambiguous interpretations discussed above do not stem from a random, interminable interplay of "mimesis without origins" (to use a term associated with Jacques Derrida) but are intentionally written into the Harry Potter story. Rowling pays close attention to the names she gives her characters, and, as critics have noticed, they clearly reveal her intentions for them.[232] The etymology and symbolism of these names are not, however, especially sophisticated or difficult to decipher. Let us look at the names of the two central characters—Harry Potter and Voldemort—to see how they relate to each other.

Aside from the vampiric name Vol-de-mort (Flight of Death), the false antagonist has yet another name, Tom Riddle. If read in reverse, Tom—"mot"—means "word" in French, which reduces the name to a "word puzzle". And what is the essence of that puzzle? Rowling has been inconstant over the years in explaining Voldemort as a character and evasive as to who or what his prototype was. At one point, she said that she did not "base Voldemort on any real person."[233] And in 2006 she acknowledged that Voldemort, whom she calls "a psychopath," was not conceived as a character at all but as an emotion, as an incarnation of the fear of death.[234]

So was Voldemort envisioned as a true character or as the embodiment of Harry's disease, his altered psychological state, and his insane delusions? This is the true "riddle" of Voldemort's name, and it explains his relation to Harry. Tom Riddle–Voldemort is a rebus of Harry's madness, which offers another possible interpretation of his ambiguous story: he commits suicide in order to return to life as a vampire, one of the living dead. Harry is a lunatic who fancies himself an omnipotent magician, a vampire (Voldemort), a giant snake, and a boy wizard all rolled into one. In his nightmares, seizures, and delusions, this sick boy sees those mortal enemies locked in an eternal struggle: "The snake rustled on the filthy, cluttered floor, and he had killed the boy, and yet he was the boy . . . (. . .) He was Harry . . . Harry, no Voldemort . . . (. . .) He opened his eyes."[235] This understanding solves "the riddle of his being" (as J. M. Barrie once said of Peter Pan). And it may be one reason why Rowling has been so hesitant to answer questions about her plots. In particular, it clarifies why, in the early days of her success, she had such a problem explaining why Voldemort was going after Harry, as in the following interview:

> JKR: When he was one year old, the most evil wizard for hundreds and hundreds of years attempted to kill him. He killed Harry's parents, and then he tried to kill Harry—he tried to curse him.
> DR: Why?
> JKR: I can't tell you. It's the 64,000 dollar question. I can't tell you. He—Harry doesn't know yet. Harry has to find out, before we find out.[236]

This also explains why, when asked in an interview, "Why do you think young children are so drawn to these books?" Rowling responds that she finds the question "hard (. . .) to answer":

> JKR: That's such a, such a very hard question to answer, because . . . without being disingenuous, I wrote what I wanted to write. [. . .] I just want to write it the way I'm writing it at the moment, and enjoy writing it, and do it my way, without trying to, you know, work to a formula.[237]

Who would suspect a writer of being "disingenuous" about the attractions of her story for children in response to a question that is normally considered flattering? There is no reason for anyone to suspect her of hiding anything from her public—"in plain sight," as it were—but of course she knows better. In her interview, she finds a way out of this difficulty, claiming that she does not want to "work to a formula." But we know from this same interview that she did have her formula ready-made and that her larger plot of all seven books had been in place since 1992.[238] So she actually does have an answer, but not one she is prepared to reveal to her audience of young readers.[239]

Now what about Harry's name?[240] One thing that we notice is that it is often coupled with the exclamation "Hurry!"[241] Is this a coincidence, or was the name chosen because of the assonance of the two words? In his seizures and nightmares, as we have seen, Harry is regularly seen fleeing from a mortal danger; he also hastens away from the scenes of his crimes. As we will see, Rowling perceives and describes death as "rushing," hurrying, as Harry hurries toward his inevitable, violent, and premature death and the story's "dying fall."[242] In the chapter titled "Flesh, Blood and Bone," he even hears that same word spoken by Voldemort: "And Harry heard the high, cold voice again: "Hurry!"[243] That parallels his name with Voldemort's and makes it a linchpin of the plot. "Hurry-to-death" is hurrying away from "Flight-of-death," a menacing, impending, "rushing death" from which there is ultimately no escape.

Harry's Death as Entertainment

We should now discuss what Rowling considers to be the series' central theme: death. Here we will explore the death-related attitudes promoted by the Harry Potter saga, and we should be prepared to encounter some unusual views and unexpected ideas in the course of that exploration. Death marches through the Harry Potter series like a conquistador, all the way to its ultimate triumph. Harry's violent death is the culmination of the story, and his death is foretold and rehearsed in the violent deaths of other characters. The death rate of the series characters is close to the mortality levels when the Black Death was rampaging through medieval Europe: along the entire plot arc, almost one character in two ends up dead. Word-use frequency is another telling indicator of how the violence escalates from book to book. For example, the verb "kill" is used three times as often in the seventh book as in the second, while the word "death" shows an even more striking fourteen-fold increase.

Representations of death and the symbolism associated with death are something of an obsession in the Harry Potter series. Death omens, prophecies about death, appear recurrently, foreshadowing horrific events to come.[244] Voldemort's allies are called Death Eaters, and the dementors are described in terms of the living dead.[245] There are also the Inferi, corpses bewitched back to "life" by Voldemort.[246] Hogwarts is a school with a high student death rate, especially during tournaments; it almost seems that students are supposed to die whenever a teacher needs them to.[247] Death is also a frequent topic of conversation among wizards. There are endless rumors of Harry's death, fatal accidents, and deliberate murders (and the wizarding world's newspaper has a field day with all this carnage). The tombs, burial sites, and cemeteries that Harry "visits" in his nightmares, classic clichés of the Gothic novel, are among the series' favorite settings for killings and other atrocities.[248]

Let us begin with the death of Harry's parents, the series' first dual death and the first such event of which readers are made aware.[249] Harry's thoughts about his parents' death are ever-present in the narrative. Among an array of similarly sentimental laments (the author leaves no stone unturned in the theme of an orphan child longing for his dead parents), *The Goblet of Fire* contains a particularly uncommon description, in which the death of Harry's parents is compared to that of a spider killed during lab experiments by "the same curse":

> So that was how his parents had died . . . exactly like that spider. Had they been unblemished and unmarked too? Had they simply seen the flash of green light and heard the rush of speeding death, before life was wiped from their bodies?[250]

What is the intended meaning of this comparison? To emphasize that killing is easy, perhaps, or that killing people and killing an insect is basically the same thing? Harry's speculations that his parents' dead bodies may have looked like the spider's reveal an unusual degree of morbid voyeurism. This is perhaps the most telling but not the only instance in the series where the death of an animal is compared with the death of wizards.

How are other deaths described in the novel? The murder of Frank Bryce, the Riddles' gardener and a secondary character, consists in him dropping his walking stick "with a clatter," then "he opened his mouth and let out a scream," a very loud scream. There is "a flash of green light, a rushing sound," and he "crumpled." He was, we are told, "dead before he hit the floor."[251] The absence of any explicitly physiological, philosophical, or even emotional reflections makes this death, which is accompanied by that iconic "rushing sound," very similar to that of the spider. Since the sound and light show is not designed to communicate the victim's feelings or fears at the moment of his death, there is little likelihood of the reader feeling any strong sympathy for that unfortunate individual. The death is far more reminiscent of a violent cartoon or a computer game than a literary description of a human tragedy.[252]

Frank Bryce was an old man. But what about younger victims? The murder of Harry's schoolmate Cedric is portrayed in a similarly objectified way, with "a blast of green light" followed by the sound of "something heavy" falling to the ground, and a view of the boy's body "lying spread-eagled" on the ground. The details, again, are astonishingly sparse. The dead Cedric is even trivialized, shown with "blank and expressionless" eyes and a "half-open mouth, which looked slightly surprised." The only literary ornament here is a trite metaphor that compares those empty eyes to "the windows of a deserted house."[253] Once again, we are shown how the body looks but have no idea how the victim might have felt, and neither the event nor the corpse, described in such a naturalistic way, is apt to engage our empathy. We are later told that Harry was terrified.[254] But the image we are left with more adequately represents the entirely voyeuristic way in which a murderous maniac might survey the body of his victim.

These are the deaths of minor characters. Now what about major ones? Are their deaths described with more compassion? Here is how Dumbledore's demise is depicted: he is killed by a "jet of green light" that hits him in the chest. Through Harry's eyes, we see how Dumbledore "was blasted into the air" and how "For a split second he seemed to hang suspended beneath the shining skull, and then he fell slowly backward, like a great rag doll, over the battlements and out of sight."[255] This is indeed an objectification beyond anything we have seen so far: the corpse of Harry's mentor and role model being compared to "a great rag doll" that is suspended in the air before slowly falling—helplessly, ridiculously—backwards. No psychological affinity is required here: people are easy to dispose of, and once they are dead, their bodies are almost comically objectivized by being portrayed as a toy flung into the air or as a spider. We are told about Dumbledore "pleading" with Snape and are informed that this "frightened" Harry. But does this rouse the reader's compassion for him? After the event, Harry is described as "shaking in every limb"; we are told that "his body ached all over, and his breath came in painful stabs."[256] As usual, readers are expected to feel more for his physical travails than for the travails of his soul.[257]

The most unsettling of all, however, is the account of a young girl's murder. Myrtle hides from a classmate's teasing in the toilets and, while she is crying in a stall, "The door was locked, and I was crying, and then I heard somebody come in and (. . .) I died."[258] At the beginning, we know very little about the circumstances of Myrtle's death. We learn that her schoolmates never liked her because to them she was just sulky and annoying: "Nobody missed me even when I was alive."[259] Her ghost, called "Moaning Myrtle" (the nickname comes from all the weeping) eventually tells her story, which is treated as broad, almost slapstick, comedy. A "gulping" creature "with swollen eyes" because she cries recollecting her death[260] ("a carnivalesque, grotesque joke of a girl," as one critic perceptively commented[261]), she spends most of her time in a toilet bowl, a location that makes it hard for Harry—and the reader—not to imagine her "zooming down a pipe to the lake with the contents of a toilet." The author does not want the reader to miss the point: this actually happens, as Myrtle explains, "[i]f someone flushes my toilet when I am not expecting it."[262] To heighten the comedy, the author exaggerates her speech, making her sound both pretentious and absurd even when she is describing her own murder:

"Myrtle's whole aspect changed at once. She looked as though she had never been asked such a flattering question. 'Ooooh, it was dreadful,' she said with relish. 'It happened right in here. I died in this very stall.'"[263] The readers are encouraged to share Myrtle's schoolmates' attitude toward her, and the message is clear: nothing could be funnier and more embarrassing from a youngster's point of view than dying in a toilet stall. So much for this excerpt from a series that one critic called "full of wonderful, spontaneous humor."[264]

We will now look at the major episodes in which Harry's death is described, since we do see this favorite children's hero on the brink of death on many occasions. Harry frequently contemplates his death and is often convinced that his end has come, that there is no hope.[265] When the basilisk bites him in *The Chamber of Secrets*, his agony is portrayed as a "white-hot pain" that spreads "slowly and steadily from the wound." His robes are soaked with blood and his vision is "foggy." He hears the voice of Riddle, who tells him, "You're dead" and promises he is going to sit there and watch him die. Gradually Harry begins to feel "drowsy" (which is, as we have seen, a common sensation during and after his seizures and psychotic breaks). "If this is dying, thought Harry, it's not so bad," which is, to say the least, an unanticipated conclusion.[266] In *The Prisoner of Azkaban*, Harry expects to die when he is attacked by dementors, the incarnations of death, and his impending death is described similarly to that of other characters. He is blinded by a "white fog," suddenly feels "a pair of strong, clammy hands" around his neck, hears his mother's scream. . . . And then he comes to his senses as usual: exhausted and lying on the grass.[267] But this is not the only time in *Azkaban* where Harry is confronted by dementors. The second time we watch as his "eyes rolled up into his head." He is "drowning in cold." He cannot see; he feels himself "being dragged downward, the roaring growing louder."[268] The description of these physical sensations is less frightening than puzzling; all the reader can do is wonder who or what is doing the "roaring" and "dragging." In *The Order of the Phoenix*, Harry imagines his death while, probably, suffering a psychotic break (and intensely painful convulsions).[269] He imagined Voldemort trying to kill him on the grave of Tom Riddle's father, while Harry was in such pain that he "no longer knew there he was."[270] This nightmare or seizure ends as many others have and will, when the exhausted Harry comes to lying on the ground with his face "pressed into grass," feeling drained and dizzy.[271]

The last time Harry finds himself on the brink of death, his unity with Voldemort is reiterated once again. Here, the Dark Lord even looks like Harry, mirroring his posture with his head "tilted to one side." Voldemort gazes at "the boy standing before him" in a way that likens him to "a curious child." What are we, the readers, supposed to see? Two children trying to kill each other or a single child who has confused one element of his split identity with his mortal enemy? Because if we are to believe that Voldemort is not just another state of Harry's consciousness but the very embodiment of evil, if we are witnessing not an attempted suicide but an imminent murder, this scene expresses a peculiar attitude toward the killer, calling him "a curious child":

> At that moment he felt that nobody mattered but Voldemort. It was just the two of them. (. . .)
>
> And still, Voldemort and Harry looked at each other, and now Voldemort tilted his head a little to the side, considering the boy standing before him, and a singularly mirthless smile curled the lip-less mouth.
>
> (. . .) Voldemort had raised his wand. His head was still tilted to one side, like a curious child, wondering what would happen if he proceeded. Harry looked back into the red eyes, and wanted it to happen now, quickly, while he could still stand, before he lost control, before he betrayed fear—
>
> He saw the mouth move and a flash of green light, and everything was gone.[272]

But what is Harry feeling? On his way to meet his death, Harry is shown to be terrified, his fingers numb, his hands sweating and "his heart throwing itself against his ribs."[273] As usual, this is physiology, not psychology: the only glimpse of what is in his mind is when he thinks about Ginny's kiss. The death itself is bluntly portrayed: "everything was gone."[274] What do we see next? Harry, as usual, is lying on the ground. So does this mean that if you kill yourself or are killed, all you have to do is close your eyes and when you open them again, you might find yourself in some other place? Is it all a matter of curiosity? Because if death is "easy" or even fun, and if it is entertaining to watch someone else die, then naturally one would be curious about exactly how it happens.

After two chapters have been spent describing his after-death experience, Harry comes back to life, as the undead should, and finally kills Voldemort, which seems redundant: Harry knows that at this point Voldemort cannot harm anyone any more.[275] Voldemort's body is shown to look very much like Cedric's and is viewed with the same degree of serene objectification; he looks exactly like the spider, like Cedric, like Harry's parents, and like everyone and everything else whose death is portrayed in this fictional massacre.[276] These descriptions represent the ultimate affirmation of the banality of a violent death.

The ambiguity of Harry's persona is fertile ground for multiple interpretations, but one thing is sure: death has been stalking the poor, sick child from the very beginning of this deathly saga—"Harry understood at last that he was not supposed to survive. His job was to walk calmly into Death's welcoming arms."[277] We learn at the end that only his death "will truly mean the end of Voldemort" and that he has been kept alive so that he can die at the right moment. More precisely, and far more graphically, he has been raised all along "as a pig for slaughter."[278] And this was, as we have heard, all "carefully planned," all programmed by the plot from the very outset.

If we believe that Voldemort is Harry's delusion, then this is a story about a progressive mental disease that drives the protagonist to a profound insanity and finally leads him to commit suicide, all the while imagining himself in a duel to the death with the omnipotent Voldemort. The plot could be interpreted as the story of how Harry obeys the voices that prompt him to murder his victims and finally kill himself. But if we believe that Harry and Voldemort are two distinct entities, this series is guiding readers to accept the role of victims. As in a vampire saga, the acceptance of violent death without resistance is even described as an act of courage.[279] And finally, the vampire mythos prevails when Harry returns to life, having won immortality in return for his obedient assumption of victimhood.

The Humble Secret of Celebrity: Death as a Party

Harry Potter is no Raskolnikov: philosophical questions and moral dilemmas about death or the afterlife do not preoccupy him on any level. Indeed, as John Pennington points out, the major death-related questions are not even hinted at in the series:

> And what of death? Does death exist? Is there an afterlife? The poltergeist Peeves, Nearly Headless Nick, and Moaning Myrtle suggest that there is no final resting place, and the Mirror of Erised suggests that the good—Harry's parents particularly—are somehow stuck in limbo, or a kind of purgatory. So where does that leave Cedric Diggory? Is he truly dead? Is there an afterlife? Or does existence just end with death? These larger concerns are left unexplored,

not because Rowling wants readers to contemplate such concerns; rather, she does not seem interested in serious speculation."[280]

The most common interpretation of the series is that Harry sacrifices himself to save the wizarding world.[281] Leaving aside the question of why it takes him so long (seven increasingly hefty tomes) to make that sacrifice, with many of his friends dying in the process, we will instead query the concept of death promoted by the Harry Potter books and explore how instrumental it has been in the commodification of death.

It should come as no surprise that in the Potter saga, death is frequently associated with or compared to a party. Here are just two examples. In *The Chamber of Secrets*, Harry attends a party organized by a ghost on the occasion of his "five hundredth deathday."[282] This party takes place on Halloween and is presented as what the author imagines to be more chic and more visually arresting than any pedestrian shindig for the living: most of the guests are "translucent," an orchestra seated on a "black-draped" platform scrapes away at its musical saws, a chandelier "blazed midnight-blue with a thousand more black candles," and the air is misted by the breath of the living.[283] (This whole scenario may have been suggested by the celebration of Halloween, whose popularity was burgeoning while Rowling was writing her books.) At the end of the series, in *The Deathly Hallows*, when Harry has died and entered the netherworld, the dead Dumbledore, "chuckling immoderately," tells him: "This is, as they say, your party."[284]

While clearly modeling some of her scenes on the danse macabre, Rowling (whose text indulges extensively in medievalism) dramatically modifies its medieval subtext.[285] In the series, images of living protagonists amid the dead are common. Harry's near-death experience after Cedric's murder is staged as a hideous cotillion in which he finds himself surrounded by Voldemort's dead victims as they manifest from his wand. These "thick gray ghosts," described as "gray as a smoky statue," surround Harry to shield him from Voldemort.[286] In the final scene of Harry's death, the dead gather around him, ready to accompany him to the final destination of this seven-volume-long nightmare: "Less substantial than living bodies, but much more than ghosts, they moved toward him." Harry imagines them all encouraging him to die; his dead mother's smile is "widest of all" and his dead father "nodded encouragement" "as he stumbled and slipped towards the end of his life."[287] Why are all the dead so eager to see Harry die? Is it just to highlight his heroism in conquering evil and saving the wizarding world? Or is it to satisfy the reader who has been expecting Harry's death from the very beginning of the story?

These associations between death and party find their parallels in *Hannibal*, the TV show. Lecter often celebrates a murder by hosting a party, in his case, though, a dinner party.[288] Cannibals and cannibalism, another fascination of 1990s Hollywood, also figure in the series.

For death to be entertaining, devoid of the moral or philosophical reflection or the profound drama that many YAL writers fear might make their books too boring or unapproachably moralistic, a dread of death cannot be part of the equation. This is why Dumbledore trains Harry after a fashion, explaining to him that fear of death and the dead is as silly as a "fear of the darkness."[289] Dying is, in fact, not "so bad" (and these are the very words that the author puts into Harry's mouth much earlier in the tale[290]). Death is not to be feared but embraced. It is not painful, the young reader learns, it does not hurt, and it is "quicker and easier than falling asleep," as the dead Sirius explains to Harry in the closing scene:

> "You are nearly there," said James. "Very close. We are . . . so proud of you."
>
> "Does it hurt?"
>
> The childish question had fallen from Harry's lips before he could stop it.
>
> "Dying? Not at all," said Sirius. "Quicker and easier than falling asleep."[291]

Once again, this attitude finds its parallel in *Hannibal*. When the cancer-stricken Bella Crawford discusses suicide with Hannibal Lecter, he calls death a "cure" (citing Socrates, no less) and encourages her to go ahead and do it.[292]

According to Rowling, Voldemort is afraid of "ignominious" death (which is precisely how Philippe Ariès describes modern attitudes toward it). She explains in an interview: "Voldemort's fear is death, ignominious death. I mean, he regards death itself as ignominious. He thinks that it's a shameful human weakness, as you know."[293] But if Voldemort is not a protagonist but a delusion, an incarnation of the fear of death, then to kill him is to kill that fear. The author therefore "liberates" Harry from the fear of death by making him commit suicide or accept being slaughtered and allowing him to "return to life" as one of the undead.

From the first book on, death is called an "adventure": "After all, to the well-organized mind, death is but the next great adventure."[294] That phrase is even repeated a few pages later, perhaps so that readers can better process the idea.[295] Leaving aside the question of how well the mind of a nine-year-old reader (Rowling considers her books appropriate for that age[296]) might be able to grasp this "adventure," let us examine what it actually involves. A possible interpretation is that the final destination of the "adventure" is to achieve immortality and join the living dead as Harry ultimately does. The epitaph on Harry's parents' headstone, which reads "The last enemy that shall be destroyed is death," and the struggle among the main characters of the series to achieve the immortality that finally falls into Harry's hands, reinforce this impression.[297] And the logical corollary of this is Dumbledore's reflection on death (which has a positively medieval ring to it): "Do not pity the dead, Harry. Pity the living, and, above all, those who live without love."[298] Should the reader conclude that anyone who wants to become "the true master of death" has to accept a violent death rather than trying to escape it and consider death as a reward?[299]

Toward the end, Rowling is writing the word "Death" with a capital D. The last book pictures life after death as a quasi-physical space distinguished only by its banality (King's Cross station!). Death is conceived as the moment when all the riddles of life—or of the books' plot line, at least—are answered, if we only ask. Does this suggest, in other words, that we satisfy our curiosity by dying? And that may also be why this netherworld is depicted as a railroad station, a straightforward metaphor for a point of departure. The pleasurable return to life after achieving the immortality of the living dead is a concept of the afterlife that is, once again, very similar to that which underpins the vampire sagas, as we observed in the previous chapter.

Death is regarded as something to be eagerly anticipated, as the ultimate act of self-accomplishment. Structurally—by its prominent place in the plot and its concluding role in the narrative—it is the final stage in a protracted coming-of-age rite. By dying, the boy in round glasses establishes himself as a bona fide adult, not only joining the dead adults as their equal but also basking in the approbation of the portraits of Hogwarts' dead headmasters and headmistresses. The last time we see him, he is the father of a growing family. These attitudes toward death are certainly reminiscent of premodern (possibly even premedieval) attitudes to death and dying. As Vladimir Propp, a Russian formalist, demonstrates in his seminal work *Morphology of the Folktale*, the adventures experienced by the protagonists in folk tales may reflect the cruel—and sometimes deadly—initiations that were part of rites of passage in premodern society.[300] Often the transition from one age group to another was associated with "death" of a boy's "old self" and his "rebirth" into a new social role as an adult.

The appeal of this new appreciation of death in contemporary culture is perhaps best reflected by the fact that an attitude toward real (not virtual) death as an "adventure" has even found its way into the discourse of studies of death and bereavement. As Colin Murray Parkes suggests, "And in the end, when even those things that remained are taken away, we embark on the greatest adventure of all."[301]

Neo-Medievalism as Politics and the Banality of Evil

Obviously, the Harry Potter books are indulgent in quasi-medieval aesthetics, witchcraft, and Gothic imagery.[302] But besides brooms, caldrons, dungeons, and ghosts, one finds more important ways in which medievalism is present in these books.

Let us consider, for example, the sense of blood and lineage. Everything about a person is determined by his or her "blood" or family origins.[303] Children usually take sides and follow political and moral choices made for them by their parents because it is "in their veins." Obsession with blood and race transmutes into an obsession with images of blood and bleeding, reminiscent of the fascination with blood in the medieval culture:[304] the parchment is "dotted with drops of blood,"[305] blood is "splattered the grass,"[306] "blood seeping down the sleeve of his turned robes," "blood blossoming over his robes."[307] A chapter titled "Flesh, Blood and Bone" speaks *altissimo voce* about this fascination.[308] Harry, his friends, other children, and adults are bleeding in the series countless times.[309]

Early in the Harry Potter publishing adventure, critics pointed out that tortures, sufferings, and psychical abuse was completely trivialized in the series.[310] However fair, this criticism has not explicated the connection between the medieval setting chosen for the novels and the value system that make tortures and atrocities fit so well into the wizard world. The images of torture play a central role in the narrative.[311] The descriptions of tortures that are exhibited in detail, with precision and at length, do not usually represent the victim's viewpoint:

> And into his mind burst the vision of an emaciated old man lying in rags upon a stone floor, screaming, a horrible drawn-out scream, a scream of unendurable agony. . . . "No! No! I beg you, I beg you." "You lied to Lord Voldemort, Ollivander!" "I did not. . . . I swear I did not." [. . .] And Harry saw the white hand raise its wand and felt Voldemort's surge of vicious anger, saw the frail old main on the floor writhe in agony.[312]

The tortures and killing are described from the point of view of the perpetrator, from the point of view of Harry, who is portrayed on these occasions, as we have seen earlier, as feeling mounting "excitement."[313]

It would be a mistake to think that only tortures of the secondary protagonists are described in an objectified way. As well as the scenes of murders, the agonies and sufferings of the tortured main protagonists are again observed externally. For example, the readers see the poisoning of Dumbledore through the eyes of his perpetrator: Harry watches the sufferings he brings upon his teacher and finally notices his victim "rolled over onto his face," which sounds anything but not tragic:

> "I want to die! I want to die! Make it stop, make it stop, I want to die!" "Drink this, Professor. Drink this. . . ." Dumbledore drank, and no sooner had he finished than he yelled, "KILL ME!" "This—this one will!" gasped Harry. "Just drink this. . . . It'll be over . . . all over!" Dumbledore gulped at the goblet, drained every last drop, and then, with a great, rattling gasp, rolled over onto his face.[314]

Even when Harry is tortured, the author keeps describing the external manifestations of his pain. She portrays his weird bodily movements, for example, "his eyes were rolling madly in his head."[315] In another scene, Harry's "agony" is presented as follows: "Harry's scar exploded with pain" and "he put his hands over his face; his knees buckled; he was on the ground and he could see nothing at all."[316] This detached observation increases voyeuristic aspect of the narrative, reinforcing an impression that we are exposed to the sentiments of a deluded maniac.

In the Harry Potter universe, torture is the main way to deal with an enemy.[317] But, as in the Middle Ages, torture is not restricted to the enemies and not only "bad guys" use torture. Harry Potter also orders his house elf to torture a betrayal suspect. Torture is used in all spheres of life; on a number of occasions, teachers torture their pupils.[318] The language the Harry Potter characters employ reflects normalization of torture and banalization of evil. Expressions such as "keeping someone in enough pain" emphasize "economical aspect" of atrocities.[319] A positive character, Hagrid, speaks about a murder of the Harry's parents to Harry using the jargon of professional killers by saying that Voldemort wanted to kill baby-Harry because he "Wanted ter make a clean job of it, I suppose, or maybe he just liked killin' by then make a clean job."[320] In the series, torture becomes a routine way to communicate and get information and also a routine form of punishment.[321] But torture is never discussed in the series as violation of human rights, human dignity, and respect. It is represented as a matter-of-fact custom, as policy, which is habitual to the point of not even being debated. For Harry and his friends, court and law are not an option for conflict resolution. Force and fight are the only way to solve problems, while the state system is described as dysfunctional and corrupt.

It could be argued that Rowling tried to fashion her series after the Brothers Grimm's tales and that the series' indulgence in medievalism comes from this source. For example, her man-eater (she has not missed a chance to include cannibalism in the series) bears a German-sounding name Fenrir. Indeed, early in her writing career, responding to criticism, Rowling compared her story to Grimms' tales, arguing that what she writes is less brutal and scary than their tales, which are considered classics for children:

> JKR: . . . and they [Grimms' tales —D.K.] are frightening. And in
> fact, I think, more frightening than anything I've written so far.
> I mean, children being murdered. There are horrible things. But
> this is centuries back, and I don't think children have changed
> that much.[322]

Clearly Rowling is not aware that medieval tales were not supposed to be "for children": the concept of childhood and related special activities did not exist in the medieval epoch.[323] Tales were created for the amusement and entertainment of the adult audience, and they revealed all kind of ghastly medieval customs and habits. Stating that "children have not changed," she ignores the fact that the moral norms and what is considered appropriate for children had indeed changed since the Middle Ages. The brutal appeal of the medieval tales to "the dark corners of human psyche" was "tamed" for children by Charles Perrault and Hans Christian Anderson precisely to imbue these ancient tales with a different system of values. The "civilization of mores," as Mircea Eliade termed this process, had made them suitable for the more humanistic ideas about individual, society, and the value of human life.

Undoubtedly, neo-medievalism has its own raison d'être in the series. Under the disguise of medieval costumes and witchcraft, the Harry Potter books express a changing attitude to people for which "neo-medievalism"—namely, an image of the Middle Ages that reduces this period to the "Dark Ages," to a system of values that radically opposes humanistic and Enlightenment ideals—becomes a potent metaphor.[324]

The Reception of a Manual on the Art of Dying

Looking through the Harry Potter bibliography, which is immense, we see that the series' reception has shifted over time. By becoming as unavoidable a part of daily consumption worldwide as soda and burgers, the series has actually been instrumental in changing our expectations of YAL. By and large, the debates about the Harry Potter series have mirrored those on violence in YAL. Early in the Harry Potter enterprise, the expectations of YAL were quite different than they are today. While some critics wondered about the "explicit threat of death" and death being "the running theme" of these books, others were content to leave the question of these books' possible influence on the YA audience open "for future research."[325] In those early days, Harry Potter admirers—soon joined by a number of intellectuals when schools, both parochial and secular, began banning Harry Potter from their libraries—have argued that "[b]leak stories are nothing new; just take a close look at *Oedipus Rex*, *The Tragedy of King Lear* or *The Grapes of Wrath*."[326] But whatever comparisons may be drawn between Sophocles, Shakespeare, and Steinbeck on the one hand and Rowling on the other, one thing is clear: those great works of art focused on the existential dilemmas and tragic circumstances of people, not of a nonhuman, a vampire, or a mentally disturbed serial killer disguised as a teenager. As sales increased from volume to volume and Pottermania swept the globe, critics objecting to the Harry Potter saga became gradually more circumspect.[327] By the end of the 2000s, critics were exploring the idea that the series is indeed about death but that this is one of its great contributions. Its educative role was seen in the way it helped children and adults to discuss death[328] and in its "ability to help young people engage with death."[329] Other critics suggested that the Harry Potter series exemplifies the "qualities of postmodern childhood"[330]: "[T]here is much darkness in these books. However, it is always rooted in the psychological darkness associated with childhood and with human development: with anger, loss, death, grief, fear, and with desire."[331] And, so the argument goes, "Children need to see their feelings, particularly the darkest ones, reflected in their stories."[332] But the questions still stands: Does every child need to picture himself or herself as a serial killer and torturer, and is "postmodern childhood" totally reducible to a litany of atrocities?

Sometimes, researchers—fans of Harry Potter—can go as far as to argue that Harry Potter helps children cultivate "anti-torture'" and "anti-violence" attitudes, develop negative attitudes to the Bush administration, and even encourage readers to support Obama in 2008.[333] There is also a claim that the "*Harry Potter* series, with its use of magic, frightening storylines, and character ambiguity, is beneficial to children who are dealing with issues related to terror and terrorism" and that its cruelties can teach children to handle physical and psychological victimization.[334] One can only guess the grounds for assuming that fictional horrors "lead children to explore important, yet frightening issues while remaining in an emotionally safe state,"[335] not to mention that this assessment completely disregards literature's formative influence on the way readers—children and adults alike—experience emotions.

Coincidentally or not, the young actors who played the key roles in the Harry Potter movies reported various psychological problems while shooting the movies: "I was hanging in rags when we finished shooting," Emma Watson is reported as saying about her time on the last two films in an article titled "Emma Watson felt 'Schizophrenic' shooting 'Harry Potter And The Deathly Hallows.'"[336] Daniel Radcliffe started drinking while shooting Harry Potter: "I can point to many scenes where I'm just gone," he said. "Dead behind the eyes."[337] Are the assurances of a journalist that "he takes an ownership of his problem," does not blame the plot explicitly for this issue, and does not relate this problem to the content of any particular one of the movies entirely convincing? Radcliffe had, in fact, been dubious at first about playing Harry. When asked if he had wanted the role at the beginning, he replied in no uncertain terms that he had not:

> His life sounded like a nightmare! I thought, "God, this poor kid."
> But I think after I got the part I then went back and read all four.
> (. . .) I read them all back to back and just became obsessed.[338]

Speaking to the *Guardian*, Radcliffe also revealed that he was thinking about giving up on Harry Potter and quitting the series after *Azkaban* (when he was fourteen years old).[339] And he has been recently reported unwilling to "be" Harry again.[340]

The question, though, persists:

> [D]o children really take the fantasy, fiction, and fables as facts? Sadly, some do. In an interview with *Newsweek*, the Potter author admitted: "I get letters from children addressed to Professor Dumbledore . . . begging to be let into Hogwarts, and some of them are really sad. Because they want it to be true so badly they've convinced themselves it's true."[341]

So can we be so sure that "No evidence was located to suggest that (. . .) reading Harry Potter (. . .) disrupts children's ability to distinguish fantasy from reality"?[342] Should we be comforted by the statement that "[a]lthough research does suggest a positive relationship between exposure to violent acts in visual forms of media (e.g., TV, movies) and engagement in aggressive behavior and positive attitudes towards violence, there is a lack of empirical evidence to suggest any connection between reading violent material and similar negative outcomes"?[343]

As psychological studies holding the opposite view on violence demonstrate, the Harry Potter series—and fandom culture in general—can trigger depression in readers, and children can even become addicted (Pottermaniacs in the truest sense of the word):

> HP fandom also produced a disruptive influence on day to day functioning of some fans in a 6 month follow-up. In sum, we found parallels between criteria used to diagnose traditional forms of addiction or dependence and some people's attachment to a phenomenon in popular culture.[344]

While these studies mostly limit themselves to exploring the series' psychological impact on their subjects and say little or nothing about the reasons for the Harry Potter phenomenon, I hope that my analysis of this text has gone some way toward filling that gap.

Indeed, death is treated in the series as a special kind of diversion: If immortality is to come through death, as it does for Harry, then death itself is no more than a brief detour. It is, additionally, easier to imagine death as a game, something not to be taken seriously, when it is someone else, a fictional character, who is dying. The disengaged and objectivized descriptions of death and pain that are so plentiful in the Harry Potter series may have been signally instrumental in this respect.

Harry Potter in Russia

We should conclude this chapter by examining the reception of the Harry Potter series in Russia. This case study will highlight the bestselling elements of the Harry Potter story from another angle and will serve to confirm my hypothesis that the series' global success is largely associated with the extent to which it indulged in the new cultural movement that I have conceptualized as the cult of death.

Harry Potter has not simply outsold everything under the sun. Back in 2008, one journalist remarked that J. K. Rowling could soon surpass the sales of Mao Zedong.[345] By now, Rowling has probably become the best-translated author of all time; her series has been translated into sixty-seven languages, with Russia coming in as the thirty-sixth country to publish an official translation of the series' first book.[346] The Rosmen Publishing House obtained the rights for the Russian translation, and *Harry Potter and the Philosopher's/Sorcerer's Stone* appeared in December 2001, three years after the publication of the English original. The series was hugely successful with the Russian audience and racked up the same extraordinary sales in Russia as everywhere else. According to experts, the first book sold 1,200,000 copies.[347] But even prior to the paper edition, an excited Russian audience (the overwhelming majority of the Russian population does not read English) was already following the events of the first book in online translation. Several Russian websites were created, and various translations were published on them, some of them protected by copyright and others not.[348]

Excitement over the books resulted in the development of Pottermania in Russia that followed basically the same pattern as in the United Kingdom and the United States. The consumption of Harry Potter merchandise in Russia, including games, toys, costumes, etc., conforms to models set elsewhere. As we saw in the case of vampire sagas, Harry Potter fandom in Russia also functions similarly to its American counterpart, one example of that being the Moscow-based Harry Potter Club.[349] Harry Potter was also added to the roster of Russian role-playing games, and Russian fans produced countless fanfics about their favorite hero.[350]

The commercial success of the series and reader enthusiasm was such that shortly after the Russian translation of Rowling's novel, a Russian version of Harry Potter appeared. In 2002, Eksmo, one of Russia's largest publishing houses, published *Tanya Grotter and the Magical Double Bass* by Russian author Dmitry Emets. According to company spokesperson Alexei Shelkhov, 100,000 copies sold out immediately.[351] International Harry Potter fandom was fascinated by his illegitimate Russian sister, and soon Byblos, a Dutch publishing house, published an English translation of *Tanya Grotter*. J. K. Rowling and Time Warner sued Eksmo and Emets for breach of copyright and secured an injunction prohibiting the translation of the Grotter novel into English. Rowling failed to obtain a court decision in Russia, however, and Eksmo has continued publishing Emets' series, arguing that his work represents a parody of Harry Potter, which is allowed under copyright law. The interesting precedent in copyright law created by this case has been discussed by legal scholars, who have debated the extent

Fig. 5. Cover of
the first edition,
*Tanya Grotter and
the Magical Double
Bass,* by Dmitry
Emets.

to which the copyright law could be applied to literary texts: "The court based its opinion on the similarities between Tanya and Harry, noting similar enemies, antics, and even eyeglasses."[352] The sixteen Tanya Grotter books that have been published to date have accumulated an enthusiastic fan base and spawned a number of computer games, much as the original Harry Potter series did.

The huge success of these books is undoubtedly attributable to their structural similarity to the Harry Potter series, so the court must have thought. What structural elements did Emets appropriate from the Harry Potter books to kickstart his success and grab his target audience's attention? At first glance at the first book—which provides the best material to answer my question because the plot of the Tanya Grotter series later diverged from the Harry Potter books—the similarities are offset by the differences. To begin with, the Tanya Grotter series reverses the gender roles of the original. Tanya is an orphan who lives with her uncle, German Durnev, aunt Ninel, and cousin Pipa (Penelope). Like Harry, she was found one morning on the doorstep of her uncle's flat, lying in the case of the magical double bass on which she will later fly through the air, much as Harry and his friends use brooms. (Emets' wizards also fly on vacuum cleaners and play Dragonball with actual dragons instead of Quidditch at their school of magic). Like Harry, she has a mark on her face, but in her case it is a birthmark on her nose, which turns out to be a protection given to her by her father in his fatal fight with Chuma-del'-Tort, a horrible witch. She is treated as badly by her relatives as Harry was, being confined to the loggia of their apartment or kept in a closet with their ugly dog. She is even made to eat from the dog's plate (remember dog biscuits offered to Harry by Aunt Marge?). Tanya also discovers her magical abilities by chance and, like Harry, is accepted into a school of magic called Tibidokhs. This school, governed by a powerful good magician Sardanapal, is also full of all kinds of magic and magical creatures from the world's folk tales. The reader will already have guessed that Tanya has an archenemy, *She Who Is Not* or Chuma-del'-Tort (chuma is a feminine Russian noun meaning "plague"). But the Tanya Grotter series differs from the Harry Potter books in that it reflects certain realities of post-Soviet society. The pretense of urban sophistication is far more typical of Emets' books than it is of the Harry Potter series. Tanya, for instance, lives in a Russian megalopolis, not in a small English town, and Emets' protagonists have a higher social status: Tanya's parents are not simply wizards but also intellectuals, musicians, and philosophers. Unlike Harry's parents, of whose great deeds we know little, Tanya's father was a great and famous magician. And Sardanapal, the headmaster of Tibidokhs, is called "Academician" by his friends. The series gathers together a number of protagonists and allusions that mean a great deal to Russians, including Russian folklore, Alexander Pushkin's tales, and even ancient Greek and Roman mythology. This "Russianness" should not conceal, however, Emets' meticulous reproduction of all major structural pillars of the Harry Potter plot.

Disgust for human beings is one of the fundamentally important features Emets imitates. In this series, people are called not Muggles but Lopukhoidy (*lopukh* being a slang word for a nitwit or a ne'er-do-well), and nothing but foolishness and nastiness can be expected of them.[353] There is even a *Dictionary of 1000 Most Disgusting Lopukhoids*.[354] Tanya's foster parents serve the same purpose as Harry's second family: as a demonstration of how horrible humans are. The Durnevs (a name derived from the Russian word for "fool") are every bit as revolting as the Dursleys. Tanya's cousin Pipa is spoiled and ugly and is compared to a gorilla, as Dudley was.[355] Aunt Ninel is mountainously fat, extremely rude and unpleasant, and "hisses like a snake."[356] Tanya's bony uncle is even more repulsive: this local politician is a cynical liar who builds his career on duping orphans and the elderly.[357] The same hierarchical gap is maintained between people and wizards here as in the Harry Potter series: one has to be born with magical capacities to avoid the miserable destiny of being a human.[358] One of the protagonists, Meduziya, a professor at Tibidokhs, expresses her deep scorn for people by almost repeating Hagrid's words: "I could not care less about what Lopukhoids need!"[359]

Nightmare hypnotics are also utilized in this story. Obedient to convention, the plot begins with a nightmare: Tanya's uncle is dreaming that Chuma is trying to strangle him with her dead hands and warning him to return what Tanya is keeping hidden from her, or else. This story makes a horrible impression on Tanya, who has a kind of fit, shakes the table and spills hot tea on her cousin. Parallels between magic and madness are drawn quite directly from the very beginning: Tanya's schoolmates call her "psycho" or "crackbrain." The institution she enters to learn magic is a School for Behaviorally-Challenged Young Witches and Wizards. As with Harry, her head spins whenever she makes close contact with the world of magic or thinks about Chuma. On occasion, she also feels like vomiting.[360] Like Harry, Tanya has hallucinations about Chuma and sees her reflection in a mirror.[361] At the very beginning, Tanya accidentally puts a spell on her uncle, and he goes insane, thinking he is a rabbit. Interestingly, Tanya's wizardly parents are also spoken of as alcoholics as Harry's father was, and her friend is the son of an alcoholic.[362]

No less than the Harry Potter series, this book, filled as it is with death omens and death prophecies, is about death and dying. Chuma-del'-Tort, the female Voldemort who killed Tanya's parents, wants to kill Tanya too. Like Voldemort, Chuma's power failed her as she tried to kill baby Tanya, so she keeps track of her as she grows, eager to disprove the prophecy that foretells that she will be killed by the offspring of this branch of the Grotter family. To murder this girl-who-lived therefore becomes the most important item on her agenda and the mainspring of the plot. From the beginning, Tanya lives under the threat of being captured by Chuma and dying a horrible death.[363] When Tanya flies for the first time on her magical double bass that she inherited from her parents, she is attacked by a dark shadow resembling a dementor that tries to kill her.

The image of Chuma bears all the essential characteristics of Voldemort. Like Voldemort, she resembles a vampire. After her unsuccessful attempt to kill Tanya, her power sapped by the magic of Tanya's father, is paralyzed and lies in a coffin, vampire-like, for ten years. Interestingly, Tanya counts Count Dracula among her ancestors on her father's side, and her uncle even looks like a vampire.[364] The vampire theme is further developed in *Tanya Grotter and Centaur's Boots* (2004), where Stikhariy, a powerful spirit, needs Tanya's blood to return to the world where he belongs. As we can see, Emets could not afford to dispense with these structural features, even when trying to avoid further similarities with the Harry Potter series due to accusations of plagiarism. Even more explicitly than Voldemort, Chuma is described with all the usual attributes of death: she has a dead body, dead hands, and dead jaws. In the final scene, when she rises from a coffin, her face "looked like a skull," and "a red light came from her empty sockets."[365] Death worship too finds a place in this book, when Shurasik, one of the students, makes animal sacrifices to Chuma, thus reanimating her and helping her rise from her coffin.[366] The book abounds in quite gruesome details and depictions of suffering.[367]

Emets' *Tanya Grotter and the Magical Double Bass* reveals attitudes toward death that are similar to those in the Harry Potter series. It culminates in Tanya's assassination, a murder that is portrayed in naturalistic and demeaning detail. Tanya is described as lying on the floor, incapable of moving, weeping uncontrollably while her tormentor watches her sufferings and recounts how she murdered her parents. What is most extraordinary is that the Emets' book, written in 2002, ends in a similar fashion to Rowling's *Harry Potter and the Deathly Hallows*, which was published five years later. All secrets are revealed to the reader at the time of Tanya's murder as they are in the "King's Cross" chapter of *The Deathly Hallows*. And after suffering the fatal blow, Tanya, like Harry, comes to in the hospital, thus ensuring that the story—and its financial success—will continue.[368] Tanya too is scheduled to suffer several times as the series progressed, letting her fans enjoy her near-death experiences as entertainment, just as Harry's fans do.

Two more Russian re-creations of Harry Potter appeared in the mid-2000s. *Larin Petr and the Factory of Magic* by Yaroslav Morozov (2004) continued to five volumes, and *Denis Kotik* by Aleksandr Zorich made it to four. These series, although containing the same basic elements as Tanya Grotter, were less successful, probably because they were published by smaller publishing houses and because they appeared on the market later.

As in the United States, several parodies were also written in Russian, which attests to the Potter series' huge success with the Russian audience. As early as 2002, Aleksandr Zvalevsky and Igor' Mit'ko put out *Porry Hatter and the Stone Philosopher*, applying to the Harry Potter plot the ideas of Russian formalists, who argued that irony is based on the structural principle of inverting meaning and turning everything upside down.[369] Porry, the protagonist, is an ordinary boy who has no magical skills. He lives the happy life of a beloved son in his well-established family of wizards. The wizarding world, however, is under threat from the hateful Lord Mordevolt. This powerful magician thinks that wizards should be stripped of their powers and transformed into ordinary people because he believes that the future of humanity lies not with magic but with scientific progress. He tries to take Porry's power away but loses his own instead. As a result, Porry becomes an enthusiastic scientist who hates magic, does not want to enroll in a school of magic, etc., etc. . . . Even in this parody, along with the iconic name Harry Potter—or something that sounds very similar—certain structural elements remain untouched, which testifies to their crucial importance to the Harry Potter story. An adult lunatic threatens and pursues the boy, and people are inferior creatures to be despised. In this parody, the wizards call people *mudly* (which calls to mind a vulgar Russian word for extreme idiots), Porry's birth is an embarrassment to the family because he has no magical powers, and people are described as "these unfortunate creatures who cannot mutate or scale walls."[370] This series was funnier and better written than some of its successors, such as Sergey Panarin's *Harry Proglotter and Magic Shawarmatrix* (2005). Although not particularly popular, this series also did produce two titles.

We should probably conclude this exploration on the reception of Harry Potter in Russia by saying that Harry Ivanovich Potter may be running in the Russian Federation's presidential elections in 2018.[371] Created by a group of political scientists in 2003 to mock the bogus election of Eduard Rossel, the notoriously corrupt pro-Putin governor of Sverdlovsk, this same personage applied to register for the presidential elections in April 2013. On that occasion, though, he was used by pro-Putin political advisors to compromise the candidacy of Alexey Navalny, the popular opposition leader.[372]

What is certainly more important to my analysis than the fate of Harry Ivanovich Potter's political career is that Harry's triumph in Russia may be explained by the same key elements that produced the Potter phenomenon in the United States. The Russian imitations and parodies confirm my hypothesis about the message in these books, re-creating the same coming-of-death scenario that reverberated with the zeitgeist of the late 1990s to the 2010s, which was bemused by the cult of death.

Harry Potter's mega-popularity, the unexpected and unprecedented success of books that are so deficient in style, philosophy, and psychological depth, is ultimately owed to their ability to leverage certain new attitudes toward humans, humanity, and human life that began to emerge in Western culture during the late 1980s. The Harry Potter books captured the formulaic features of Gothic Aesthetic—a plot that imitates nightmare and nonhuman principal characters who despise humankind (those repulsive Muggles) as an inferior race—when that new and powerful trend was still in its infancy. The series combined features of the new, most prominent, and most marketable character types—maniac, vampire, serial killer—in its main protagonist. This new school novel created a new market and tapped into a new audience that reveled in the fresh excitements of the rising cult of death. Throughout the Harry Potter books, the celebration of death emerges as a new strategy in entertainment and a prominent element in the culture of nightmare consumption, which presents violent virtual death as fun for the whole family.

Conclusion

The cult of death, a movement in popular culture, originates from complex aesthetic, intellectual, and historical sources. To summarize the results of my study, I will highlight the main stages of its development over the past decades.

The *aesthetic* factor crucial to its formation was Gothic Aesthetic. This powerful trend in fiction and movies laid the groundwork for the aestheticization of violent death as an expression of disapprobation of humans as a species. Gothic Aesthetic emerged in the 1980s and early 1990s, when two tendencies—depicting nonhuman monsters on the one hand and describing nightmares on the other—amalgamated in popular fiction and movies. The idealization of the monster as a new cultural hero acting in manmade nightmares produced a new formula that proved highly successful. Gothic Aesthetic transformed the undead into the indispensable protagonists of movies and fiction, providing sine qua non conditions for the contemporary ascent of the cult of death.

Gothic Aesthetic is deeply rooted in the Western culture of the past two centuries.[1] Authors of Gothic novels experimented with literary nightmares and developed literary devices that helped them induce in their readers a nightmarish trance. It should be stressed, however, that the Gothic novelists were not exactly robust predecessors of Gothic Aesthetic. Most Gothic novelists were not daring enough to break away from the anthropocentric ideals of the Enlightenment, a tendency exemplified by Mary Shelley's Frankenstein: the opposition between man and monster is clear-cut in her novel.[2] Even the Gothic revival in the late nineteenth and early twentieth centuries did not produce the kind of monsters we routinely encounter today. At that time, the protagonists who captures the writer's full attention and with whom readers were supposed to identify—as in Bram Stoker's paradigmatic *Dracula*—were still humans, not monsters.

The true nonhumans of Gothic Aesthetic were pioneered by J. R. R. Tolkien. He created an aesthetic universe that exemplified antihumanism: readers of Tolkien's epic were expected to identify firmly with his distinctly nonhuman hobbits. H. P. Lovecraft's mesmeric aesthetics offered literary nightmare as means of hedonistic self-indulgence in delightful horror and horrible delight, and as a direct alternative to the world of people.[3] The works of Tolkien and Lovecraft laid the foundations of the contemporary culture of nightmare consumption and facilitated the nightmare's penetration into the everyday life of millions of readers, viewers, and gamers.

The cult of death rode the wave of Gothic Aesthetic. Monsters "feeding" on humans exemplified a fascination with violent fictional death as an expression of the ultimate contempt for humans and humanity. The audience's willingness to identify with monsters was facilitated by the nightmarish trance into which those works plunge their readers and viewers by distorting their normal perceptions, using tried-and-true literary devices as well as new technologies to generate the illusion that the reader or viewer himself or herself feels endowed with nonhuman powers. If the Gothic novel, which protested against the aesthetics of the Enlightenment, was fundamentally a revolt against rationality, the present day Gothic Aesthetic could be regarded as a reaction to a crisis of rationality prompted by the questioning of the foundations of Western philosophy and aesthetics of modernity in the late twentieth century. The collapse of the master narratives (or *grands paradigmes*) of the social sciences and humanities in the 1970s and 1980s was an important dimension of this crisis.

The *intellectual* origins of the cult of death are traced back to two philosophical ideas: the critique of European humanism and the rejection of human exceptionalism. Both ideas found a new popularity with intellectuals and philosophers in the 1960s and 1970s before going on to penetrate into popular culture. This transition profoundly changed their meaning, deprived them of their initial critical impulse, and transformed them into fashionable cultural commodities.

French Theory, which greatly influenced Western thinking in the second half of the twentieth century, held those ideas in high regard. The French intellectuals' critique of humanism, in which they followed Marx and Nietzsche, was subordinate to their major intellectual goal, which was to dismantle the transcendental subject of classical Western philosophy. The critique of the ideology of the Enlightenment and of bourgeois society was also important to them, serving as it did to reinforce their stance on humanism. Ultimately, positioning monsters or animals at the center of their inquiry was a radical gesture that eloquently symbolized their approach to humanism and human exceptionalism. In the same period, anglophone ethical philosophers and intellectuals were laying the theoretical foundations of the animal rights movement. They insisted that animals had moral rights and propagated the term "speciesism" to denounce the idea of human exceptionalism and human supremacy over all other living organisms.

Two other movements—transhumanism and posthumanism—contributed greatly to the rejection of human exceptionalism and the dissolution of the boundaries between humans, animals, and monsters in the popular imagination. They acquired prominence and popularity in the late 1990s and early 2000s and played an important role in commodification of the ideas they espoused. Transhumanism, which emerged toward the end of the 1970s among scientists and engineers, promoted the idea that humanity's purpose is to create an artificial intelligence that will permeate the universe. The human race is here regarded as a transitional step in the process of evolution, one that will be transcended by "god-like" machines many millions of times more powerful than the human intelligence. The transhumanists converted the abstract critique of humanism and the rejection of human exceptionalism into an applied scientific project and a pragmatic policy for future research. While transhumanists are indifferent regarding the destiny of the human race, other scientists consider superseding of the human race as a must for any meaningful future development. Posthumanism, a trend in humanities that developed in the 1990s and appropriated the heritage of French Theory, attempts to erase the human presence from philosophy and the humanities altogether.

The animal rights movement, transhumanism, and posthumanism benefited from the general intellectual atmosphere of the late twentieth century, shaped as it was by the legacy of French Theory. This is not to say that all these movements were driven by the same philosophical ideas that had inspired the French thinkers. But they did share with French Theory certain important presuppositions about the place of humans in the value system. In contrast to French Theory, the animal rights movement, transhumanism, and posthumanism cannot be regarded as mere philosophical schools. From the late 1970s on, animal rights defenders became a powerful social force that actively promoted the rejection of human exceptionalism. Posthumanism and especially transhumanism became highly popular social movements in the 2000s. The popularity of transhumanism has grown significantly due to advancements in artificial intelligence, nanotechnology, bioengineering, and genetic engineering, while posthumanism has acquired considerable influence in cultural criticism and cultural studies and has proven successful in advocating its ideas beyond the confines of academia.

The ideas supported by those movements filtered into popular culture through political discourse, cultural criticism, technological innovations, and academic debate. Countless novels and films were created based on them, as the denunciation of humanism and human exceptionalism became an increasingly popular cultural commodity that entailed new ways of dealing with the human characters in literature and art. And the changing attitudes to people articulated in blockbusters, in their turn, informed the rising cult of death.

I would suggest that Europe's Unmasterable past could be seen as an important *historical* premise of the cult of death. The experience of the concentration camp universe[4] brought about a deep disillusionment with human beings and humanity. It compromised the Enlightenment belief in human nature and the human race as the one uniquely moral species, and it created favorable preconditions for a mass disenchantment with human nature. In the 1960s and 1970s, almost thirty years after the fact, new generations in the Western democracies began to process the historical legacy of Auschwitz, which the previous generation had sought to erase from its memory. With regard to Soviet communism, the publication of Aleksandr Solzhenitsyn's *Gulag Archipelago* in the West in 1973 dramatically improved the understanding of the scale of the crimes against humanity committed in Russia under the Soviets and marked a decisive stage in the process of disillusionment with communism. And the "crisis of the future"—the mass disenchantment with traditional future-oriented political ideologies based on a "religion of progress"—began in the West in the 1970s, largely due to what Theodor Adorno called "working through the past."[5] The concentration camp universe can be seen as an irreducible common legacy of today's society, including the United States, a country that has no firsthand familiarity with totalitarian regimes, either Nazism or communism.[6]

As we have seen, this experience was important to the French avantgarde thinkers' stand on humanism. By the early 1990s, however, their philosophical critique of humanism and questioning of human exceptionalism had acquired a new meaning in the process of commodification. No longer a philosophical expression of tragic experience, antihumanism laid the groundwork for the acceptance of violent death as a popular theme in mass entertainment. The rejection of human exceptionalism prompted the normalization and idealization of monsters and opened the way to the refutation of humanity and human beings in contemporary popular culture.

Based on these premises, we are finally in the position to document the cult of death as a unique popular culture movement and to identify the most important stages in its development over past decades. This historical overview will discern complex relations and intersections between the facts and phenomena in various spheres of social and cultural life that constitute the cult of death. Most importantly, it will demonstrate that changing attitudes to human protagonists in fiction and movies were indeed interconnected with changes in death-related social and cultural practices.

The formation of the cult of death began in the 1970s, when several important developments laid the groundwork for its future triumph. The 1970s were marked by the emergence of young adult literature as a new genre that came to place an unprecedented emphasis on unmotivated violence, and by a resurgence of horror films that continued into the following decades. The late 1970s and early 1980s also witnessed the first stirring of interest in serial killers. The spike in Tolkien's popularity, manifested by the translation of *The Lord of the Rings* into most European languages in the 1970s, signaled a nascent public interest in nonhuman monsters as trendy protagonists of fiction and movies. Gothic rock, heavy metal, and rap, which originated in the 1970s, were frequently focused on violence and on death-related themes. The Goth youth subculture concentrated on the macabre while *The Lord of the Rings* inspired a slew of role-playing games that taught their users to identify with nonhuman monsters. The first journals concerned with thanatology and death studies appeared at this time, manifesting the growing public and academic interest in death.

The period from the 1980s to the late 1990s was crucial to the development of the cult of death. Here we observe the first palpable signs of the cult of death taking over the popular culture, and we witness the first stages in the commodification of the critique of humanism. During this period, an important shift occurred in the representation of the monster, which emerged as a new aesthetic ideal. Along with the exponentially growing popularity of vampire sagas, zombie apocalypses, and other tales of the undead, this period is also marked by a fascination with serial killers and cannibals. By the late 1980s, the images of vampire, serial killer, and cannibal began to fuse in popular culture, creating a roster of trend-setting protagonists. Two books of primary importance to these developments were also published at this time: The first book of the Harry Potter series, which promoted new attitudes toward human protagonists and death, appeared in the United Kingdom in 1997 and in the United States in 1998, and Nina Auerbach's *Our Vampires, Ourselves* (1999) successfully promoted the idea that the difference between humans and monsters is ambiguous and that the murderous monster is actually the Other and thus deserves our sympathy and understanding. In the late 1980s through the early 1990s, when computer game technology entered a new era, cutting-edge technologies provided unique opportunities for the representation of nonhuman monsters and the dissemination of the culture of nightmare consumption. Experiments in sound and visuals were beginning to justify previously voiced suspicions that these technologies were now being employed to induce an unconscious dream state in users. This period was marked by an increasing number of cartoons and movies featuring violent death and attacks on humans, and the incidence of violence in prime-time television programs that was far higher than in real life. By the early 1990s, Gothic Aesthetic had taken over fiction and movies, which now regularly featured the undead in manmade nightmares.

The idealization of monsters in fiction and movies, which signaled a radical rejection of human exceptionalism, corresponded to the changes in social and cultural practices that were taking place in this period. The vampire subculture gained a firm foothold, rivaling the Goth and Emo subcultures in popularity. The fascination with the serial killer gave birth to a celebrity culture centered on real serial killers. Changes in the celebration of Halloween also find their counterparts in these trends in movies and fiction. The spread of sadistic urban legends about Halloween in the United States that began in the late 1970s and caused a nationwide panic in the 1980s served to attract unprecedented public attention to this holiday. Those sadistic hoaxes conditioned the rapid growth of Halloween's popularity by positioning this holiday as a high-profile expression of anti-humanism and a new and compellingly fashionable commodity. During its transformation into an astonishingly successful holiday, Halloween's focus shifted from children to adults and came to be explicitly centered on death-related symbolism and the undead. Death rites too had begun to evolve, as reflected in the popularity of such new practices as green funerals and cryonization in the United States and Europe, which signaled a growing dissatisfaction with existing rituals and traditions. And finally, death studies and thanatology studies developed into academic fields in their own right in the 1990s, moving death to the center of the academic research agenda in various fields of the social sciences and humanities.

As the new millennium dawned, the extent to which the cult of death had taken over popular culture became increasingly clear. Violent entertainment broke new grounds in the commodification of antihumanism. Death had acquired such prominence on television that researchers began to speak of "death as a public spectacle." In the early 2000s, the secular apocalypse, which proclaimed and even celebrated the end of human civilization, became an extremely prominent genre in entertainment. The horror genre developed three new species, BDSM, "slashers," and torture porn, the last of which had taken over genres other than horror by the mid-2000s. Horror merged with the Gothic genre, whose most macabre variations gained a new prominence. Popular culture developed yet another important trend in this period, namely, a fascination with cannibalism. In movies and fiction, cannibalism, once the expression of the ultimate act of inhumanity, acquired the new status of a fashionable diversion. In concert with descriptions of vampires "feeding on humans" and of serial killers "hunting humans," these representations signify a questioning of the fundamental food taboo. The obsession with food as a theme of public debate and research that characterized the 2000s, on the one hand, and the constant comparisons of people with animals, and even specifically with livestock, on the other, served greatly to reinforce that questioning. And this enhanced the appreciation of the unbridgeable gap between the idealized monster and undistinguished humankind, now considered food for monsters and an inferior race that is to be superseded in the process of evolution.

In the 2000s, dramatic changes continued to impact all death-related social practices, in a way that may be understood as a manifestation of postmodernity and an after-effect of the crisis of tradition. But could it also be that the commodification of death has forced death-related practices and industries into the same pattern of diversification as typifies any other commodity? In the 2000s, Halloween continued its inroads into global culture, becoming a major American, European, and Russian holiday that rivals only Christmas in the amount of money spent on decorations and parties. The further development of this holiday, which, according to observers, was "becoming more openly horrific,"[7] had begun to affect other festivals, with Christmas and Valentine's Day haunted houses becoming increasingly common. Another important sign of the times was the spread of the cult of Santa Muerte, which had been restricted to domestic ceremonials in the suburbs of Mexico but in the early 2000s began branching out into the American metropolis and swiftly expanding far beyond Mexican immigrant milieu. Several new entertainment industries exploiting death as their major attraction emerged during this time. Dark tourism—visits to the sites of mass crimes and murders—developed as a new offering from the tourist industry and has since then been successfully growing in America, Europe, and Russia. The market for the artwork of serial killers and for murderabilia—collectibles related to violent crimes and serial killings—quickly developed a huge international following. In the new millennium, "death education" entered secondary school curriculums in the United States and gained a significant foothold in higher education.[8] And thanatography—the recounting of symptoms and thoughts by a dying person—took its place as a new narrative genre. Traditional funerals were by now giving way to a wide range of new forms: ashes jewelry, the scattering of ashes, roadside memorials, death parties, etc., while green funerals and cryonization continued to grow in popularity. This most conservative of rituals was undergoing an unprecedented degree of individualization and diversification. Some of these new trends in funeral practices may stem from a general confusion as to the meaning of death. But they also could be regarded as a sign of the breakdown of the "social glue." If rituals are to be seen as expressions of belonging to a certain collectivity, these changes may express growing disappointment in human collectivity and frustration with the idea of belonging to any human community. Fashion, the international industry par excellence, caught up with other death-related industries and festivities in this decade by inventing the new trends of corpse chic, "to die for" style and "skull style." Representations of the aftermath of a violent death were now routinely featured in fashion advertisements.

These major trends in social and cultural practices, all elements in the cult of death, may relate to a new understanding of the place and role of humans. The meaning of violent death has been transformed from a tragedy to a source of entertainment, a "violent delight" and even a "party." The general public has grown accustomed to the idea—in the context of fiction and movies at least—that humanity is not an ultimate value and can easily be consigned to evolutionary obsolescence. The mass demand for those ideas is a major trademark of the popular culture bestsellers, and their wide dissemination has been taken on by the entertainment industry, along with several other commercial and cultural initiatives, as a kind of cause.

The cult of death transforms violent death into a popular culture commodity and an acceptable form of entertainment. Its specificity consists in the dehumanization of humanity in general, rather than of any particular social group or ethnicity, as it was in the case of communism and fascism in the previous century. Surfacing throughout several cultural and social phenomena and practices, it offers antihumanism as a popular commodity, rather than as a political project for the future. The cult of death expresses a nascent cultural paradigm—a profound contempt for the human race.

Notes

INTRODUCTION

1. Data from Centers for Disease Control and Prevention and the World Bank: http://www.cdc.gov/nchs/data/nvsr/nvsr60/nvsr60_09.pdf; http://www.cdc.gov/mmwr/preview/mmwrhtml/mm5842a7.htm; http://www.cdc.gov/nchs/data/nvsr/nvsr52/nvsr52_14.pdf; http://www.cdc.gov/nchs/deaths.htm; http://ec.europa.eu/eurostat/statistics-explained/index.php/File:Life_expectancy_at_birth_and_at_age_65,_EU-28,_2002–13_(¹)_(years)_PF15.png; http://data.worldbank.org/indicator/SP.DYN.LE00.IN/countries/1W?display=graph

2. On life expectancy in these countries in this period, see Clayne. L. Pope, "Adult Mortality in America before 1900: A View from Family Histories," in *Strategic Factors in Nineteenth Century American Economic History: A Volume to Honor Robert W. Fogel*, ed. Claudia Goldin and Hugh Rockoff (Chicago: Chicago University Press, 1992), 280–84; H. O. Lancaster, *Expectations of Life: A Study in the Demography, Statistics, and History of World Mortality* (New York: Springer, 1990), 8, 29, 44, 338–96. See also: http://www.mortality.org; http://www.unece.org/fileadmin/DAM/stats/documents/ece/ces/ge.11/2013/WP_5.4.pdf; https://ourworldindata.org/life-expectancy/. On premodern demographic regime, see Pierre Goubert, *Louis XIV et vingt millions de Français* (Paris: Fayard, 1966).

3. Geoffrey Gorer, "The Pornography of Death," *Encounter*, October 1955, 49–52.

4. Ernest Becker, *The Denial of Death* (New York: Free Press Paperbacks, 1973).

5. Philippe Ariès, *The Hour of Our Death* (New York: Vintage Books, 1982), 13.

6. Barney Galland Glaser and Anselm Leonard Strauss, eds., *Awareness of Dying* (New Brunswick, NJ: Transaction, 1966), 3. See also Elisabeth Kübler-Ross, *Questions and Answers on Death and Dying* (New York: Macmillan, 1974). A discussion on death and dying was stimulated by the publication of Jessica Mitford's *The American Way of Death* in 1963, but it was short-lived.

7. http://tinyurl.com/o7c6rkp

8. Ronald L. Grimes, *Deeply into the Bone: Re-inventing Rites of Passage* (Berkeley: University of California Press, 2000), 258. On silence on death in America see also Robert Kastenbaum, *Death, Society, and Human Experience* (1977) (Upper Saddle River, NJ: Pearson, 2011).

9. "Views on End-of-Life Medical Treatment," PEW Research: Religion and Public Life Project, November 21, 2013, http://tinyurl.com/ljrtnsh. See also *The Project on Death in America*, http://www.opensocietyfoundations.org/publications/transforming-culture-dying-project-death-america-1994-2003

10. Craig Bowron, "Our Unrealistic Attitudes about Death through a Doctor's Eyes," *Washington Post*, February 17, 2012 http://tinyurl.com/6t4gh8c

11. Douglas David, *A Brief History of Death* (Hoboken, NJ: John Wiley & Sons, 2008), 170.

12. Geoffrey C. Bowker and Susan Leigh Star, *Sorting Things Out: Classification and Its Consequences* (Cambridge, MA: MIT Press, 2000), 72–74, 123–24. See also https://public.health.oregon.gov/BirthDeathCertificates/RegisterVitalRecords/Documents/Death/cdelderly.pdf

13. Allan Kellehear, *A Social History of Dying* (Cambridge: Cambridge University Press, 2007), 253.

14. Norbert Elias, *The Loneliness of the Dying* (1985) (London: Bloomsbury Publishing USA, 2001), 85.

15. Michael C. Kearl, "What Death Means," in *Endings: A Sociology of Death and Dying* (Oxford: Oxford University Press, 1989), 47.

16. Colin Murray Parkes, Pittu Laungani, and William Young, eds., *Death and Bereavement Across Cultures* (London: Routledge, 2003), 234.

17. Vladimir Leskin, "To Die in Russia," *Mir v Rossii*, no. 4 (2010): 124–61, http://demoscope.ru/weekly/2010/0443/analit02.php. For attitudes toward death among Russian elderly people, see also http://www.emissia.org/offline/2013/2047.htm

18. Leskin, "To Die in Russia," 135.

19. Although there are no reliable statistics, these figures are estimates that are accepted by the majority of the historians of this period.

20. Patricio V. Marques, "Dying Too Young: Addressing Premature Mortality and Ill Health Due to Non-Communicable Diseases and Injuries in the Russian Federation," Europe and Central Asia Human Development Department, The World Bank, http://tinyurl.com/omytv86

21. See, for example, Evgeny Andreev and Alexander Vishnevsky, "The Challenge of High Mortality in Russia," *Narodonaselenie*, no. 3 (2004): 75–84. See also http://vestnik.mednet.ru/content/view/479/30/lang,ru/

22. On the revival of the interest in death, especially in the social sciences, humanities, and media, see Tony Walter, *The Revival of Death* (Hove: Psychology Press, 1994), 2–5; and Folker Hanusch, *Representing Death in the News: Journalism, Media and Mortality* (London: Palgrave Macmillan, 2010), 2.

23. Keith F. Durkin, "Death, Dying, and the Dead in Popular Culture," in *Handbook of Death & Dying*, ed. Clifton D. Bryant (Thousand Oaks, CA: Sage Publications, 2003), 1:47. A number of scholars have documented the various ways in which Americans attempt to deny death (see, for example, Lynne Ann DeSpelder and Albert Lee Strickland, *The Last Dance: Encountering Death and Dying*, 6th ed.

[New York: McGraw-Hill, 2002]). In *Understanding Dying, Death, and Bereavement*, 6th ed. (Belmont, CA: Thomson Publishing, 2007), Michael R. Leming and George E. Dickinson also demonstrate that the United States is a death-denial society.

24. For a study of violence and especially sexual violence in post-Soviet culture, see Elliot Borenstein, *Overkill: Sex and Violence in Contemporary Russian Popular Culture* (Ithaca: Cornell University Press, 2007), where he analyzes the violence in popular culture as an expression of and response to Russia's national collapse. On the representations of death in Russian postmodernism, see Marc Lipovetsky, *Russian Postmodernist Fiction: Dialogue with Chaos* (Armonk, NY: M. E. Sharpe, 1999), 10–11, 12, 63, 239.

25. Dolf Zillmann, "The Psychology of the Appeal of Portrayals of Violence," in *Why We Watch*, ed. Jeffrey Goldstein (New York: Oxford University Press, 1998), 180. Vivian Sobchack has also discussed violent death as having been "naturalized" in our culture in response to the changing perception of death and acknowledges the difference between contemporary culture and the 1950s: "Death in movies may have been quick but it was dramatic, meaningful. Those who died did so for a reason. In those days, we didn't even think in term of assassination (. . .), or about junkies, madmen, snipers" (Sobchack, "The Violent Dance: A Personal Memoir of Death in the Movies," in *Screening Violence*, ed. Stephen Prince [London: Athlone Press], 112). Sobchack speaks about contemporary fascination with senseless and random violence and death on the screen as reflecting our "increasingly uncivil society" (125). See also Sobchack, *Meta Morphing: Visual Transformation and the Culture of Quick-Change* (Minneapolis: University of Minnesota Press, 2000).

26. Leming and Dickinson, *Understanding Dying, Death, and Bereavement*, 4.

27. Durkin, "Death, Dying, and the Dead," 41.

28. As *A Report of the Surgeon General* of 2001 states, at the end of the 1990s, 61 percent of television programs contained violent content, 44 percent of perpetrators of violence were depicted as attractive, and no immediate punishment was depicted in nearly 75 percent of the violent scenes (http://www.ncbi.nlm.nih.gov/books/NBK44293/). S. L. Smith and E. Donnerstein, "Harmful Effects of Exposure to Media Violence: Learning of Aggression, Emotional Desensitization, and Fear," in *Human Aggression: Theories, Research, and Implications for Social Policy*, ed. R. G. Green and E. Donnerstein (New York: Academic Press, 1998), 167–202.

29. "Crime in prime time is at least 10 times as rampant as in the real world": George Gerbner, Lary Croos, Michael Morgan, and Nancy Signorelli, "Living with Television: The Dynamic of the Cultivation Process" in *Perspectives on Media Effects*, ed. Jennings Bryan and Dolf Zillman (Hillsdale, NJ: Lawrence Erlbaum Associates, 1986), 26.

30. Zillmann, "The Psychology of the Appeal," 180 (he references here his study conducted with James Weaver in 1993).

31. On the impact of television on the perception of death as "public spectacle," see Charlton D. McIlwain, *When Death Goes Pop: Death, Media, and the Remaking of Community* (New York: Peter Lang, 2005). On the high level of representations of death in the media as well as on the ritualized aspect of death of celebrities, see Johanna Sumiala, *Media and Ritual: Death, Community and Everyday Life* (London: Routledge, 2012).

32. On torture porn as a new powerful genre see Steve Jones, *Torture Porn: Popular Horror after Saw* (New York: Palgrave Macmillan, 2013).

33. Durkin, "Death, Dying, and the Dead," 44–45. One specific genre of horror film, the slasher movie, has become especially popular in recent years. According to Fred Molitor and Barry S. Sapolsky ("Sex, Violence, and Victimization in Slasher Films," in *Journal of Broadcasting and Electronic Media* 37 [2014]: 235), "The accentuation in these films is on extreme graphic violence."

34. David Buckingham, *After the Death of Childhood* (Cambridge: Polity, 2000), 127.

35. Rebecca Shillabeer, "The Fascination with Torture and Death in Twenty-First-Century Crime Fiction," in *The Power of Death: Contemporary Reflections on Death in Western Society*, ed. Maria-Jose Blanco and Ricarda Vidal (New York: Berghahn Books, 2014), 104.

36. Sara Mosle, "The Outlook's Bleak," *New York Times Magazine*, August 2, 1998.

37. Nolan Feeney, "The 8 Habits of Highly Successful Young-Adult Fiction Authors," *The Atlantic*, October 22, 2013. http://tinyurl.com/mts4f9p

38. Meghan Cox Gurdon, "Darkness Too Visible," *Wall Street Journal*, June 4, 2011, http://tinyurl.com/nfzg755

39. For the psychological studies of violence in entertainment, which deals with the reasons why death exerts such an enthrallment on ordinary people, see Jeffrey A. Kottler, *The Lust for Blood: Why We Are Fascinated by Death, Murder, Horror, and Violence* (Amherst, NY: Prometheus Books, 2010). His focus is on death as real-life event. Although engagingly written, this book does not provide a distinctively new intellectual perspective on its subject matter. See also David Trend, *The Myth of Media Violence: A Critical Introduction* (Malden, MA: Blackwell, 2007). On psychological theories of entertainment, see *Psychology of Entertainment*, ed. Jennings Bryant and Peter Vorderer (London: Routledge, 2013). For an anthropological perspective on violence, see Melvin Konner, "Sacred Violence, Mimetic Rivalry, and War," in *Mimesis and Science: Empirical Research on Imitation and the Mimetic Theory of Culture and Religion*, ed. Scott R. Garrels (East Lansing: Michigan State University Press, 2011), 155–74.

40. On issues pertaining to media violence and the debate on censorship and freedom of expression, see, for example, Martin Barker and Julian Petley, "Introduction," in *Ill Effects: The Media/Violence Debate*, ed. Martin Barker and Julian Petley (Hove: Psychology Press, 1997), 1–11.

41. Durkin, "Death, Dying, and the Dead," 47–48.

42. Vicki Goldberg, "Death Takes a Holiday, Sort Of," in *Why We Watch*, 29.

43. Catherine Jenkins, "Life Extension, Immortality and the Patient Voice," in *The Power of Death*, 215.

44. On pro and contra of the theory of empathy and counterempathy see Clark McCauley, "When Screen Violence Is Not Attractive," in *Why We Watch*, 202, 205.

45. For example, John Taylor's *Body Horror: Photojournalism, Catastrophe, and War* (New York: New York University Press, 1998) follows John Keane's idea that representations of violence create "public spheres of controversy" (*Reflections on Violence* [London: Verso, 1996]), encouraging people to "find remedies to savagery" (4). Taylor believes that photojournalism of violence may result in moments of "identification," "reflection," and interest in "the dreadful fates of others."

46. Susan D. Moeller, *Compassion Fatigue: How The Media Sell Disease, Famine, War, and Death* (New York: Routledge, 1999).

47. Norbert Elias and Eric Dunning, *Quest for Excitement: Sport and Leisure in the Civilizing Process* (Oxford: Blackwell, 1986), 31. See also Dolf Zillmann, "The Psychology of the Appeal of Portrayals of Violence," 192–96.

48. "As it happens, 40 years ago, no one had to contend with young-adult literature because there was no such thing." Gurdon, "Darkness Too Visible."

49. Alan Warren, Dale Salwak, Daryl F. Mallett, *Roald Dahl: From the Gremlins to the Chocolate Factory* (San Bernardino, CA: Borgo Press, 1994), 26. Also, on Dahl's perception of adults as enemies, see Jeremy Treglown, *Roald Dahl: A Biography* (New York: Farrar, Straus & Giroux, 1994). Roald Dahl saw the key to his success as an author of children's books in his ability "to conspire with children against adults" (Warren, Salwak, and Mallett, *Roald Dahl*, 237). His approach was followed: "Rather than channeling our efforts into ways of instrumentalizing narrative violence and placing it in the service of a pedagogy of fear, we need to think about interrogating (with the child) the attractiveness of violence." Maria Tatar, "Violent Delights in Children Literature," in *Why We Watch*, ed. Jeffrey Goldstein, 87.

50. Willa Petschek, "Roald Dahl at Home," *New York Times*, December 25, 1977. On the primitive urge for retributive justice as a root of fictional violence, see Henry Bacon, *The Fascination of Film Violence* (New York: Palgrave Macmillan, 2015).

51. On uses of violence in YAL, see Perri Klass, "A Bambi for the 90's, via Shakespeare," *New York Times*, June 19, 1994. For reflections on the nature of child criminality see: Carol Anne David, *Children Who Kill: Profiles of Teen and Pre-teen Killers* (London: Allison & Busby, 2004).

52. Gurdon, "Darkness Too Visible."

53. "These results suggest that playing violent video games does not constitute a significant risk for future violent criminal acts." Christopher J. Ferguson et al., "Violent Video Games and Aggression: Causal Relationship or Byproduct of Family Violence and Intrinsic Violence Motivation?" *Criminal Justice and Behavior* 35, no. 3 (March 2008), 20. On the "catalyst theory," see also Christopher J. Ferguson, "Does Movie or Video Game Violence Predict Societal Violence? It Depends on What You Look at and When," *Journal of Communication* 65 (2015): 193–212. On the absence of correlation between media violence and crime, and on the argument about the decrease in violent crime see: Jonathan L. Freedman, *Media Violence and Its Effect on Aggression: Assessing the Scientific Evidence* (Toronto: University of Toronto Press, 2002). According to Ian Vine, "The 'harmful effects' approach to the media is moribund and reactionary" (Vine, "The Dangerous Psycho-Logic of Media 'Effects'," in *Ill Effects: The Media/Violence Debate*, ed. Martin Barker and Julian Petley [Hove: Psychology Press, 1997], 121).

54. "A fear of crime, for example, of the kind that is sometimes thought to be induced by television reporting, can lead to an illogical desire to retreat from the outside world; but it may also be a necessary prerequisite for crime prevention." David Buckingham, "Electronic Child Abuse? Rethinking the Media's Effects on Children," in Martin Barker and Julian Petley, ed., *Ill Effects: The Media/Violence Debate*, 34. "We instrument for game sales with game characteristics, game quality

and time on the market, and estimate that, while a one percent increase in violent games is associated with up to a 0.03% decrease in violent crime, non-violent games appear to have no effect on crime rates." Scott Cunningham, Benjamin Engelstätter, and Michael R. Ward, "Understanding the Effects of Violent Video Games on Violent Crime," *Social Science Research Network*, April 7, 2011 (http://papers. ssrn.com/sol3/papers.cfm?abstract_id=1804959). George Gerbner, the author of cultivation theory, holds that media violence has an undeniable influence on the audience and may "cultivate exaggerated notions of the prevalence of violence and risk out in the world." George Gerbner and Larry Gross, "Living With Television: The Violence Profile," *Journal of Communication* 26, no. 2 (1976): 173–99. See also George Gerbner and Nancy Signorielli, *Violence and Terror in the Mass Media* (Paris: UNESCO, 1988), no. 102, *Reports and Papers in Mass Communication*.

55. This is one possible way of interpreting the theory of "psychological reversal" and "protective frames." Michael J. Apter (*The Dangerous Edge: The Psychology of Excitement* [New York: Free Press, 1992]).

56. Durkin, "Death, Dying, and the Dead," 47. See also Philip Stone and Richard Sharpley, "Consuming Dark Tourism: A Thanatological Perspective," *Annals of Tourist Research* 35, no. 2 (2008): 587.

57. On the positive outcomes of computer game play by young people, see Keith Durkin and Bonnie Barber, "Not So Doomed: Computer Game Play and Positive Adolescent Development," *Journal of Applied Developmental Psychology* 23 (2002): 373–92. For criticism of catharsis hypothesis, see Douglas A. Gentile, "Catharsis and Media Violence: A Conceptual Analysis," *Societies* 3, no. 4 (2013): 491–510.

58. "Over the past 50 years, a large number of studies conducted around the world have shown that watching violent television, watching violent films, or playing violent video games increases the likelihood for aggressive behavior." Media Violence Commission, International Society for Research on Aggression (ISRA), "Report of the Media Violence Commission," *Aggressive Behavior* 38 (2012): 335–41. These issues were discussed with a focus on video games. Craig A. Anderson, Douglas A Gentile, and Katherine E. Buckley, *Violent Video Game Effects on Children and Adolescents: Theory, Research, and Public Policy* (New York: Oxford University Press, 2007). See also Craig A. Anderson and Brad J. Bushman, "Effects of Violent Video Games On Aggressive Behaviour, Aggressive Cognition, Aggressive Affect, Physiological Arousal, and Prosocial Behavior: A Meta-Analytic Review of the Scientific Literature," *Psychological Science* 12, no. 5 (September 2005): 353–59.

59. L. Rowell Huesdmann, "The Impact of Electronic Media Violence: Scientific Theory and Research" *Journal of Adolescent Health* 41, no. 7 (2007), http://www. ncbi.nlm.nih.gov/pmc/articles/PMC2704015/. See also Dorothy G. Singer and Jerome L. Singer, *Handbook of Children and the Media* (Thousand Oaks, CA: Sage Publications, 2001), 224.

60. Tony Walter, Jane Littlewood, and Michael Pickering ("Death in the News: The Public Invigilation of Private Emotion," in *Death, Dying and Bereavement*, ed. Donna Dickenson, Malcolm Johnson, Jeanne Samson Katz ed. [London: SAGE, 2000], 20), however, caution against interpreting thanatological content in the news media solely in this light. On sadism as a motivating force behind crime novels featuring gore and graphic details of murder, see Shillabeer, "The Fascination with Torture and Death," 110.

61. Keith Hawton, Kathryn Williams, "Influences of the Media on Suicide," *BMJ* (Dec 14, 2002), 325 (7377): 1374–75. See also Ritva Levo-Henriksson, *Media and Ethnic Identity: Hopi Views on Media, Identity, and Communication* (London: Routledge, 2007), 20.

62. World Health Organization (WHO), "Preventing Suicide: A Global Imperative," http://tinyurl.com/ozflr4c; http://www.who.int/mental_health/suicide-pre vention/en/; http://www.befrienders.org/suicide-statistics

63. Joel Black, *The Aesthetics of Murder* (Baltimore: Johns Hopkins University Press, 1991).

64. Laura Frost, "Black Screens, Lost Bodies," in *Horror after 9/11: World of Fear, Cinema of Terror,* ed. Aviva Briefel and Sam J. Miller (Austin: University of Texas Press), 15.

65. Including economic growth, commercialization, new advertising technologies, advanced communications, the Internet, and globalization. *Understanding Dying, Death, and Bereavement,* 3. See also Hanusch, *Representing Death in the News,* 145; Buckingham, *After the Death of Childhood,* 127.

66. These features distinguish my approach from the recent collection of essays *The Power of Death: Contemporary Reflections on Death in Western Society,* published by Maria-Jose Blanco and Ricarda Vidal. In that collection, scholars in various fields examine death from an interdisciplinary perspective that includes burial customs in Europe, the fascination with death in crime fiction, the phenomenon of serial killer art, the way the movies show how the bereaved behave and how the movies depict death. The essays seek to contrast death as entertainment with death as a natural life event (to "combine the study of the contradictory aspects of death as entertainment and death as natural end of life" (*The Power of Death,* 4) and therefore do not consider these discrete elements as a single cultural movement inspired by the changing attitudes to humans. Also, the contributors to this collection of highly relevant essays do not share a common intellectual perspective on the causes of the phenomena they describe.

67. Robert Hertz, *Death and The Right Hand* (1907), trans. Rodney and Claudia Needham (Glencoe, IL: The Free Press, 1960), 78, http://tinyurl.com/pvsofn7

68. Pierre Nora, "L'Ère de la commemoration," in *Les Lieux de mémoire,* vol. III, ed. Pierre Nora (Paris: Gallimard, 1992).

69. On the spread of illiteracy and the importance of magic in the "other America," see Chris Hedges, *Empire of Illusion: The End of Literacy and the Triumph of Spectacle* (New York: Nation Books, 2010).

70. The commodification of death is often understood in sociology and anthropology as the monetization of funeral-related costs and services; I use this term to describe a process of commodification of violent death in fiction and movies. For examples of the commodification of funerals and rise of the coffin industry, see *Commodifying Everything: Relationships of the Market,* ed. Susan Strasser (New York: Routledge, 2013).

71. Max Horkheimer and Theodor Adorno, "The Culture Industry: Enlightenment as Mass Deception," in *Dialectic of Enlightenment* (New York: Herder and Herder, 1972); Theodor Adorno, "On Popular Music," *Studies in Philosophy and Social Sciences* 9, no. 1 (1941).

72. Theodor Adorno, "Culture Industry Reconsidered," *New German Critique,* no. 6 (1975): 12–13.

73. In my understanding of the concept of human exceptionalism, I follow a tradition running from Aristotle to Ludwig Wittgenstein who asserts that an onto-logical gap separates humans from other living beings. In *Philosophical Investiga-tions* ([1953], trans. G. E. M. Anscomb [Oxford: Blackwell Publishing, 2009]), 223, Wittgenstein famously argues that "[i]f a lion could speak, we could not understand him," and that applying to animals the concepts that describe human psychological conditions has no meaning. See also Raimond Gaita, who speaks of human beings as unique and irreplaceable due to their reflectivity, which is unique among other living organisms, and as "precious as nothing else we know in nature." Gaita, *The Philosopher's Dog* (Melbourne: Text Publishing, 2002), 199.

74. Speaking of popular culture, I seek to emphasize less the distinction between high and low culture than its ubiquity. On a breakdown of the distinction between high and low culture at the age of postmodernity, see Fredric Jameson, *Postmodern-ism or, the Cultural Logic of Late Capitalism* (London: Verso, 1991).

75. As Francis Fukuyama argues, the concept of human exceptionalism that rests upon a shared understanding of the uniqueness of human nature remains cru-cial because "much of our political world rests on the existence of a stable human 'essence' with which we are endowed by nature, or rather, on the fact that we believe such an essence exists." Fukuyama, *Our Posthuman Future: Consequences of the Biotechnology Revolution* (New York: Farrar, Straus & Giroux, 2002), 217. For a political critique of Fukuyama's views, see John Gray, *Black Mass: Apocalyptic Religion and the Death of Utopia* (New York: Farrar, Straus & Giroux, 2007).

76. Dina Khapaeva, *Nightmare: From Literary Experiments to Cultural Project*, trans. Rosie Tweddle (Amsterdam: Brill, 2013).

77. The studies offer various explanations, including parallels between Ancient Greek tragedy and horror and a psychological desire for the sublime, the response (inadequate) to the fear of change and modern uncertainties, technological prog-ress, and Otherness; the accommodation of general social anxieties and escapism, for example, Noel Carroll, *The Philosophy of Horror: Or, Paradoxes of the Heart* (1990) (New York: Routledge, 2003); Joseph Grixti, *Terrors of Uncertainty: The Cultural Contexts of Horror Fiction* (London: Routledge, 1989); Paul Wells, *The Horror Genre: From Beelzebub to Blair Witch* (London: Wallflower Press, 2000); Jason Colavito, *Knowing Fear: Science, Knowledge and the Development of the Horror Genre* (Jefferson, NC: McFarland, 2008); and Mark A. Vieira, *Hollywood Horror: From Gothic to Cosmic* (New York: Harry N. Abrams, 2003).

78. As the content of movies coming under that label has become increasingly horrific, "slashers" and torture porn, as we discussed earlier, have separated out of the horror genre.

79. On the Gothic novel, see David Punter, *The Literature of Terror: A History of Gothic Fictions from 1765 to the Present Day*, 2 vols. (Harlow, Essex: Longman, 1996); Fred Botting, *Gothic* (London: Routledge, 1996); George E. Haggerty, *Gothic Fiction/Gothic Form* (University Park: Pennsylvania State University Press, 1989); Markman Ellis, *The History of Gothic Fiction* (Edinburgh: Edinburgh University Press, 2000); Christian Grunenberg, ed., *The Gothic: Transmutations of Horror in Late Twentieth Cen-tury Art* (Cambridge, MA: MIT Press, 1997); Jerrold E. Hogle, ed., *The Cambridge Companion to Gothic Fiction* (Cambridge: Cambridge University Press, 2002).

80. Punter, *The Literature of Terror*, 1:1.

81. Punter, *The Literature of Terror*, 1:2–3. On the Neogothic as an American genre, see Irving Malin, *New American Gothic* (Carbondale: Southern Illinois University Press, 1962). There is also a tradition of applying the concept of Gothic to Soviet literature and culture. Eric Naiman applied the notion of Gothic to Soviet culture in his book *Sex in Public: The Incarnation of Early Soviet Ideology* (Princeton: Princeton University Press, 1997) where he predominantly addresses the Soviet sexuality. On psychoanalytical interpretation of Soviet prose and its Gothic themes, see Lilya Kaganovsky, *How the Soviet Man Was Unmade: Cultural Fantasy and Male Subjectivity under Stalin* (Pittsburgh: University of Pittsburgh Press, 2008). On grotesque trend in the late Soviet and post-Soviet literature of the 1980s and the 1990s, see Kevin M. F. Platt, *History in a Grotesque Key: Russian Literature and the Idea of Revolution* (Stanford, CA: Stanford University Press, 1997).

82. "This is not, of course, to say that all twentieth-century horror fiction has its roots in the Gothic: but it is remarkable how much of it does, how much of it relies on themes and styles which, by rights, would seem to be more than a century out of date." Punter, *The Literature of Terror*, 1:3. Punter proposes to isolate Gothic narratives from "the surrounding culture" (146).

83. Allan Lloyd-Smith, David Punter, eds., *A Companion to the Gothic* (Oxford: Blackwell, 2000). On the Gothic genre, see Robert Miles, *Gothic Writing 1750–1820: A Genealogy*, 2nd ed. (Manchester: Manchester University Press, 2002) and Peter K. Garrett, *Gothic Reflections: Narrative Force in Nineteenth-Century Fiction* (Ithaca: Cornell University Press, 2003).

84. Fred Botting, *The Gothic*, Essays and Studies (Cambridge: D. S. Brewer, 2001) 3.

85. Botting, *The Gothic*, 1.

86. Louis S. Gross, *Redefining the American Gothic: From Wieland to Day of the Dead* (Ann Arbor: UMI Research Press, 1989).

87. On the debates regarding the genre theory, and on the essentialist approach to genre see Joseph Farrell, "Classical Genre in Theory and Practice," *New Literary History* 34, no. 3 (Summer 2003), and especially Thomas Pavel, "Literary Genres as Norms and Good Habits," *New Literary History* 34, no. 2 (Spring 2003): 202. See also the criticism of this position by Hayden White, "Commentary: Good of Their Kind," *New Literary History* 34, no. 2 (Spring 2003): 367–68, and "Anomalies of Genre: The Utility Theory and History for the Study of Literary Genres," *New Literary History* 34, no. 2 (Spring 2003): 598, 600. On the uses of genre as an important classification tool, see Michael Prince, "Mauvais Genres," *New Literary History* 34, no. 2 (Spring 2003): 475. Genre fusion seems to sit well with the antiessentialist trend in genre theory initiated by Russian formalists Yury Tynyanov and Victor Shklovsky on the one hand and Mikhail Bakhtin on the other, and further developed by Jacques Derrida (Jacques Derrida, "The Law of Genre," trans. Avital Ronell, *Critical Inquiry* 7, no. 1, 55–81) and Tzvetan Todorov (*The Fantastic: A Structural Approach to a Literary Genre*, trans. Richard Howard [Cleveland, OH: Case Western Reserve University Press, 1973]).

88. Although nightmares are sometimes mentioned by scholars in relation to the Gothic genre, prior to my study *Nightmare: From Literary Reality to Cultural Project*, nightmare has not been evaluated as a unique literary device that changes and transforms the relationship between author and reader and dramatically affects the

reader's perception. Sandra Gilbert and Susan Gubar have noted the "nightmare confessional mode of the gothic genre" but did not develop the concept further (*The Madwoman in the Attic: The Woman Writer and the Nineteenth-Century Literary Imagination* [New Haven: Yale University Press, 2000], xii, 314). Their discussion actually revolves around genre issues and female sensuality. They did not consider imitation of nightmare in those frightening or revolting narratives important in classifying or explaining the cultural products defined as the horror genre. The feminist reading of the Gothic continues in *Art of Darkness: A Poetics of Gothic* by Anne Williams, who follows Yulia Kristeva's reading of the Gothic as a male/female opposition and discusses the Gothic as the poetic and "nightmare" as "nightmère." Anne Williams, *Art of Darkness: A Poetics of Gothic* (Chicago: University of Chicago Press, 1997).

89. Philip Simpson was arguably the first to notice that shift in the twentieth-century Gothic: "Paradoxically and destabilizing enough, the 'threatened maiden' may now even be the killer himself in losing flight from his self-destructive socio-pathology." Philip Simpson, *Psycho Paths: Tracking the Serial Killer Through Contemporary American Film and Fiction* (Carbondale: Southern Illinois University Press, 2000), 34. Simpson did not, however, acknowledge the cultural significance and consequences of this shift.

90. Clive Bloom in "Introduction: Death's Own Backyard," and "Epilogue: Further Thoughts on Gothic" emphasized the "withdrawal of God" and occultists roots of Gothic:[Clive Bloom, ed., *Gothic Horror: A Guide for Students and Readers*, 2nd. ed. (New York: Palgrave MacMillan, 2007], 18, 291–97).

91. On the demonic in literature, see, for example, Robert Muchembled, *Une histoire du diable, XIIe–XXe siècle* (Paris: Editions du Seuil, 2000), Ewan Fernie, *The Demonic: Literature and Experience* (New York: Routledge, 2012).

92. For example, an evolutionary dead end (Peter Watts, *Blindsight* [New York: Tor Books, 2006]) or a virus (Guillermo del Toro and Chuck Hogan, *The Strain* [New York: HarperCollins, 2009]).

93. Mikhail Bakhtin, *Problems of Dostoevsky's Poetics*, trans. Caryl Emerson (Minneapolis: University of Minnesota Press, 1984). Hans Ulrich Gumbrecht describes Stimmung, or moods of reading, as producing somewhat similar effects on the reader, challenging the reader's powers of discernment and description (Hans Ulrich Gumbrecht, *Atmosphere, Mood, Stimmung: On A Hidden Potential of Literature*, trans. Erik Butler (Stanford, CA: Stanford University Press, 2012).

94. On the culture of nightmare consumption, see Khapaeva, *Nightmare*, 280–86.

CHAPTER ONE

1. On the history of the concept and the philosophical foundations of humanism, see Nicolas Walter, *Humanism: What's in the Word* (London: Rationalist Press Association, 1997); Paul Kurtz, *Forbidden Fruit: The Ethics of Humanism* (Amherst, NY: Prometheus Books, 1988) and Tony Davies, *Humanism* (Oxford: Routledge, 2006).

2. I follow François Cusset's "common denominator" for French philosophers (Cusset, *French Theory: How Foucault, Derrida, Deleuze, & Co Transformed the Intel-*

lectual Life of the United States [Minneapolis: University of Minnesota Press, 2008]). On the concept of structuralism as common denominator for the movement, see Allan Megill, *Prophets of Extremity: Nietzsche, Heidegger, Foucault, Derrida* (Berkeley: University of California Press, 1985), 204.

3. For a critique of these French thinkers' stand on humanism and an attempt to defend the values of the Enlightenment through rethinking the question of the subject, see Luc Ferry and Alain Renaut, *La pensée 68. Essai sur l'anti-humanisme contemporain* (Paris: Gallimard, 1985), xvi and 98–99. Unlike these authors, however, I do not believe that we have re-established "a consensus on morality based on human rights," the "autonomy of the subject," etc. (16)

4. These ideas were widely adopted by those who considered themselves the intellectual heirs of French Theory: "Because in the concluding pages of Foucault's book, the king's place becomes the place of a dead—or at least a dying—humanity (. . .) must we lose all our composure, as some of those we count among the best minds of the day seem to have done? (. . .) must one behave like an academician embittered by the imminence of his replacement in the position of mastery? Are we going to witness the creation of a League of the Rights of Man to be the Subject and Object of Philosophy, under the motto 'Humanists of All Parties, Unite!'?" Georges Canguilhem, "The Death of Man, or, Exhaustion of the Cogito?" in *The Cambridge Companion to Foucault*, ed. Gary Gutting (Cambridge: Cambridge University Press, 2005), 72. For a critique of humanism, see also Martin Halliwell and Andrew Mousley, *Critical Humanisms: Humanist/Anti-Humanist Dialogues* (Edinburgh: Edinburgh University Press, 2003).

5. Jean-François Lyotard, *Le Tombeau de l'intellectuel, et autres papiers* (Paris: Galilée, 1984), 65. See also his further reflections on the issue in "The Inhuman": "(. . .) what if human beings, in humanism's sense, were in the process of, constrained into, becoming inhuman, [. . .] what if what is 'proper' to humankind were to be inhabited by the inhuman?" Jean-François Lyotard, *The Inhuman. Reflections on Time*, trans. Geoffrey Bennington and Rachel Bowlby (Cambridge: Polity Press, 1991), 2.

6. See François Furet, *Atelier de l'histoire* (Paris: Flammarion, 1982), vol. 2, and Nikolay Koposov, "L'Univers clos des signes: Vers une histoire du paradigme linguistique," in *De Russie et d'ailleurs: Mélanges Marc Ferro*, ed. Martine Godet (Paris: Institut d'études slaves, 1995), 501–13.

7. Louis Althusser, *For Marx* (1965), trans. Ben Brewster (London: Verso, 1969), 11. On Althusser and his ties with structuralism, see Camille Robcis, "'China in Our Heads': Althusser, Maoism, and Structuralism," *Social Text* 30, no. 1/110 (March 20, 2012): 51–69.

8. Louis Althusser, *For Marx*, 221 (first published as "Marxisme et humanisme," *Cahiers de l'ISEA*, June 1964).

9. Maksim Gorky, "Proletarian Humanism," *Pravda*, May 23, 1934; *Izvestia*, May 23, 1934 (my translation—D.K.).

10. Stalin used this concept in his speech of May 4, 1935, published by *Literaturnaya Gazeta* on July 9, 1935.

11. On the French structuralists' "assault on humanism," see Richard Wolin, *The Seduction of Unreason: The Intellectual Romance with Fascism* (Princeton: Princeton University Press, 2006), 7ff.

12. Friedrich Nietzsche, *"On the Genealogy of Morality" and Other Writings*, ed. Keith Ansell-Pearson, trans. Carol Diethe (Cambridge: Cambridge University Press, 2007), 92.

13. These reflections on the resurrection of humanism were popular during the war and immediately after. C. S. Lewis, for example, wrote *The Abolition of Man* in 1943.

14. Quoted from *The Cambridge Companion to Lévi-Strauss*, Boris Wiseman ed. (Cambridge: Cambridge University Press, 2009), 26.

15. See David Farrell Krell, "Analysis," in Martin Heidegger, *Nietzsche*, vol. 1: *The Will to Power as Art*, trans. David Farrell Krell (San Francisco: Harper and Row, 1979), 241.

16. François Dosse, *History of Structuralism: The Rising Sign, 1945–1966* (Minneapolis: University of Minnesota Press, 1997).

17. Christopher Johnson, *Claude Lévi-Strauss: The Formative Years* (Cambridge: Cambridge University Press, 2003), 145. On the "false humanism" and "democratic humanism" in Lévi-Strauss, see Denis Kambouchner, "Lévi-Strauss and the Question of Humanism Followed by a Letter from Claude Lévi-Strauss," in *The Cambridge Companion to Lévi-Strauss*, 26 ff.

18. Claude Lévi-Strauss, *Structural Anthropology*, trans. Monique Layton (Chicago: University of Chicago Press, 1983), vol. 2, 41, see also 53.

19. Lévi-Strauss proclaims "a democratic humanism in opposition to those preceding it and created from privileged civilizations for the privileged classes." Claude Lévi-Strauss, "Three Humanisms" (1956), *Structural Anthropology*, vol. 2, 274. Marcel Hénaff, *Claude Lévi-Strauss and the Making of Structural Anthropology* (Minneapolis: University of Minnesota Press, 1998), 243.

20. Claude Lévi-Strauss, *The Savage Mind* (Chicago: University of Chicago Press, 1966), 247.

21. "In Sartre's terminology I am therefore to be defined as a transcendental materialist and aesthete. I am a transcendental materialist because I do not regard dialectical reason as *something other than* analytical reason, upon which the absolute originality of a human order would be based, but as *something additional* in analytical reason: the necessary condition for it to venture to undertake the resolution of the human into the nonhuman." Lévi-Strauss, *The Savage Mind*, 246. On Lévi-Strauss' "scientific humanism," see also Roland A. Champagne, *Claude Lévi-Strauss* (Woodbridge, CT: Twayne Publishers, 1987).

22. On the critique of anti-humanism in Foucault, see Graham Good, *Humanism Betrayed: Theory, Ideology and Culture in the Contemporary University* (Montreal: McGill-Queen's University Press, 2001). Graham Good calls the Foucauldian concept of power "dehumanizing" (83–84). On other aspects of Foucault's philosophical system, see François Gros, *Michel Foucault* (Paris: Presse universitaire de France, 1996); François Gros, *Le courage de la vérité* (Paris: Presses Universitaires de France, 2002); and Béatrice Han, *L'ontologie manquée de Michel Foucault: entre l'historique et le transcendantal* (Paris: Jérôme Millon, 1998).

23. "He [Nietzsche—D.K.] took the end of time and transformed it into the death of God and the odyssey of the last man; he took up anthropological finitude once again, but in order to use it as a basis for the prodigious leap of the superman; he took up once again the great continuous chain of History, but in order to bend

it round into the infinity of the eternal return. [. . .] It was Nietzsche, in any case, who burned for us, even before we were born, the intermingled promises of the dialectic and anthropology." Michel Foucault, *The Order of Things* (New York: Vintage Books, 1994), 262–63.

24. Hayden White, *The Content of the Form: Narrative Discourse and Historical Representation* (Baltimore: Johns Hopkins University Press, 1990), 109. White emphasizes that Foucault's attacks on humanism were based on "his refusal to credit the idea of a human subject" (105, 138). As Allan Megill puts it, "It is well known that structuralism, in its search for a stable object of investigation, concentrates on language (*langue*) rather than on the human speaker, and Foucault's attack on subjectivism and anthropologism did seem to fit within this framework." (Megill, *Prophets of Extremity*, 204).

25. On Foucault's notion of the episteme, see Ian Maclean, "Foucault's Renaissance Episteme Reassessed: An Aristotelian Counterblast," *Journal of the History of Ideas* 59, no. 1 (January 1998): 149–66, and Béatrice Han, *Foucault's Critical Project: Between the Transcendental and the Historical*, 61ff.

26. Foucault, *The Order of Things*, 344.

27. Foucault, *The Order of Things*, 385.

28. This connection between Nietzsche and Foucault's thinking is underlined by Megill: "The 'death of God' is also, at the same time, a death of man, of author, and of artists" (Megill, *Prophets of Extremity*, 160).

29. Foucault, *The Order of Things*, 342.

30. "[O]n the one hand, it is already pointing in the direction of an anthropology that will call into question man's very essence (his finitude, his relation with time, the imminence of death[. . .]." Foucault, *The Order of Things*, 225.

31. Foucault, *The Order of Things*, 387. And "man is in the process of disappearing" (385).

32. On Foucault's deconstruction of humanism and his controversy with Jürgen Habermas, see David Ingram, "Foucault and Habermas," in *The Cambridge Companion to Foucault*, 250, 249.

33. David Ingram, "Foucault and Habermas," in *The Cambridge Companion to Foucault*, 245. On the Marxist critique in Foucault, see also Hubert L. Dreyfus and Paul Rabinow, *Michel Foucault: Beyond Structuralism and Hermeneutics* (Chicago: University of Chicago Press, 1982), xxii, 34, 115, 139 (although they emphasize more Nietzsche's heritage in his thinking).

34. Michael S. Roth, "Foucault's 'History of the Present,'" *History and Theory* 20, no. 1 (February 1981): 35–37.

35. Paul A. Bové, "The End of Humanism: Michel Foucault and the Power of Disciplines," *Humanities in Society*, no. 3 (1980): 23–40.

36. For example, Mike Gane, "Introduction: Michel Foucault" in *Towards a Critique of Foucault: Foucault, Lacan and the Question of Ethics*, ed. Mike Gane (New York: Routledge, 1986), 8. Paden showed the contradiction between Foucault's antihumanism and his attempts to lay down groundwork for the humanities. Roger Paden, "Foucault's Antihumanism," *Human Studies* 10, no. 1 (Foucault Memorial Issue, ed. Dordrecht et al.) (1987): 123–41. On Foucault's "humanism," see also Paul A. Bové, *Intellectuals in Power: A Genealogy of Critical Humanism* (New York: Columbia University Press, 1986). And, as Hayden White maintains, "volumes 2

and 3 of the *History of Sexuality* must be seen as parts of his more general project of contributing to that 'death of Man' that he announced at the end of *The Order of Things*." Hayden White, *The Content of the Form: Narrative Discourse and Historical Representation* (Baltimore: Johns Hopkins University Press, 1990), 138.

37. Richard Rorty, *Consequences of Pragmatism* (Minneapolis: University of Minnesota Press, 1982); "Méthode: science sociale et espoir social," *Critique* (1986) no. 42, 71–72, 879–97; Richard Rorty, *Michel Foucault: Du monde entier* (Paris: Minuit, 1986), 873–97; Richard Rorty, "Moral Identity and Private Autonomy: The Case of Foucault," in *Essays on Heidegger and Others. Philosophical Papers*, vol. 2 (Cambridge: Cambridge University Press, 1991). On contradictions regarding Foucault's stand on humanism between "The Order of Things" and "Dits et écrits," see François Gros, "Foucault face à son œuvre," in *Lectures de Michel Foucault*, vol. 3 (Lyon: ENS Éditions, 2003), 96. For a discussion of Rorty's position on Dewey and postmodernism, see Martin Jay, *Songs of Experience. Modern American and European Variations on a Universal Theme* (Berkeley: University of California Press, 2005), 299–311. Among attempts to liberate Foucault from the liberal reading, see Andrew Zimmerman, "Foucault in Berkeley and Magnitogorsk: Totalitarianism and the Limits of Liberal Critique," *Contemporary European History* 23, no. 2 (2014): 225–36. For a useful guide to Foucault's statements on humanism and the death of man, see Clare O'Farrell, *Michel Foucault* (New York: Sage Publications, 2005).

38. Jacques Bouveresse, "L'objectivité, la connaissance et le pouvoir," in *L'infréquentable Michel Foucault. Renouveaux de la pensée critique*, ed. Didier Eribon (Paris: Actes du Colloque au Centre Georges-Pompidou, 21–22 juin 2000), 33–14, and especially on Foucault's misrepresentations of Nietzsche: Jacques Bouveresse, *Nietzsche contre Foucault. Sur la vérité, la connaisance et le pouvoir* (Paris: Agone, 2016), 62, 44.

39. Roland Barthes, "The Death of the Author," in Roland Barthes, *Image Music Text*, trans. Stephen Heath (New York: Hill and Wang, 1977), 148. Foucault delivered his lecture entitled "Qu'est-ce qu'un auteur?" [What Is an Author?] in February 1969. On the relations between Barthes' and Foucault's ideas regarding the death of the author, see Seán Burke, *The Death and Return of the Author: Criticism and Subjectivity in Barthes, Foucault and Derrida* (Edinburgh: Edinburgh University Press, 1992); Michael North, "Authorship and Autography," in *Theories and Methodologies. PMLA* 116, no. 5 (October 2001), 1377–85; and Allen Graham, *Roland Barthes* (London: Routledge, 2003).

40. For the criticism of the concept, see Burke, *The Death and Return of the Author*.

41. On Baudrillard's intellectual trajectory, see Marc Poster, "Introduction," in *Jean Baudrillard, Selected Writings* (Stanford, CA: Stanford University Press, 2001).

42. Jean Baudrillard, *Symbolic Exchange and Death*, trans. Ian H. Grant (New York: Sage Publications, 1993), 4.

43. Baudrillard, *Symbolic Exchange and Death*, 5.

44. Jean Baudrillard, *Fatal Strategies*, trans. Phil Beitchman and W. W. J. Neisluchowski (Cambridge MA: MIT Press, 2008).

45. Jean Baudrillard, *The Transparency of Evil* (London: Verso, 1993).

46. Dosse, *History of Structuralism*, XX.

47. Gabrielle M. Spiegel, *The Past as Text: The Theory and Practice of Medieval Historiography* (Baltimore: Johns Hopkins University Press, 1997), 42.

48. Richard Bessel and Dirk Schumann, "Introduction. Violence, Normality, and the Construction of Postwar Europe," in Richard Bessel and Dirk Schumann, *Life After Death: Approaches to a Cultural and Social History of Europe* (Cambridge: Cambridge University Press, 2003).

49. Tony Judt, *Postwar: A History of Europe Since 1945* (New York: Penguin Books, 2006).

50. "Indeed, one dominant theme in French intellectual life since the late 1970s has been the moral inadequacy of the French intellectual of the previous generation." Tony Judt, *Past Imperfect: French Intellectuals, 1944–1956* (Oakland: University of California Press, 1994), 3.

51. For example, Erich Fromm, a representative of the Frankfurt School, asserted that "[i]n the nineteenth century the problem was that God is dead; in the twentieth century the problem is that man is dead." Erich Fromm, *The Sane Society* (New York: Henry Holt and Company, 1955), 360. Further, "In the nineteenth century inhumanity meant cruelty; in the twentieth century it means schizoid self-alienation. The danger of the past was that men became slaves. The danger of the future is that men become robots. True enough, robots do not rebel. But given man's nature, robots cannot live and remain sane, they become 'Golems,' they will destroy their world and themselves because they cannot stand any longer the boredom of a meaningless life" (91).

52. On the influence of French Theory on popular culture, see Cusset, *French Theory*.

53. Cusset, *French Theory*, 266.

54. Luc Ferry and Alain Renaut, *French Philosophy of the Sixties. An Essay on Anti-humanism*, trans. Mary H. S. Cattani (Amherst: University of Massachusetts Press, 1990), XXV.

55. James M. Jasper, *The Art of Moral Protest: Culture, Biography, and Creativity in Social Movements* (Chicago: University of Chicago Press, 1999), 137, 246.

56. Foucault, *The Order of Things*, 156–57.

57. Foucault, *The Order of Things*, 157.

58. Alex Neville Sharpe, *Foucault's Monsters and the Challenge of Law* (Oxford: Routledge-Cavendish, 2009), 12.

59. Patrick Llored has reinterpreted his 1968 essay "La pharmacie de Platon" from the perspective of animality: Llored, *Jacques Derrida: Politique et éthique de l'animalité* (Paris: Sils Maria, 2012).

60. Jacques Derrida, "Violence Against Animals," in *For What Tomorrow . . . A Dialogue*, ed. Jacques Derrida and Élisabeth Roudinesco, trans. Jeff Fort (Stanford, CA: Stanford University Press, 2004); Jacques Derrida, *The Animal That Therefore I Am*, trans. David Wills (New York: Fordham University Press, 2008), especially 394–95.

61. Llored, *Jacques Derrida: Politique et éthique de l'animalité*.

62. Derrida, "Violence Against Animals," 66.

63. Steven Best, "The Rise of Critical Animal Studies: Putting Theory into Action and Animal Liberation into Higher Education," *Journal for Critical Ani-*

mal Studies VII, no. 1 (2009). Since killing animals can be potentially the first step toward killing humans, it also presupposes discrimination against the Other. Cary Wolfe, *What Is Posthumanism?* (Minneapolis: University of Minnesota Press, 2010), 7, 8.

64. Joanna Bourke, *What It Means to Be Human: Historical Reflections from the 1800s to the Present* (Berkeley, CA: Counterpoint, 2013), 371.

65. Marc Bekoff, *The Animal Manifesto: Six Reasons for Expanding Our Compassion Footprint* (Novato, CA: New World Library, 2010). See also Kelly Oliver, *Animal Lessons: How They Teach Us to Be Human* (New York: Columbia University Press, 2009).

66. Bourke, *What It Means to Be Human*, 384.

67. Bourke, *What It Means to Be Human*, 378.

68. For more details on the animal rights movement see Gary Francione, *Rain Without Thunder: The Ideology of the Animal Rights Movement* (Philadelphia: Temple University Press, 1996).

69. Richard D. Ryder, "Experiments on Animals," in *Animals, Men and Morals*, ed. Roslind Godlovitch, Stanley Godlovitch, and John Harris (London: Gollancz, 1971).

70. Peter Singer, *Rethinking Life and Death: The Collapse of Our Traditional Ethics* (Melbourne: Text Publishing, 1994), 4.

71. Singer, *Rethinking Life and Death*, 105. "On the other hand, perhaps it is not wrong to take the life of a brain-damaged human infant—after all, many people think such infants should be allowed to die, and an infant who is 'allowed to die' ends up just as dead as one that is killed." Peter Singer, "Ethics and the New Animal Liberation Movement," in *In Defense of Animals*, ed. Peter Singer (New York: Basil Blackwell, 1985), 6.

72. Following Bernard Williams' critique of Singer's "speciesism" (Williams, "The Human Prejudice," in *Philosophy as a Humanistic Discipline*, ed. A. Moore [Princeton: Princeton University Press, 2005], 135–54), one can argue that humans may treat their species membership as a morally significant property.

73. Peter Singer, "To Defame Religion Is a Human Right," *The Guardian*, April 15, 2009, http://www.theguardian.com/commentisfree/belief/2009/apr/15/religion-islam-atheism-defamation

74. Boria Sax, *Animals in the Third Reich: Pets, Scapegoats, and the Holocaust* (London: A & C Black Publishers, 2000) 113.

75. "Hitler (. . .) appeared to enjoy films of people being killed and beaten, but he could not endure depictions of animals being harmed. Himmler, head of the SS, also had, in the words of his doctor, a 'positively hysterical' reaction to hunting. 'How can you find pleasure . . . ,' asked the man who directed the concentration camps, 'in shooting from behind cover at poor creatures browsing on the edge of a wood, innocent, defenseless, and unsuspecting? It's really pure murder'": Sax, *Animals in the Third Reich*, 121.

76. Sax, *Animals in the Third Reich*, 123. On "anthropologization" of the animal by the Nazi regime, see Roberto Esposito, *Bios: Biopolitics and Philosophy (Posthumanities)* (Minneapolis: University of Minnesota Press, 2008), 130–31.

77. The history of the law on the transportation of animals demonstrates how this legislation justified the idea that selected groups of humans—who are not con-

sidered useful and whose lives, therefore, may be considered "not worth living"—can be treated more cruelly than useful animals: Sax, *Animals in the Third Reich*, 115.

78. Sax, *Animals in the Third Reich*, 115.

79. Sax, *Animals in the Third Reich*, 150.

80. Julian Huxley, "Transhumanism," in *New Bottles for New Wine* (London: Chatto & Windus, 1957), 13–17, reprinted by the World Transhumanist Association, http://www.transhumanism.org/index.php/WTA/more/huxley (by "Peking man," Huxley means Homo erectus pekinensis).

81. In his "A History of Transhumanist Thought," Nick Bostrom seeks to tie transhumanism directly to the Renaissance humanists and the Enlightenment. Nick Bostrom, "A History of Transhumanist Thought," *Journal of Evolution and Technology* 14, no. 1 (April 2005). More important for my thesis is Lyotard's lengthy discussion of manufacturing "hardware capable of 'nurturing' software at least as complex (or replex) as human brain," in Jean-François Lyotard, "Can Thought Go on Without a Body?" in Jean-François Lyotard, *The Inhuman: Reflections on Time*, 14.

82. Ray Kurzweil, *The Singularity Is Near: When Humans Transcend Biology* (New York: Viking, 2005), 241.

83. Hugo de Garis, *The Artilect War: Cosmists vs. Terrans: A Bitter Controversy Concerning Whether Humanity Should Build Godlike Massively Intelligent Machines* (Palm Springs, CA: ETC Publications, 2005), 254; Hugo de Garis, *Multis and Monos: What the Multicultured Can Teach the Monocultured: Towards the Creation of a Global State* (Palm Springs, CA: ETC Publications, 2010), 514; Hugo de Garis, *Artificial Brains: An Evolved Neural Net Module Approach* (Vancouver: World Scientific, 2010), 400.

84. Nicholas D. Kristof, "Robokitty," *New York Times*, August 1, 1999, http://www.nytimes.com/1999/08/01/magazine/robokitty.html?src=pm&pagewanted=3

85. Kristof, "Robokitty." By "gigadeath war," de Garis is referring to a war in which "billions of people will be killed."

86. For a survey of posthumanism, see Neil Badmington, *Alien Chic: Posthumanism and the Other Within* (New York: Routledge, 2004); for his analysis of antihumanism, see 34–40.

87. Andy Miah, "A Critical History of Posthumanism," in *Medical Enhancements and Posthumanity*, ed. Bert Gordijn, Ruth Chadwick (New York: Routledge, 2007).

88. Andy Miah, "A Critical History of Posthumanism," 16.

89. Vernor Vinge, "The Coming Technological Singularity: How to Survive in the Post-Human Era," https://www-rohan.sdsu.edu/faculty/vinge/misc/singularity.html

90. For example, see Cary Wolfe, *What Is Posthumanism?* XII. See also a review by Catherine Ingraham (Ingraham, "What Is Posthumanism?" *Future Anterior* 7, no. 1 [Summer 2010]: 96–103).

91. Donna Haraway, "Cyborg Manifesto: Science, Technology, and Socialist-Feminism in the Twentieth Century," in *Simians, Cyborgs and Women: The Reinvention of Nature* (New York: Routledge, 1991), 149–81.

92. "But the posthuman does not really mean the end of humanity. It signals instead the end of a certain conception of the human who (. . .) had the wealth, power and leisure to conceptualize themselves as autonomous beings exercising

their will through individual agency and choice. What is lethal is not the posthuman as such but the grafting of the posthuman onto a liberal humanist view of the self." N. Katherine Hayles, in *How We Became Posthuman* (Chicago: University of Chicago Press, 1999), 287.

93. These distinctions are drawn by Cary Wolfe in *What Is Posthumanism?* xv. On the ongoing debates between posthumanists of various schools, see, for example, "Theory of a Different Order: A Conversation with Katherine Hayles and Niklas Luhmann," in *Observing Complexity: Systems Theory and Postmodernity*, ed. Cary Wolfe and William Rasch (Minneapolis: University of Minnesota Press, 2000). See also Hans Moravec, *Robot: Mere Machine to Transcendent Mind* (New York: Oxford University Press, 1999).

94. See his webpage at http://www.kevinwarwick.com/. See also Kurzweil, *The Singularity Is Near*, 241.

95. Jonathon Keats, "The $1.38B Quest to Build a Supercomputer Replica of a Human Brain," *Wired*, 05.14.13, http://www.wired.com/2013/05/neurologist-markam-human-brain/all/

96. www.extremetech.com/extreme/152240-what-is-transhumanism-or-what-does-it-mean-to-be-human

97. Kurzweil, *The Singularity Is Near*, 241.

98. Marios Kyriazis, *Anti-Aging Medicines* (Loughborough: Thoth Publications, 2005).

99. Dale Carrico, "The Politics of Morphological Freedom," http://ieet.org/index.php/IEET/more/carrico20060803

100. Zoltan Istvan, *The Transhumanist Wager* (n.p.: Futurity Imagine Publishing, 2013), http://media.lanecc.edu/users/borrowdalej/TW/TW.pdf. See also http://tinyurl.com/o2wwah4

101. This sits well with Martha Nussbaum's notion that that almost every human value is incompatible with immortality. Nussbaum, "Mortal Immortals: Lucretius on Death and the Voice of Nature," *Philosophy and Phenomenological Research* 50 (1989): 337–38. Brendan Shea develops these arguments in relation to the vampire's immortality as described in *Twilight*, arguing that if vampires existed they would not care less about human values. Shea "To Bite or Not to Bite: Twilight, Immortality and the Meaning of Life," in *Twilight and Philosophy: Vampires, Vegetarians, and the Pursuit of Immortality*, ed. Rebecca Housel, J. Jeremy Wisnewski, and William Irwin (Hoboken: John Wiley & Sons, 2009), 89–90.

102. Francis Fukuyama identifies "posthuman stage of history" as a radical attempt to transcend human nature in the name of nonhuman future: Fukuyama, *Our Posthuman Future*, 7.

103. Samuel Moyn, *The Last Utopia: Human Rights in History* (Cambridge, MA: Belknap Press, 2012).

104. On popular culture's fascination with end of the world, see Kylo-Patrick R. Hart and Annette M. Holba, eds., *Media and The Apocalypse* (New York: Peter Lang Publishing, 2009). However, some transhumanists and some posthumanists also believe that superhuman machine intelligence could be friendly to humans ("friendly AI").

105. Christopher Norris, *Derrida* (Cambridge, MA: Harvard University Press, 1987), 227; Jacques Derrida, "Of an Apocalyptic Tone Recently Adopted in Philosophy," *Oxford Literary Review* 6, no. 2 (1984): 3–37.

106. White, *The Content of the Form*, 107, 130.

107. Veronica Hollinger, "Apocalypse Coma," in *Edging into the Future: Science Fiction and Contemporary Cultural Transformation*, ed. Veronica Hollinger and Joan Gordon (Philadelphia: University of Pennsylvania Press, 2002), 165. Julia Kristeva even claims that "literature as such, represents the ultimate coding of our . . . most serious apocalypses." Julia Kristeva, *Powers of Horror: An Essay on Abjection*, trans. Leon S. Roudiez (New York: Columbia University Press, 2012), 208.

108. Peter Yoonsuk Paik, *From Utopia to Apocalypse: Science Fiction and the Politics of Catastrophe* (Minneapolis: University of Minnesota Press, 2010).

109. Krishan Kumar, "Apocalypse, Millennium and Utopia Today," in *Apocalypse Theory and the Ends of the Earth*, ed. Malcolm Bull (Oxford: Blackwell, 1995), 205. On apocalypse as the end of history (but in the literal sense of ending and the prevalence of violent death in the mass media in the United States), see Catherine Russell, *Narrative Mortality: Death, Closure, and New Wave Cinemas* (Minneapolis: University of Minnesota Press, 2010), 175, 191.

110. Even in Clifford D. Simak's *City* (1952), which comes closest to the contemporary apocalypses, humanity is not destroyed by dogs but willingly abandons the Earth. On the apocalyptic genre, see Nancy A. Schaefer, "Y2K as an Endtime Sign: Apocalypticism in America at the fin-de-millennium," *Journal of Popular Culture* 38, iss. 1 (2004): 82–105.

111. "The serial killer seeks transcendental meaning in the traditional manner of idealistic truth seekers but is thwarted by the indeterminacy of experience." Philip L. Simpson, *Psycho Paths: Tracking the Serial Killer through Contemporary American Film and Fiction* (Carbondale: Southern Illinois University Press, 2000), 17. In her review of Simpson's book, Karen Beckman points out that he is one of those who conflate acts of cognition and acts of murder. Beckman, "Review of *Psycho Paths: Tracking the Serial Killer through Contemporary American Film and Fiction by* Philip L. Simpson (Southern Illinois University Press, 2000)," *Journal of Criminal Justice and Popular Culture* 8, no. 1 (2001): 61–65.

112. C. Richard King "(Mis)uses of Cannibalism in Contemporary Cultural Critique," *Diacritics* 30, no. 1 (Spring 2000): 106.

113. Grace M. Jantzen, *Foundations of Violence* (New York: Taylor & Francis, 2008), vii, viii. The lines of argument summarized here are developed by Jantzen on pages 1, 4, 5, 6, 10, 12, 14, and 33.

114. As an example of this discourse, see Tammy Bruce, *The Death of Right and Wrong* (Roseville, CA: Prima Publishing, 2003).

115. On the crisis of the concepts of the right and the left, see Olivier Mongin, *Face au scepticisme. Les mutations du paysage intellectuel (1976–1998)* (Paris: Hachette, 1998).

116. Wolin, *The Seduction of Unreason*, 14. See also Richard Wolin, *The Wind from the East: French Intellectuals, the Cultural Revolution, and the Legacy of the 1960s* (Princeton: Princeton University Press, 2004).

CHAPTER TWO

1. On cemeteries and funerals in Soviet everyday life, see Catriona Kelly, *St. Petersburg: Shadows of the Past* (New Haven: Yale University Press, 2014), 313–32.

2. I. A. Kremleva, "Documenting Burial and Memorial Customs and Rituals,"

in *The Russians: Everyday Life in the Family and Society* (Moscow: Nauka, 1989), 307–27.

3. Richard Huntington and Peter Metcalf, *Celebrations of Death: The Anthropology of Mortuary Ritual* (Cambridge: Cambridge University Press. 1979), 187.

4. Grimes, *Deeply into the Bone,* 269; see also 265.

5. Grimes, *Deeply into the Bone.* On the history of cremation in the 20th century and on the cultural history of the burial rituals, see Thomas W. Laqueur, *The Work of the Dead: A Cultural History of Mortal Remains* (Princeton: Princeton University Press, 2015).

6. Jack Santino, "Introduction: Festivals of Life and Death," in *Halloween and Other Festivals of Death and Life,* ed. Jack Santino (Knoxville: University of Tennessee Press, 1994), xix.

7. David Clark, *Transforming the Culture of Dying: The Work of the Project on Death in America* (Oxford: Oxford University Press, 2013).

8. Joshua Slocum and Lisa Carlso, *Final Rights: Reclaiming the American Way of Death* (Hinesburg, VT: Upper Access Books, 2011), 129.

9. Douglas Davies says that the ecological concerns of green funerals "reflect something of a potential paradigm shift in the understanding of death." Davies, *A Brief History of Death* (Hoboken, NJ: Wiley-Blackwell, 2005), 83, 79, 125. On the cultural meaning of burials in the Western world, see Robert Pogue Harrison, *The Dominion of the Dead* (Chicago: University of Chicago Press, 2003).

10. www.promessa.se/

11. Kathy Garces-Foley, *Death and Religion in a Changing World* (Armonk, NY: M. E. Sharpe, 2006), 112–13.

12. Garces-Foley, *Death and Religion in a Changing World,* 113.

13. A. Sokolova, "'Funerals Without a Corpse': Transformations in the Traditional Burial Ritual," *Antropologicheskii forum,* no. 15 (2011): 187–202; I. A. Kremleva, "Burial and Memorial Customs and Rituals," in *The Russians: Folk Culture, Then and Now,* vol. 3: *Family Life* (Moscow: IEA RAN, 2000), 231–65.

14. On an ideological vacuum in post-Soviet society after the collapse of communism, see Dina Khapaeva, *Portrait critique de la Russie: Essais sur la société gothique,* trans. Nina Kehayan (La Tour d'Aigues: Éditions de l'Aube, 2012), 115–16.

15. I. Pulya, "Held Hostage by the 'Black Agent,'" *Rossiiskaya gazeta,* January 25, 2010.

16. V. E. Dobrovol'skaya, "Conventions among Cemetery Workers," in *The Folklore of Small Societal Groups* (Moscow: State Center of Russian Folklore, 2008), 126–33; S. V. Filippova, "Structural Changes in Ritual Services in Contemporary Russian Society," *Vestnik Saratovskogo gosudarstvennogo tekhnicheskogo universiteta* 3, no. 34 (2008): 276–82; A. S. Antonova and G. N. Syutkin, "Regional Problems in the Regulation of Burial Rituals," *Vestnik akademii* 1, no. 31 (2012): 73–76; M. E. Elyutina and S. V. Filippova, "Ritual Burial Practices: Substantive Changes," *Sotsiologicheskie issledovaniya* no. 9, (2010). These new funerals have been poorly studied because the whole experience is still novel.

17. Meike Heessels, "Every Funeral Unique in (Y)our Way! Professionals Propagating Cremation Rituals," in *Emotion, Identity, and Death,* ed. Douglas Davies and Chang-Won Park (Burlington: Ashgate, 2012), 134.

18. They are becoming popular in Europe too. One telling example is a descrip-

tion of this ritual by Michel Houellebecq in his novel *Elementary Particles*, where he gives his heroine, Annabelle, just such a burial. Houellebecq, *Les particules élémentaires* (Paris: Flammarion, 1998).

19. Elyutina and Filippova, "Ritual Burial Practices," 86–94.

20. *Understanding Dying, Death, and Bereavement*, 10.

21. Mirjam Klaassens and Maarten J. Bijlsma, "New Places of Remembrance: Individual Web Memorials in the Netherlands," *Death Studies* 38, no. 5 (2014). See also Tony Walter, Rachid Hourizi, Wendy Moncur, and Stacey Pitsillides, "Does the Internet Change How We Die and Mourn?" *Omega* 64, no. 4 (2011–12): 275–302. On Russians' ideas about virtual memorials see, for example, http://www.woman. ru/psycho/medley6/thread/4010243/. Tim Hutchings, "Wiring Death: Dying, Grieving and Remembering on the Internet," in *Emotion, Identity, and Death*, 43–58.

22. Douglas Davies, Chang-Won Park, "Introduction," in *Emotion, Identity, and Death*, 4.

23. Raf Vanderstraeten, "Burying and Remembering the Dead," *Memory Studies* 7, no. 4 (2014): 457.

24. For example, S. V. Bondarenko, *Rituals Available to Residents of a Major City: Author's Abstract of a Dissertation for the Degree of Candidate of Economic Sciences* (Moscow: Nauka, 2008).

25. Heessels, "Every Funeral Unique in (Y)our Way," 125.

26. Slocum and Carlso, *Final Rights*, 129.

27. On the extent of changes in "meaning-making practices," see Leen Van Brussel and Nico Carpentier, eds., *The Social Construction of Death: Interdisciplinary Perspective* (London: Palgrave, 2014).

28. On "woodland burials" as the ritual that runs counter to the entire Western burial tradition, see Douglas Davies, *A Brief History of Death* (Hoboken, NJ: Wiley-Blackwell, 2005), 169. See also Davies, *Death, Ritual and Belief* (London: Continuum International, 2002). For an example of what a natural burial site looks like in the US, see http://natural-burial.typepad.com/.a/6a00d83534a43169e2011168ff64 9f970c-pi; see also a telling flyer, "Recycle me," at http://environmental.lilithezine. com/Green-Burials.html

29. Over the past thirty years, the social sciences and humanities have been slow in inventing powerful ideas and concepts capable of explaining what was happening in contemporary society and of engaging scholars and the general public alike. (On the silence of the intellectuals, see Mongin, *Face au scepticisme*.) Metaphorically, it is best expressed in the recycling of old concepts through the prefixes *post-*, *neo-*, *meta-* and so forth. Our intellectual universe abounds in these second-hand concepts: post-communism, post-modernism, post-structuralism, neo-liberalism, neo-medievalism. See Dina Khapaeva, "Break of Language: A Russian French Comparison," *Journal of Russian Communications* 4, nos. 1/2 (2011): 94–113.

30. On structuring thanatology as an academic field, with the first thanatological journals appearing in the 1970s, see Leming and Dickinson *Understanding Dying*, 1. "Despite—or perhaps because of—the American tendency to avoid talking about or preparing for death, the 'American way of death' and 'death and dying' became popular topics, selling books and spawning university courses." Grimes, *Deeply into the Bone*, 259.

31. "[I]f death often appears as a strange thing to people so also does the slightly

more abstract notion of mortality, and so too the developing field of 'death studies.'" Davies and Park, *Emotion, Identity, and Death: Mortality across Disciplines*, 5.

32. *The Project on Death in America*, a program of the Open Society Institute funded by George Soros 2001–2003, 5 (www.opensocietyfoundations.org/sites/default/files/a_complete_7.pdf).

33. *Understanding Dying, Death, and Bereavement*, 12.

34. On Facebook memorial pages, virtual legacies, and online educative resources, see Carla Sofka, Kathleen Gilbert, and Illene C. Noppe, eds., *Dying, Death, and Grief in an Online Universe: For Counselors and Educators* (New York: Springer Publishing, 2012).

35. Philip R. Stone, "Dark Tourism Experience: Mediating Between Life and Death," in *Tourist Experience: Contemporary Perspectives* (Advances in Tourism), ed. Richard Sharpley and Philip R. Stone (Oxford: Routledge, 2010); Richard Sharpley and Philip R. Stone, eds., *The Darker Side of Travel: The Theory and Practice of Dark Tourism* (Bristol: Channel View Publications, 2009).

36. Durkin, "Death, Dying, and the Dead in Popular Culture," 46.

37. Ricarda Vidal, "Death and Visual Culture," in *The Power of Death: Contemporary Reflections on Death in Western Society*, ed. Maria-Jose Blanco and Ricarda Vidal (New York: Berghahn Books, 2014), 115–26.

38. As, for example, in Mitch Albom's *Tuesdays with Morrie* (New York: Broadway Books, 2002).

39. On black humor in America, see Durkin, "Death, Dying, and the Dead in Popular Culture," 46. See also Trevor J. Blank, *The Last Laugh: Folk Humor, Celebrity Culture, and Mass-Mediated Disasters in the Digital Age* (Folklore Studies in a Multicultural World) (Madison: University of Wisconsin Press, 2013). The constant presence of dark humor in Soviet Russia may be linked to a cynical contrast between the optimistic normativity of Soviet propaganda, the officially proclaimed "merry life" (as Stalin infamously announced in a speech at the First All-Union Meeting of Stakhanovists on November 17, 1935), and the systematic mass destruction of the USSR's population by the Soviet regime. Black humor stood in opposition to the official Soviet discourse, emphasizing those aspects of Soviet life that contradicted the image of "happiness for all people" under Soviet rule. Black humor and macabre jokes are still popular in post-Soviet Russia.

40. Colin Murray Parkes, "Conclusions II: Attachments and Losses in Cross-Cultural Perspectives," in *Death and Bereavement Across Cultures*, ed. Colin Murray Parkes, Pittu Laungani, and William Young (London: Routledge, 2003), 234.

41. Halloween consumer spending survey from the National Retail Federation (NRF), https://nrf.com/resources/halloween-headquarters

42. Nicholas Rogers, *Halloween: From Pagan Ritual to Party Night* (Oxford: Oxford University Press, 2002), 6. See also the National Retail Foundation's statistics on Halloween spending, https://nrf.com/sites/default/files/Halloween%20 2011_0.pdf

43. David J. Skal, *Death Makes a Holiday: A Cultural History of Halloween* (New York: Bloomsbury USA, 2002).

44. Lisa Morton, *Trick or Treat: A History of Halloween* (London: Reaktion Books, 2013).

45. On the celebration of this holiday in the 2000s, see Roseanne Montillo, *Halloween and Commemorations of the Dead* (New York: Infobase Publishing, 2009), 81. See also Malcolm Foley and Hugh O'Donnell, eds., *Treat or Trick? Halloween in a Globalising World* (Cambridge: Cambridge Scholars Publishing, 2009).

46. Santino, "Introduction: Festivals of Life and Death," xvii.

47. Santino, "Introduction: Festivals of Life and Death," xviii.

48. Santino, "Introduction: Festivals of Life and Death," xviii.

49. Russell W. Belk, "Halloween: An Evolving American Consumption Ritual," in *Advances in Consumer Research*, ed. Marvin E. Goldberg, Gerald Gorn, and Richard W. Pollay (Provo: Association for Consumer Research, 1990), 17:509 ff. For arguments against linking Samhain to human sacrifice, see Ronald Hutton, *The Stations of the Sun: A History of the Ritual Year in Britain* (Oxford: Oxford University Press, 1996). See also Robert Lee Ellison, *The Solitary Druid: Walking the Path of Wisdom and Spirit* (New York: Citadel Press, 2005), 92–93, and James MacKillop, *Dictionary of Celtic Mythology* (Oxford: Oxford University Press, 1998).

50. Edward Muir, *Ritual in Early Modern Europe* (Cambridge: Cambridge University Press, 2005), 71, 131.

51. Ralph Linton and Adeline Linton, *Halloween through Twenty Centuries* (New York: Schuman, 1950).

52. Morton, *Trick or Treat*, 198.

53. Stanley Brandes, "The Day of the Dead, Halloween, and the Quest for Mexican National Identity," *Journal of American Folklore* 111, no. 442 (1998): 359–80. See also Elizabeth Carmichael and Chloe Sayer, *The Skeleton at the Feast: The Day of the Dead in Mexico* (Austin: University of Texas Press, 2001).

54. This recently transferred holiday remains poorly researched. Among research articles on Halloween celebration in Russian schools, see Valentina Prokhorova, "Halloween in Russia: What Makes an Unwelcomed Guest Stay?" in Foley and O'Donnell, *Treat or Trick?*

55. Halloween was banned in Karelia in 2011 and in Kuban in 2012. www.gazeta.ru/social/2013/10/30/5730345.shtml
See also "Minister of Culture Asked to Ban the Celebration of Halloween in Russia," *Izvestia*, October 22, 2014, http://izvestia.ru/news/578323

56. www.peterburg.biz/26-oktyabrya-halloween-v-leningradskom-zooparke.html; www.newsru.com/religy/28oct2013/helloween_print.html; http://tinyurl.com/q4bhtmc; http://tripsmile.ru/kalendar/361-hjellouin-v-rossii-data-i-kak-budem-prazdnovat#toc1

57. See, for example, "Day of the Dead: America's Newest Holiday," www.mexicansugarskull.com/support/events.html

58. Regina M. Marchi, *Day of the Dead in the USA: The Migration and Transformation of a Cultural Phenomenon* (New Brunswick, NJ: Rutgers University Press, 2009).

59. David Alexandros, "The FBI's Growing Concern with the Cult of 'Holy Death' (Santa Muerte)," http://tinyurl.com/nte2azp

60. Pamela Bastante and Brenton Dickenson, "Nuestra Señora de las Sombras: The Enigmatic Identity of Santa Muerte," *Journal of the Southwest* 55, no. 4 (Winter 2013): 435–71.

61. Pamela L. Bunker, Lisa J. Campbell, and Robert J. Bunker, "Torture, Beheadings, and Narcocultos," *Small Wars & Insurgencies* 21, no. 1 (2010): 145–78; Deborah A. Sibila and Andrea J. Weiss, "The Death Cult of the Drug Lords: Mexico's Patron Saint of Crime, Criminals, and the Dispossessed," *Foreign Military Studies Office Report*, http://tinyurl.com/qbr8w89

62. R. Andrew Chesnut, *Devoted to Death: Santa Muerte, the Skeleton Saint* (Oxford: Oxford University Press, 2012), 191.

63. Robert J. Bunker, "Santa Muerte: Inspired and Ritualistic Killings," *FBI Law Enforcement Bulletin*, February 2013, http://tinyurl.com/o2t6knh

64. Jesper Aagaard Petersen, "Contemporary Religious Satanism: Who Serves Satan?" in *Contemporary Religious Satanism: A Critical Anthology* (Controversial New Religions), ed. Jesper Aagaard Petersen (London: Ashgate, 2009).

65. On the development of violent style in haute couture in the 1990s and the interpretation of this trend as anxieties about consumer culture, see Caroline Evans, *Fashion at the Edge: Spectacle, Modernity and Deathliness* (New Haven: Yale University Press, 2003); on this trend in cheap fashion, see David Colman, "The Heyday of the Dead," *New York Times*, July 27, 2006, http://www.nytimes.com/2006/07/27/fashion/27SKULLS.html?pagewanted=all&_r=0

66. See, for example, this advertisement of "Infant Boy Skeleton Romper" from Target: http://www.target.com/p/infant-boy-skeleton-romper/-/A-39600596#pro dSlot=medium_1_10&term=kids+skeleton+clothes; or this home décor: https://s3.amazonaws.com/rebelsmarket_production/images/5382/original/how_to_accessorize_your_home_with_skulls.jpg?1430845119. See also Sarah Jost, "Necromanticism and the New Devotion: Death, Religion, and the Occult in Pop Culture," http://tinyurl.com/qdrby4f

67. Jacque Lynn Foltyn, "Fashions: Exploring Critical Issues," Mansfield College, Oxford, September 25–27, 2009.

68. The high online profile of such images is striking. See, for example, the cover of *Vogue Italia*: "The Latest Wave" (August 2010).

69. www.amazon.com/The-Corpse-Bride-Fashion-Doll/dp/B000A6U676

70. www.skullspiration.com/short-history-skulls-art/

71. Colman, "The Heyday of the Dead." See, for example, sculptural decoration on the front door of the Vortex pub in Atlanta: https://en.wikipedia.org/wiki/The_Vortex_Bar_%26_Grill#/media/File:Atlanta_010.jpg

72. www.damienhirst.com/for-the-love-of-god

73. Jacques Lynn Foltyn, "Dead Famous and Dead Sexy: Popular Culture, Forensics and the Rise of the Corpse," *Mortality* 13, no. 2 (2008): 153–73.

74. Robert S. Gottfried, *The Black Death* (New York: Simon & Schuster, 2010), xiii. See also Joseph Patrick Byrne, *The Black Death* (Portsmouth: Greenwood Publishing Group, 2004), 126.

75. ". . . scholarly estimates range from 45% to an incredible 75% of Florence's total population." Robert S. Gottfried, *The Black Death*, 46.

76. Jean-Baptiste Bertran, *Relation historique de la peste de Marseille, en 1720* (Cologne: Pierre Marteau, 1723), 407. See also Philippe Joutard, ed., *Histoire de Marseille en treize événements* (Marseille: Jeanne Laffitte, 1988).

77. Feodor Derbek, *A History of Plague in Russia* (St. Petersburg, [s.n.], 1905);

Konstantin Vasiliev and Andrei Segal, *A History of Epidemics in Russia* (Moscow: Medgiz, 1960).

78. J. W. Thompson, "The Plague and World War: Parallels and Comparisons," in *The Black Death: A Turning Point in History?* ed. William M. Bowsky (New York: Holt, Rinehart and Winston, 1971).

79. Emmanuel Le Roy Ladurie, *Les paysans de Languedoc* (Paris: S.E.V.P.E.N., 1966).

80. Ariès, *The Hour of Our Death*, 45.

81. Roger Chartier, "Les arts de mourir, 1450–1600," *Annales. Économies, Sociétés, Civilisations* 31, iss. 1 (1976): 51, 52.

82. Paul Lacroix, *Manners, Custom and Dress During the Middle Ages and During the Renaissance Period* (1878) (New York: Kessinger Publishing, 2010). On public executions as a rite of inhumation, see Vivas Mathieu, "Les lieux d'exécution comme espaces d'inhumation. Traitement et devenir du cadavre des criminels (XIIe.-XIVe. siècle)," *Revue historique* 2, no. 670 (2014): 295–312.

83. Johan Huizinga, *The Autumn of the Middle Ages*, trans. Rodney J. Payton and Ulrich Mammitzsch (Chicago: University of Chicago Press, 1996), 124.

84. Paul Binski, *Medieval Death: Rituals and Representation* (Ithaca: Cornell University Press, 1996), 152. "The deceased [are shown] in the state of perfection that they would attain at the Resurrection" (94). On the presentations of death in medieval culture, see also James M. Clark, *The Dance of Death in the Middle Ages and Renaissance* (Glasgow: Jackson, 1950); Patrick J. Geary, *Living with the Dead in the Middle Ages* (Ithaca: Cornell University Press, 1994).

85. Huizinga, *The Autumn of the Middle Ages*.

86. Ariès, *The Hour of Our Death*, 49.

87. Ariès, *The Hour of Our Death*, 103–6.

88. Mikhail Bakhtin, *Rabelais and His World*, trans. Helene Iswolsky (Bloomington: Indiana University Press, 2009).

89. Bakhtin, *Rabelais and His World*, 221–35.

90. On Romanticism's fascination with death see Nicholas Saul, "Love, Death and Liebestad in German Romanticism," in *The Cambridge Companion to German Romanticism*, ed. Nicholas Saul (Cambridge: Cambridge University Press, 2009), 172.

91. Folker Hanusch suggests that American tabloids began creating horrifying images of death to draw readership away from the weeklies. Hanusch, *Representing Death in the News*, 28.

92. Goldberg, "Death Takes a Holiday, Sort Of," 27–52.

93. On moral themes even in the penny press, see Kate Bates, "Empathy or Entertainment? The Form and Function of Violent Crime Narratives in Early-Nineteenth Century Broadsides," *Law, Crime and History* 2 (2014): 1–27. For late-19th-century trends in French press, see Christina Staudt, *Picturing the Dead and Dying in Nineteenth Century L'Illustration* (New York: Columbia University, 2001).

94. On the fixation on decay and degeneration in English literature in the last decade of the nineteenth century and for a discussion of "hybrid literary monstrosities," see Susan J. Navarette, *The Shape of Fear: Horror and the Fin de Siècle Culture of Decadence* (Lexington: University Press of Kentucky, 1998). On the representa-

tion of death in Victorian literature, see Catherine Gallagher, *The Body Economic: Life, Death, and Sensation in Political Economy and the Victorian Novel* (Princeton: Princeton University Press, 2008); Mary Elizabeth Hotz, *Literary Remains: Representations of Death and Burial in Victorian England* (Albany: State University of New York Press, 2009); Deborah Lutz, *Relics of Death in Victorian Literature and Culture* (Cambridge: Cambridge University Press, 2015). In contrast, the lack of interest in death as a research topic among scholars of Victorian times in the first half of the twentieth century is manifested by the fact that the very word "death" is absent from the books on this period. See, for example, Walter E. Houghton, *The Victorian Frame of Mind* (New Haven: Yale University Press, 1957).

95. Michael Wheeler, *Heaven, Hell, and the Victorians* (Cambridge: Cambridge University Press, 1994), 28.

96. On the English love of keeping mementos of the dead, see Peter Metcalf and Richard Huntington, eds., *Celebrations of Death: The Anthropology of Mortuary Ritual*, 2nd ed. (Cambridge: Cambridge University Press, 1991).

97. Wheeler, *Heaven, Hell, and the Victorians*, 29, n. 90.

98. On the photographs of dead bodies taken by these journalists, especially Mathew Brady, see Maggi M. Morehouse and Zoe Trodd, eds., *Civil War America: A Social and Cultural History* (New York: Routledge, 2012), 219. On Civil War photographs see also Mark S. Schantz, *Awaiting the Heavenly Country: The Civil War and America's Culture of Death* (Ithaca: Cornell University Press, 2008), 192, 184, 187; Lisa A. Long, *Rehabilitating Bodies: Health, History, and the American Civil War* (Philadelphia: University of Pennsylvania Press, 2004), 251. See also Bonnie Brennen and Hanno Hardt, eds., *Picturing the Past: Media, History, and Photography* (Champaign: University of Illinois Press, 1999), 135. On the influence of mortality during the Civil War on the American culture, see Drew Gilpin Faust, *This Republic of Suffering: Death and the American Civil War* (New York: Vintage Books, 2009).

99. On war memorials, and especially on the "political cult of the dead' in modern times, see Reinhart Koselleck, "War Memorials: Identity Formations of the Survivals," in Reinhart Koselleck, *The Practice of Conceptual History: Timing History, Spacing Concepts* (Stanford: Stanford University Press, 2002), 317–20.

100. Eugen Weber, *France—Fin de siècle* (Cambridge, MA: Harvard University Press, 1986), 9–26; Ruth Harris, *Murders and Madness—Medicine, Law and Society in the Fin de Siècle* (Oxford: Clarendon Press, 1989). Thomas Laqueur, "Why The Margins Matter: Occultism and the Making of Modernity," *Modern Intellectual History* 3, no. 1 (April 2006): 111–35.

101. Jeffrey Brooks, "Marvelous Destruction: The Left-Leaning Satirical Magazines of 1905–1907," *Experiment* 19, iss. 1 (2013): 33.

102. The commission concluded that spiritualism was either fraud or superstition. The results were published in Mendeleev's volume *Materials for a Consideration of Spiritualism*. On the importance of spiritualism in late-19th-century Russia, see Ilya Vinitsky, *Ghostly Paradoxes: Modern Spiritualism and Russian Culture in the Age of Realism* (Toronto: University of Toronto Press, 2009).

103. Gorky parodied pessimism of Russian Symbolists in his verses "Poems by poet Smertyashkin (the Dead) from Russian tales" in 1912.

104. On Fedorov's 'smertobozie' see Mikhail Epstein, *Faith and Image. Religious Unconscious in Russian Culture of the Twentieth Century* (Tenafly: Hermitage, 1994).

105. Brooks, "Marvelous Destruction," 30.

106. Brooks, "Marvelous Destruction," 30.

107. With the exception of the writings of Sigmund Krzuzhanovsky and Feodor Sollogub.

108. Brooks, "Marvelous Destruction," 35.

109. For an outstanding overview of Soviet history, see Ronald Grigor Suny, *The Soviet Experiment: Russia, the USSR, and the Successor States* (New York: Oxford University Press, 1998).

110. François Furet, *The Passing of an Illusion: The Idea of Communism in the Twentieth Century* (Chicago: University of Chicago Press, 2000), 60.

111. Holger H. Herwig, "The Cult of Heroic Death in Nazi Architecture," in *War Memory and Popular Culture: Essays on Modes of Remembrance and Commemoration*, ed. Michael Keren and Holger H. Herwig (Jefferson, NC: McFarland, 2009), 105. On a highly developed sense of bloody sacrifice and political martyrdom in Nazi Germany described as a "cult of death," see Roger Moorhouse, *Berlin at War* (New York: Basic Books, 2010), 258. See also Stanley G. Payne, *A History of Fascism, 1914–1945* (Oxford: Routledge, 2005), 23–24.

112. In relation to the Nazi regime, Jay W. Baird observes formation of "the spiritual union" of the dead with the living "in the eternal present of the nation." Jay W. Baird, *To Die for Germany: Heroes in the Nazi Pantheon* (Bloomington: Indiana University Press, 1990), 11.

113. On the intellectual origins of fascism, see Georg G. Iggers, *The German Conception of History: The National Tradition of Historical Thought from Herder to the Present* (Middletown, CT: Wesleyan University Press, 1968).

114. Saul Friedländer, *Reflections of Nazism: An Essay on Kitsch and Death* (Bloomington: Indiana University Press, 1993), 169.

115. Friedländer, *Reflections of Nazism*, 43.

116. Herwig, "The Cult of Heroic Death," 108.

117. Friedländer, *Reflections of Nazism*, 43.

118. Christian Goeschel, *Suicide in Nazi Germany* (Oxford: Oxford University Press, 2009), 8, 154.

119. Friedländer, *Reflections of Nazism*, 169.

120. Paul Garson, *New Images of Nazi Germany: A Photographic Collection* (New York: McFarland, 2012), 420.

121. Goeschel, *Suicide in Nazi Germany*, 8.

122. Nicholas Goodrick-Clarke, *The Occult Roots of Nazism* (Wellingborough, Northamptonshire, UK: Aquarian Press, 1985), 218.

123. Guido von List's (1848–1919) ideas were based on distorted interpretations of the Edda and the runes. See Goodrick-Clarke, *The Occult Roots of Nazism*, 39.

124. Goodrick-Clarke, *The Occult Roots of Nazism*, 5; see also vi.

125. Goodrick-Clarke, *The Occult Roots of Nazism*, 49.

126. Goodrick-Clarke, *The Occult Roots of Nazism*, 187.

127. The only instance when the word "cult" was applied to the Soviet experience in the official discourse was in Nikita Khrushchev's Secret Report to the Twentieth Party Congress in 1956, which accused Stalin of creating a "cult of personality." The word "cult" was selected at that time with the clear intent of emphasizing how alien that entire phenomenon was to the materialistic and atheist ideology of Marxism.

128. A. S. Abramov, *By the Kremlin Wall* (Moscow: Politizdat, 1978).

129. Christel Lane, *The Rites of Rules: Ritual in Industrial Society* (Cambridge: Cambridge University Press, 1981).

130. Nina Tumarkin, *Lenin Lives: The Lenin Cult in Soviet Russia* (Cambridge, MA: Harvard University Press, 1983).

131. See, for example, Robert Conquest, *Stalin and the Kirov Murder* (Oxford: Oxford University Press, 1989).

132. Dina Khapaeva and Nicolaï Kopossov, "Les demi-dieux de la mythologie soviétique," *Annales: Economies, Sociétés, Civilisations* 47, nos. 4–5 (1992): 963–89.

133. See Dina Khapaeva, "Charmed by the Stalinism: Russian Mass Historical Consciousness on Eve of Elections," *Neprikosnovenny Zapas*, n. 5 (2007).

134. William H. Sewell, *Logics of History: Social Theory and Social Transformation* (Chicago: University of Chicago Press, 2005), 56.

135. Among several such opinions, see, for example, Amity Shlaes, "Halloween's Pagan Themes Fill West's Faith Vacuum," *Bloomberg Business Week*, October 19, 2011, http://tinyurl.com/qdcv4te

136. See, for example, Lesley Pratt Bannatyne, *Halloween Nation: Behind the Scenes of America's Fright Night* (New Orleans: Pelican Publishing Company, 2011).

137. Kimberly Armadeo, "Halloween Retail Spending Trends and Statistics," *About News*, http://useconomy.about.com/od/demand/f/Halloween-Retail-Spending-Trends.htm

138. Skal, *Death Makes a Holiday*.

139. Neo-paganism is discussed as a new wave in the folk movement by Sabina Magliocco. Magliocco, *Witching Culture: Folklore and Neo-Paganism in America* (Philadelphia: University of Pennsylvania Press, 2004).

140. Skal, *Death Makes a Holiday*.

141. Santino, "Introduction," xxv–xxiv.

142. Belk, "Halloween: An Evolving American Consumption Ritual," 508–17, http://www.acrwebsite.org/volumes/7058/volumes/v17/NA-17

143. Belk, "Halloween: An Evolving American Consumption Ritual," 508–17.

144. Belk, "Halloween: An Evolving American Consumption Ritual," 508–17.

145. Bill Ellis, "Safe Spooks. New Halloween Traditions in Response to Sadism Legends," in *Halloween and Other Festivals of Death and Life*, 25.

146. Belk, "Halloween: An Evolving American Consumption Ritual."

147. Wood (1986) quoted in Belk, "Halloween: An Evolving American Consumption Ritual," 510.

148. Morton, *Trick or Treat*, 198.

149. Ellis, "Safe Spooks," 24.

150. Ellis, "Safe Spooks," 40; see also 32, 39.

151. See, for example, these pictures: http://www.cleveland.com/parma/index.ssf/2015/10/too_bloody_gory_or_just_hallow.html

152. From an online description of Ruth Owen, *The Halloween Gross-Out Guide* (New York: Rosen Publishing, 2013), http://tinyurl.com/kzc2hjm

153. On the importance of rituals and beliefs for everyday life and for consumer behavior, see Dennis W. Rook, "The Ritual Dimension of Consumer Behavior," *Journal of Consumer Research* 12, (1985): 251–64.

154. Morton, *Trick or Treat*, 198.

155. Malcolm Foley and J. John Lennon, "JFK and Dark Tourism: A Fascination with Assassination," *International Journal of Heritage Studies* 2 (1996), 198–211.

156. Grimes, *Deeply into the Bone*, 3.

157. Grimes, *Deeply into the Bone*, 3.

158. Jameson, *Postmodernism or, the Cultural Logic of Late Capitalism*.

159. "There is growing suspicion that the so-called Western way of life has reached a precipice," concludes Grimes after examining the drastic change in rituals around the turn of the millennium. He does not, however, narrow down the reasons for this new "decline of the West." Among his suggested explanations are a need for "bodily and collective ways of making meaning" and globalization (Grimes, *Deeply into the Bone*, 13). On the emergence of new practices and beliefs about death due to dissatisfaction with the old, see Glennys Howart, *Death and Dying: A Sociological Introduction* (Cambridge: Polity, 2007), 266.

CHAPTER THREE

1. J. R. R. Tolkien, "Beowulf: The Monsters and the Critics," (1936) in *Beowulf: New Verse Translation*, trans. Seamus Heaney (New York: W.W. Norton, 2002), 106.

2. Tolkien, "Beowulf: The Monsters and the Critics," 107.

3. Tolkien, "Beowulf: The Monsters and the Critics," 109.

4. Erwin Panofsky, *Gothic Architecture and Scholasticism* (1951) (Latrobe, PA: Archabbey Publications, 2005).

5. Tolkien, "Beowulf: The Monsters and the Critics," 129.

6. Tolkien, "Beowulf: The Monsters and the Critics," 109.

7. Tolkien, "Beowulf: The Monsters and the Critics," 105.

8. Tolkien, "Beowulf: The Monsters and the Critics," 118.

9. Tolkien, "Beowulf: The Monsters and the Critics," 127.

10. Tolkien, "Beowulf: The Monsters and the Critics," 115.

11. Among studies praising Tolkien as a devoted humanist see Patrick Curry, *Defending Middle-Earth: Tolkien: Myth and Modernity* (Wilmington, MA: Mariner Books, 2004); Tom Shippey, *The Road to Middle-Earth: How J. R. R. Tolkien Created a New Mythology* (New York: HarperCollins, 2005); Roger Sale, *Modern Heroism: Essays on D. H. Lawrence, William Empson, and J. R. R. Tolkien* (Berkeley: University of California Press, 1973); and Colin Duriez, *Tolkien and C. S. Lewis: The Gift of Friendship* (Mahwah, NJ: Paulist Press, 2003). For an understanding of Tolkien's works as a coming-of-age novel, where the main character, Bilbo, "represents the reader," see Matthew Grenby, *Children's Literature* (Edinburgh: Edinburgh University Press, 2008),151–52. On Christian morality in Tolkien, see Jane Chance, *Tolkien's Art: A Mythology for England* (Lexington: University Press of Kentucky, 2001), 53–56; and Kurt Bruner and Jim Ware, *Finding God in The Lord of the Rings* (Wheaton: Tyndale House, 2001).

12. Duriez, *Tolkien and C. S. Lewis*, 106–8.

13. On the importance of the medievalism to Tolkien's writings, see J. S. Ryan, "Folktale, Fairy Tale, and the Creation of a Story," in *Tolkien and the Critics: Essays on J. R. R. Tolkien's The Lord of the Rings*, ed. N. D. Isaacs and Rose Abdelnour Zim-

bardo (South Bend, IN: University of Notre Dame Press, 1968); K. J. Battarbee, ed., *Scholarship and Fantasy: The Tolkien Phenomenon* (Finland: University of Turku Press, 1993); T. A. Shippey, "Creation from Philology in *The Lord of the Rings*," in *J. R. R. Tolkien, Scholar and Storyteller: Essays in Memoriam*, ed. Mary Salu and Robert T. Farrell (Ithaca: Cornell University Press, 1979); Shippey, *The Road to Middle-Earth*; and *Tolkien The Medievalist*, Jane Chance ed. (London: Routledge, 2003).

14. The popularity of both TV series is proven by their continuous renewal over the years.

15. David Punter and Glennis Byron, *The Gothic* (London: Wiley, 2004), 268.

16. See the following websites of Russian vampire fans: vampireDiaries-tv.ru; truebloodsite.org; and www.delenadiaries.com

17. See, for example, http://vk.com/topic-375595_24085526 (a Russian Facebook page that asks "Would you like to be a vampire?" At the time of writing, more than 60 percent had replied in the positive) or those exclamations: "i want 2 become a vampire and i'm 13 is there such thing? i read about vampires and i really wish i was 1," http://answers.yahoo.com/question/index?qid=20081013202105AA0h6MH

18. Timothy K. Beal, "Our Monsters, Ourselves," *The Chronicle*, November 9, 2001, 2. For studies of the American vampire subculture, see Katherine Ramsland, *Piercing the Darkness: Undercover with Vampires in America Today* (New York: HarperTorch, 1999).

19. On the Gothic influence on the Russian literature, see Vadim Vatsuro, *The Gothic Novel in Russia* (Moscow: Novoe literaturnoe obozrenie, 2002), and Neil Cornwell, ed., *The Gothic-Fantastic in Nineteenth-Century Russian Literature* (Amsterdam: Rodopi, 1999).

20. On the key features of Social Realism in Soviet literature, see Jeffrey Brooks, "Socialist Realism in Pravda: Read All about It!" *Slavic Review* 53, no. 4 (1994): 973–91; Evgeny Dobrenko, *The Making of the State Reader: Social and Aesthetic Contexts of the Reception of Soviet Literature*, trans. Jesse M. Savage (Stanford, CA: Stanford University Press, 1997).

21. On the history of the vampire in Russian and Soviet cinema, see Greg Dolgopolov, "High Stakes. The Vampire and the Double in Russian Cinema," in *Transnational Horror Across Visual Media: Fragmented Bodies*, ed. Dana Och and Kirsten Strayer (London: Routledge, 2013).

22. Originally published in Russian as *Nochnoi dozor* (Moscow: AST, 2006). For a more detailed interpretation of this novel, see Dina Khapaeva, *Gothic Society: A Morphology of Nightmare* (Moscow: Novoe literaturnoe obozrenie, 2007) (2nd ed., 2008), 35–38.

23. Viktor Pelevin, *Empire V* (Moscow: Eksmo, 2006).

24. Victor Pelevin, *The Sacred Book of the Werewolf*, trans. Andrew Bromfield (London: Faber and Faber, 2008); Viktor Pelevin, *Batman Apollo* (Moscow: Eksmo, 2013); Viktor Pelevin, "A Werewolf Problem in the Middle Region," in *The Blue Lantern* (Moscow: Tekst, 1991).

25. The point about a monster becoming a first-person narrator has been made by Philip Jenkins in relation to serial killers (Jenkins, *Using Murder: The Social Construction of Serial Homicide* [Social Problems and Social Issues] [Chicago: Aldine-Transaction, 1994]) and by Cecil Greek and Caroline Joan Picart in "The Com-

pulsion of Real/Reel Serial Killers and Vampires: Toward a Gothic Criminology," *Journal of Criminal Justice and Popular Culture* 10 , no. 1 (2003): 39–68. We will discuss this issue in more details later in this chapter.

26. For how to kill vampires, particularly in Slavic fashion, see Bruce A. McClelland, *Slayers and Their Vampires. A Cultural History of Killing the Dead* (Ann Arbor: University of Michigan Press, 2006).

27. Bram Stoker, *Dracula* (New York: Grosset & Dunlap, 1897), 47.

28. Stoker, *Dracula*, 17.

29. Sheridan Le Fanu, *Carmilla: A Critical Edition* (1872) (Syracuse, NY: Syracuse University Press, 2013), 96. See also 94.

30. Alexis Tolstoï, *La famille du Vourdalak* (Geneva: Age d'homme, 1993), 51. The English translation appears in Alexis Tolstoy, *Vampires: Stories of the Supernatural*, trans. Fedor Nikanov, ed. Linda Kuel (Portsmouth: Hawthorn, 1969).

31. Pelevin, *Empire V*, 153.

32. Stoker, *Dracula*, 33.

33. Carol Senf, *Bram Stoker* (Cardiff: University of Wales Press, 2010), 64; also 65–66.

34. Stoker, *Dracula*, 285.

35. Stephenie Meyer, *Twilight* (New York: Little, Brown and Company, 2005), 18–19.

36. Meyer, *Twilight*, 260.

37. Meyer, *Twilight*, 256.

38. Sergei Lukyanenko, *Night Watch*, trans. Andrew Bromfield (New York: Miramax Books/Hyperion, 2006), 16. [Here and unless otherwise indicated, translation is by Andrew Bromfield].

39. Pelevin, *Empire V*, 163 [the translation is mine—D.K.].

40. http://tinyurl.com/o7jzozj

41. For example, http://nameberry.com/list/331/Vampire-Baby-Names

42. *The Vampire Diaries*, season 1, episode 21.

43. Rebecca Housel interprets Bella Swan as a victim of both sexual and economic abuse, and draws convincing parallels between the violence against women and the vampire saga. See Housel, "The 'Real' Danger: Fact vs. Fiction for the Girl Audience," in *Twilight and Philosophy: Vampires, Vegetarians, and the Pursuit of Immortality*, ed. Rebecca Housel, J. Jeremy Wisnewski, and William Irwin (Hoboken, NJ: John Wiley & Sons, 2009), 177–92.

44. Meyer, *Twilight*, 1.

45. Meyer, *Twilight*, 449.

46. Meyer, *Twilight*, 413.

47. Natasha Bertrand, "'Fifty Shades of Grey' started out as 'Twilight' fan fiction before becoming an international phenomenon," *Business Insider*, February 15, 2015, www.businessinsider.com/fifty-shades-of-grey-started-out-as-twilight-fan-fiction-2015-2

48. For "Twilight's girl-appeal," see Joyce Ann Mercer, "Vampires, Desire, Girls and God: Twilight and the Spiritualities of Adolescent Girls," *Pastoral Psychology* 60 (2011): 16; Melissa Ames, "Twilight Follows Tradition: Analyzing 'Biting' Critiques of Vampire Narratives for Their Portrayals of Gender and Sexuality," in *Bitten by*

Twilight: Youth Culture, Media, & the Vampire Franchise, ed. Melissa A. Click, Jennifer Stevens Aubrey, and Elizabeth Behm-Morawitz (New York: Peter Lang, 2010), 38–53. For alternative interpretations of this saga see Natalie Wilson, *Seduced by Twilight: The Allure and Contradictory Messages of the Popular Saga* (Jefferson, NC: McFarland, 2011); Amy M. Clarke and Marijane Osborn, eds., *The Twilight Mystique: Critical Essays on Novels and Films* (Jefferson, NC: McFarland, 2010).

49. According to Gabriel and Young, this identification with vampires or wizards expresses a "basic human need for connection." S. Gabriel and A. F. Young, "Becoming a Vampire Without Being Bitten: The Narrative Collective-Assimilation Hypothesis," *Psychological Science* 22 (2011): 990–94. This concept of young women identifying with Bella Swan in the *Twilight* series has been discussed by Natalie Wilson in *Seduced by Twilight*). On vampire fans immersing themselves in the fantasy and escaping the reality of their lives, see also Karen Backstein, "(Un)safe Sex: Romancing the Vampire," *Cineaste* 35, no. 1 (2009): 38–41 who nevertheless considers the female protagonists of contemporary vampire genre "strong and smart."

50. For the Gallup poll data see www.gallup.com/poll/16915/three-four-ameri cans-believe-paranormal.aspx

51. For the discussion of Pelevin's hypnotics see Khapaeva, *Nightmare*, 61–82.

52. Pelevin, *Empire V*, 152.

53. Pelevin, *Empire V*, 103, 168.

54. Pelevin, *Empire V*, 168.

55. Lukyanenko, *Night Watch* [the translation is mine—D.K.], 165.

56. Lukyanenko, *Night Watch*, 56.

57. Lukyanenko, *Night Watch*, 49.

58. Lukyanenko, *Night Watch*, 67.

59. The prototype of the Light vampires' organizations is the KGB or the Mafia. As one vampire explains to his human acquaintance, "[my] work is similar to that of the KGB but is much more serious." Lukyanenko, *Night Watch*, 51.

60. Lukyanenko, *Night Watch*, 199.

61. Lukyanenko, *Night Watch*, 30.

62. On the comparison between post-Soviet and US vampires, see Dina Khapaeva, "The International Vampire Boom and Post-Soviet Gothic Aesthetic," in *Gothic Topographies: Language, Nation Building and "Race"*, ed. P. M. Mehtonen and Matti Savolainen (London: Ashgate, 2013), 143–69.

63. *The Vampire Diaries*, season 2, episode 2. On "sympathetic" vampires, see, for example, Tim Kane, *The Changing Vampire of Film and Television: A Critical Study of the Growth of a Genre* (Jefferson, NC: McFarland, 2006).

64. Meyer, *Twilight*, 263.

65. Meyer, *Twilight*, 267. One critic affirms: "Edward's experience isn't entirely strange to us, because erotic and romantic longings really do seem to share something in common with physical hanger. And who can doubt that this food analogy—the way that a vampire feeding on his victim can serve as a metaphor for an amorous conquest—accounts for a considerable part of the eroticism of vampire fiction?" (George A. Dunn, "You Look Good Enough to Eat," in *Twilight and Philosophy*, 9).

66. *True Blood*, season 5, episode 12.

67. Meyer, *Twilight*, 413.

68. *The Vampire Diaries*, season 2, episode 13.

69. *The Vampire Diaries*, season 4, episode 2.

70. Elizabeth Hand, "In 'The Wolf Gift,' Anne Rice Embraces a Hairy Horror," *Washington Post*, February 13, 2012.

71. On the new status of people in vampire saga, see Khapaeva, "The International Vampire Boom and Post-Soviet Gothic Aesthetic," 119–37; Khapaeva, "The Vampire, a Hero of Our Time," *Novoe literaturnoe obozrenie* 109 (2011): 44–61; Khapaeva, *Portrait critique de la Russie*, 174–190; Khapaeva, "From a Vampire's Point of View," *Kinokultura*, iss. 32 (April 2011), www.kinokultura.com/articles.html

72. *The Vampire Diaries*, season 4, episode 23.

73. *The Vampire Diaries*, season 4, episode 16.

74. *The Vampire Diaries*, season 1, episode 3.

75. *The Vampire Diaries*, season 1, episode 21.

76. Lukyanenko, *Night Watch*, 322.

77. Marilyn Butler, "Frankenstein and Radical Science," in *Mary Shelley, Frankenstein*, ed. J. Paul Hunter (New York: W.W. Norton, 1996), 302–13.

78. Jean-Marie Schaeffer, *La Fin de l'exception humaine* (Paris: Seuil, 2007). See also the discussion of Schaeffer's book in *Le Débat*, no. 152 (2008) and Bruno Latour, *Reassembling the Social: An Introduction to Actor-Network-Theory* (Oxford: Oxford University Press, 2005). For more detailed analysis of the French debates concerning "*la paradigm pragmatique*," see Dina Khapaeva, *Dukes of the Republic in the Age of Translation: Humanities and the Conceptual Revolution* (Moscow: Novoe literaturnoe obozrenie, 2005), 13–75.

79. Kelley Armstrong, *No Humans Involved (Women of the Otherworld)* (New York: Bantam, 2007).

80. On Soviet propaganda in literature, see Jeffrey Brooks, *Thank You, Comrade Stalin! Soviet Public Culture from Revolution to Cold War* (Princeton: Princeton University Press, 1999).

81. http://tinyurl.com/njb4rol; on various aspects of childhood education under the Soviet regime, see Catriona Kelly, *Children's World: Growing Up in Russia, 1890–1991* (New Haven: Yale University Press, 2007).

82. *Alive* was unsuccessfully imitated in at least two films that failed to make much of an impression, Pavel Ruminov's *Dead Daughters* (2007) and Aleksandr Kot's *Brest Fortress* (2010), a state-sponsored commemoration of the sixty-fifth anniversary of the Second World War.

83. At the time of writing, *The Twilight Saga* has 1.41 million followers; *The Vampire Diaries* 864,000; *True Blood* 714,000. The most popular ghost shows and movies do not come even close to these numbers: *Ghost Adventures* has 458,000 followers; *Ghost Hunters* 202,000; and *Paranormal State* 59,100.

84. Interestingly enough, this function persists in contemporary YAL; see, for example, Tom McNeal's *Far Far Away* (New York: Knopf, 2013). For a recent study of ghosts and their deconstruction and psychoanalytical interpretations, see Colin Davis, *Haunted Subjects: Deconstruction, Psychoanalysis and the Return of the Dead* (London: Palgrave McMillan, 2007).

85. On various representations of ghosts, see R. C. Finucane, *Appearances of the Dead: A Cultural History of Ghosts* (London: Junction Books, 1982).

86. Stephenie Meyer, *Eclipse*, 282.

87. Vampires, for example, are said to incarnate humankind's enduring dream of living forever, which became acute in the times of AIDS: Nina Auerbach, *Our Vampires, Ourselves* (Chicago: University of Chicago Press, 1999). 178–79.

88. This represents Huw Fullerton's opinion: www.cherwell.org/culture/film/2013/02/13/review-warm-bodies

89. To mention only one of those interpretations, Steven Zani and Kevin Meaux hold that zombies were spawned by "the failure of social institutions and the cannibalistic nature of human relations". Steven Zani and Kevin Meaux, "Lucio Fulci and the Decaying Definition of Zombie Narratives," in *Better Off Dead: The Evolution of the Zombie as Post-Human*, ed. Deborah Christie and Sarah Juliet Lauro (New York: Fordham University Press, 2011), 98–115.

90. Katherine Ramsland, "Serial Killers Only," www.psychologytoday.com/blog/shadow-boxing/201402/serial-killers-only

91. David Schmid, *Natural Born Celebrities: Serial Killers in American Culture* (Chicago: University of Chicago Press, 2005), I.

92. Jenkins, *Using Murder*, 93.

93. David Schmid, "Idols of Destruction: Celebrity and the Serial Killer," in *Framing Celebrity: New Directions in Celebrity Culture*, ed. Su Holmes and Sean Redmond (London: Routledge, 2012), 302.

94. Terrence Rafferty, "Love and Pain and the Teenage Vampire Thing," *New York Times*, October 31, 2008.

95. Simpson, *Psycho Paths*, 43. On the Gothic as a driving force behind celebrity culture, and on the collapse of the difference between fame and notoriety, see Mark Edmundson, *Nightmare on Main Street: Angels, Sadomasochism, and the Culture of Gothic* (Cambridge, MA: Harvard University Press, 1999), 9, 12.

96. Jenkins, *Using Murder*, 19–20.

97. Jenkins, *Using Murder*, 113.

98. Jenkins, *Using Murder*, 118.

99. Jenkins, *Using Murder*, 114.

100. Greek and Picart, "The Compulsion of Real/Reel Serial Killers and Vampires," 43, 62, 64.

101. Greek and Picart, "The Compulsion of Real/Reel Serial Killers and Vampires," 45.

102. Schmid, *Natural Born Celebrities*, 24, 25.

103. Joel Achenbach, "Serial Killers Shatter Myths of Fact, Fiction," *Washington Post*, April 28, 1991.

104. Lukyanenko, *Night Watch*, trans. Bromfield, 182.

105. Lukyanenko, *Night Watch*, trans. Khapaeva, 271, 277.

106. Jenkins (*Using Murder*, 212–15) claims that in the 1990s, the FBI deliberately encouraged public panic about serial killers. Schmid (*Natural Born Celebrities*, 26) makes the same point and also emphasizes the media's role in constructing the image of the serial killer (221–23).

107. Jenkins, *Using Murder*, 81.

108. Greek and Picart, "The Compulsion of Real/Reel Serial Killers and Vampires," 51.

109. Schmid, *Natural Born Celebrities*, 23.

110. Jenkins observes that these concepts of primitivism saturated the studies of serial murder in the 1980s and 1990s (*Using Murder*, 115–17).

111. Greek and Picart, "The Compulsion of Real/Reel Serial Killers and Vampires," 52.

112. Todd R. Ramlow, "Hannibal Lecter, C'est Moi," *PopMatters* (2001), www.popmatters.com/tools/print/36097/

113. Greek and Picart, "The Compulsion of Real/Reel Serial Killers and Vampires," 52.

114. "Sorbet," www.nbc.com/hannibal/episode-guide/season-1/sorbet/106

115. www.youtube.com/watch?v=uv1cDiF9dUk

116. "Kō No Mono," www.nbc.com/hannibal/episode-guide/season-2/ko-no-mono/211; "Futamono," www.nbc.com/hannibal/episode-guide/season-2/futamono/206

117. "Amuse-Bouche," www.nbc.com/hannibal/episode-guide/season-1/amuse-bouche/102

118. "Kaiseki," www.nbc.com/hannibal/episode-guide/season-2/kaiseki/201; "Kō No Mono," www.nbc.com/hannibal/episode-guide/season-2/ko-no-mono/211

119. The message of the movie appears to be well attuned to the argument of researcher Richard Sugg, who applies Lévi-Strauss' "raw" versus "cooked" dichotomy to cannibalism as an act of choice and concludes that "ritual cannibalism (. . .) is eminently cultural" (contrasting it with what he calls "famine cannibalism"). Sugg, *Mummies, Cannibals and Vampires: The History of Corpse Medicine from the Renaissance to the Victorians* (New York: Taylor & Francis, 2012), 115, and he also calls cannibalism "a cosmically meaningful ritual" of the past: Richard Sugg, "Eating Your Enemy," *History Today* 58, no. 7 (2008): http://www.historytoday.com/richard-sugg/eating-your-enemy

120. To quote just one review of "We Are Who We Are": "Out of nowhere, Grau conjures an epiphany of goodness that somehow floats free from this murky stew of revulsion: a clever moment in an intestine-manglingly memorable film." www.theguardian.com/film/2010/nov/11/we-are-what-we-are-film-review

121. Alan Sepinwall, "Review: NBC's 'Hannibal,' a riveting 'Silence of the Lambs' prequel," http://tinyurl.com/bwqwnde

122. Brian Lowry, "TV Review: 'Hannibal,'" *Variety*, March 29, 2013, http://variety.com/2013/tv/reviews/hannibal-nbc-bryan-fuller-1200330510

123. Eric Goldman, "Delicious Television," www.ign.com/articles/2013/03/30/hannibal-aperitif-review

124. http://eclipsemagazine.com/hannibal-returns-in-february/

125. http://deadline.com/2014/05/ratings-rat-race-hannibal-finale-up-what-would-you-do-debuts-even-735624/

126. www.youtube.com/watch?v=qWAF9PgDg2c

127. G. A. Hauser, *The Vampire & The Man-Eater* (CreateSpace Independent Publishing Platform, 2010). "Monsters Revolution" may be accessed at www.dailygames.com/games/monster-revolution.html

128. René Girard defines the victims in the following way: "the outsiders or marginal who can never build the analogous bonds with the community such as other members establish between themselves. It could be their quality of being a stranger, or an enemy, or underage that prevents them from integrating completely into this

community" (René Girard, *La violence et le sacré* (Paris: Bernard Grasset, 1972), 27 [translation mine—D.K.]. For an example of further development of this approach, see Jules Zanger, "A Sympathetic Vibration: Dracula and the Jews," *English Literature in Transition 1880–1920* 34, no. 1 (1991): 33–45.

129. On the use of the vampiric metaphor in *Das Kapital*, see Terrell Carver, "Making Capital out of Vampires," *The Times Higher Educational Supplement* 15 (June 1984), and Terrell Carver, *The Postmodern Marx* (Manchester: Manchester University Press, 1998), 14; Jacques Derrida, *Specters of Marx: The State of the Debt, the Work of Mourning, and the New International*, trans. Peggy Kamuf (London: Routledge, 1994), 155. Among recent efforts to return back to the Marxist concept of vampire, see Aspasia Stephanou, *Reading Vampire Gothic Through Blood: Bloodlines* (New York: Palgrave Macmillan, 2014).

130. Gilles Deleuze and Félix Guattari, *A Thousand Plateaus: Capitalism and schizophrenia*, trans. Brian Massumi (London: A&C Black, 2004), 266. On Deleuze and Guattari's uses of the vampire metaphor, see Erik Butler, *Metamorphoses of the Vampire in Literature and Film: Cultural Transformations in Europe, 1732–1933* (New York: Camden House, 2010), 6.

131. For example, Donna Haraway continues the same line of postmodern reflections about vampire initiated by Deleuze: "The vampire is the one who drinks and infuses blood in a paradigmatic act of infecting whatever is pure. . . . The vampire seems to be one of the most potent figures of our narrative practices because it is the one who infects the cosmos, the closed and organic community" (Donna Jeanne Haraway and Thyrza Nichols, *How Like a Leaf: An Interview with Thyrza Nichols Goodeve* (New York: Psychology Press, 2000), 150. See also Donna J. Haraway, *Modest_Witness@Second_Millennium: FemaleMan©_Meets_Onco MouseTM* (London: Routledge, 1997), 214–15.

132. Jennifer Fay, "Dead Subjectivity: White Zombie, Black Baghdad," *New Centennial Review* 8, no. 1 (Spring 2008): 82. On the horror film's "radical potential to subvert social hierarchies and decompose relations of power," see Steven Shaviro, *The Cinematic Body* (Minneapolis: University of Minnesota Press, 1993), 65. Shaviro later backtracked on some of his points here. See Shaviro, "The Cinematic Body Redux." www.shaviro.com/Othertexts/Cinematic.pdf

133. See, for example, Richard Dyer, "Children of the Night: Vampirism as Homosexuality, Homosexuality as Vampirism," in *Sweet Dreams: Sexuality, Gender and Popular Fiction*, ed. Susannah Radstone (London: Lawrence & Wishart, 1988), 47–72; Barbara Creed, *The Monstrous-Feminine: Film, Feminism, Psychoanalysis* (London: Routledge, 1993); Hale Hudson, "Vampires of Color and The Performance of Multicultural Whiteness," in *The Persistence of Whiteness: Race and Contemporary Hollywood Cinema*, ed. Daniel Bernardi (London: Routledge, 2008); Peter Day, ed., *Vampires: Myths and Metaphors of Enduring Evil* (Amsterdam: Rodopi, 2006); David A. Kirby and Laura A. Gaither, "Genetic Coming of Age: Genomics, Enhancement, and Identity in Film," *New Literary History* 36, no. 2 (2005) 263–82.

134. Mary Y. Hallab, *Vampire God: The Allure of the Undead in Western Culture* (New York: State University of New York Press, 2009), 33, 135; Carmen Terrell, "The Supernatural in *Twilight* and *Harry Potter*," http://tinyurl.com/pes7awa

135. Her title draws from that of the groundbreaking book on female health and sexuality, *Our Bodies Ourselves* (first published in 1971).

136. Priscilla L. Walton, *Our Cannibals, Ourselves* (Champaign: University of Illinois Press, 2004); Victoria L. Smith, "Our Serial Killers, Our Superheroes, and Ourselves: Showtime's Dexter," *Quarterly Review of Film and Video* 28, no. 5 (2011): 390–400; James Parker, "Our Zombies, Ourselves: Why We Can't Get the Undead Off Our Brains," *The Atlantic*, April 2011; and Justin E. H. Smith, "Our Animals, Ourselves," *Chronicle of Higher Education*, November 27, 2011. Among the most recent studies suggesting that vampires express our fears, moral struggles, and our environmental concerns, see Margot Adler, *Vampires Are Us: Understanding Our Love Affair with the Immortal Dark Side* (Newburyport: Weiser Books, 2014).

137. On the monster as other, see Richard Kearney, *Strangers, Gods, and Monsters: Interpreting Otherness* (London: Routledge, 2003), who focuses on achieving ethical and hospitable relations with monster as the Other; and Maria Beville, *The Unnameable Monster in Literature and Film: The 'Thing' as Itself* (London: Routledge, 2013), who emphasizes in monstrosity "a valuable experience of absolute Otherness," (xii), and that "denying the monster its status as absolute Other, means that we ultimately fail to recognise its real cultural and social significance" (7; see also pages 8 and 13). For an understanding of monsters as symbolic expressions of cultural unease see Jeffrey Jerome Cohen, "Monster Culture (Seven Theses)," in *Monster Theory: Reading Culture*, ed. Jeffrey Jerome Cohen (Minneapolis: University of Minnesota Press, 1996), 3–25.

138. David Gilmore, *Monsters: Evil Beings, Mythical Beasts, and All Manners of Imaginary Terrors* (Philadelphia: University of Pennsylvania Press, 2003).

139. Camille Paglia, *Vamps & Tramps: New Essays* (New York: Knopf Doubleday, 2011).

140. For example: "Society [of vampires in *I Am Legend*—D.K.] has evolved beyond humanity, mutating to accommodate a new-life form that both is and is not identifiably human, which proved most clearly that it is our definition and even prioritization of humanity that has been flawed from the outset." Deborah Christie, "Richard Matheson and the Modern Zombie," in *Better Off Dead*, 68.

141. Jenkins, *Using Murder*, 7.

142. Jenkins, *Using Murder*, 16.

143. Jenkins, *Using Murder*, 113. See also "Images of primitivism, savagery and the jungle (. . .) are frequently symbolized by the theme of cannibalism, which pervades the literature on serial murder" and "The Other is par excellence a cannibal" (113–14).

144. Caroline Joan (Kay) S. Picart, "Media Myths Surrounding Serial Killers: A Gothic Criminology," in *The Poetics of Crime: Understanding and Researching Crime and Deviance Through Creative Sources*, ed. Michael Hviid Jacobson (Farnham: Ashgate, 2014), 176, 178.

145. Vladimir Sorokin, *Blue Lard* (Moscow: Ad Marginem, 1999).

146. The expression "Unmasterable Past" was coined by Charles S. Mayer in *The Unmasterable Past: History, Holocaust, and German National Identity* (Cambridge, MA: Harvard University Press, 1988).

147. Fabio Parasecoli, *Bite Me: Food in Popular Culture* (Oxford: Berg Publishers, 2008), 65.

148. From an abstract of Val Plumwood's article "Tasteless: Towards a Food-Based Approach to Death," *Environmental Values* 17, no. 3 (2008).

149. For example, Kenny Paul Smith, "Vampire Churches, Vampire Images, and Invented Religions", www.equinoxpub.com/blog/2012/03/vampire-churches-vampire-images-and-invented-religions/

150. C. Richard King, "(Mis)uses of Cannibalism in Contemporary Cultural Critique," *Diacritics* 30, no. 1 (2000): 106–23.

151. Khapaeva, *Gothic Society*. See also Khapaeva, "L'esthétique gothique: Essai de compréhension de la société postsoviétique," trans. Chris Martin, *Le Banquet* 26 (2009): 53–77; and Khapaeva, "Historical Memory in Post-Soviet Gothic Society," *Social Research* 76, no. 1 (2009): 359–94. For data published in March 2015 by the Levada Center, see http://www.themoscowtimes.com/article/was-stalins-terror-justified-poll-shows-more-russians-think-it-was/518298.html

152. On the similarities between the Soviet camps and the social structure of the Germanic tribes as described by Tacitus on the one hand, and several features of Soviet society on the other, see Lev Samoilov, *A Journey to an Upside-Down World* (St. Petersburg: FARN, 1993).

153. On the trends in historical memory under Putin, see Khapaeva, "Triumphant Memory of the Perpetrators: Putin's Politics of Re-Stalinization," *Communist and Post-Communist Studies* 49 (2016): 61–73.

CHAPTER FOUR

1. In this chapter, references to the Harry Potter books will be made by page/book number, as follows:

1 *Harry Potter and the Sorcerer's Stone* (New York, Toronto: Scholastic, 1998)

2 *Harry Potter and the Chamber of Secrets* (New York, Toronto: Scholastic, 1999)

3 *Harry Potter and the Prisoner of Azkaban* (New York, Toronto: Scholastic, 1999)

4 *Harry Potter and the Goblet of Fire* (New York, Toronto: Scholastic, 2000)

5 *Harry Potter and the Order of the Phoenix* (New York, Toronto: Scholastic, 2003)

6 *Harry Potter and the Half-Blood Prince* (New York: Scholastic, 2005)

7 *Harry Potter and the Deathly Hallows* (New York: Scholastic, 2007)

2. Stephen Brown, "Marketing for Muggles: The Harry Potter Way to Higher Profits," *Business Horizons* 45, no. 1 (2002): 6–14.

3. Patrick Lee, "Pottermania Lives On in College Classrooms," http://edition.cnn.com/2008/SHOWBIZ/books/03/25/cnnu.potter/; "Harry Potter Course to Be Offered at Durham University," www.guardian.co.uk/books/2010/aug/19/harry-potter-course-durham-university

4. Katherine L. Cohen, "Dr. Kat's List: 5 Campuses If You Want the Harry Potter Experience," http://applywise.com/jul09_harry_potter.aspx

5. Valerie Estelle Frankel, ed., *Teaching with Harry Potter: Essays on Classroom Wizardry from Elementary School to College* (New York: McFarland, 2013); and Allyson Foreman, "The Boy Who Lived to Lead," http://cnu.edu/leadershipreview/pdf/v2%20i2%20foreman.pdf

6. Neil Mulholland, "Introduction" in *The Psychology of Harry Potter: An Unauthorized Examination of the Boy Who Lived*, ed. Neil Mulholland (New York: Smart Pop Books, 2007), 3. For praise of the series as a formative experience and an examination of "a sense of hope for meaning," see, for example, Sharon Black, "The Magic of Harry Potter: Symbols and Heroes of Fantasy," *Children's Literature in Education* 34, no. 3 (September 2003), 237. On Harry Potter as "neostoic" see Edmund M. Kern, *The Wisdom of Harry Potter: What Our Favorite Hero Teaches Us about Moral Choices* (Amherst, NY: Prometheus, 2003), 119, 37. On Harry as a true hero see Mary Pharr, "In Media Res. Harry Potter as Hero-in-Progress," in *The Ivory Tower and Harry Potter: Perspectives on a Literary Phenomenon*, ed. Lana A. Whited (Columbia: University of Missouri Press, 2004), 56–66. For the series as a cosmic battle between good and evil that expresses real-life concerns, see Giselle Liza Anatol, "Introduction," in *Reading Harry Potter: Critical Essays*, ed. Giselle Liza Anatol (Westport, CT: Praeger, 2003), x–xiii, and Gail A. Grynbaum, "The Secrets of Harry Potter," *San Francisco Jung Institute Library Journal* 19, no. 4 (February 2001): 17–48. This reading is supported even by those scholars who address the question of ideology of Rowling's writings, for example Farah Mendlesohn, "Crowning the King: Harry Potter and the Construction of Authority," in *The Ivory Tower*, 159–81. For a perspective on the series as a morality tale, see Shira Wolosky, *The Riddles of Harry Potter: Secret Passages and Interpretive Quests* (New York: Palgrave Macmillan, 2010). Wolosky views the series as political and social critique and a serious work of literature. See also http://tinyurl.com/psnbqrl

7. 371/3.

8. John Pennington, "From Elfland to Hogwarts, or the Aesthetic Trouble with Harry Potter," *The Lion and the Unicorn* 26, no. 1 (January 2002). Joan Acocella contends that "part of the secret of Rowling's success is her utter traditionalism. The Potter story is a fairy tale, plus a bildungsroman, plus a murder mystery, plus a cosmic war of good and evil, and there's almost no classic in any of those genres that doesn't reverberate between the lines of Harry's saga." Acocella, "Under the Spell," *The New Yorker*, July 31, 2000, 74. See also Philip Nel, "Is There a Text in This Advertising Campaign? Literature, Marketing, and Harry Potter," *The Lion and the Unicorn* 29, no. 2 (April 2005), http://muse.jhu.edu/journals/uni/summary/v029/29.2nel.html

9. A. S. Byatt, "Harry Potter and the Childish Adult," *New York Times*, July 7, 2003.

10. Victoria Peterson-Hilleque, *J.K. Rowling, Extraordinary Author* (Edina: ABDO, 2010); John Granger, *Potter's Bookshelf: The Great Books Behind the Hogwarts Adventures* (New York: Berkley Books, 2009). See also Stephen King, "Wild About Harry," *New York Times*, July 23, 2000. Diana Peterson compares Rowling to Dickens and speaks about the "epic quality of the work" ("Preface" in *Harry Potter's World Wide Influence*, ed. Diana Peterson (Cambridge: Cambridge Scholars Publishing, 2009), vii–xi, especially vii and xi.

11. Anthony Holden, "Why Harry Potter Doesn't Cast a Spell Over Me," *The Guardian*, June 25, 2000. For the view that the protagonists do not change and never grow older, see Maria Nikolaejeva, "Harry Potter and the Secrets of Children's Literature," in *Critical Perspectives on Harry Potter*, ed. Elizabeth E. Heilman

(New York: Taylor & Francis, 2008), 235, and Ron Charles, "Harry Potter and the Death of Reading," *Washington Post*, July 15, 2007.

12. Harold Bloom, "Can 35 Million Book Buyers Be Wrong? Yes," *Wall Street Journal*, July 11, 2000.

13. *Critical Perspectives on Harry Potter*, 3. On Harry Potter as an exemplum in overcoming anxiety in children, see, for example, Eli R. Lebowitz and Haim Omer, *Treating Childhood and Adolescent Anxiety: A Guide for Caregivers* (Hoboken, NJ: John Wiley & Sons, 2013). See also Giselle Liza Anatol, "Introduction," in *Reading Harry Potter: Critical Essays*, xv.

14. For example, Harry's stomach "turn over," "clench," gives " a funny jolt" 5/3; 3/5; 281/3, 27/3; it "lurched" 107/3; he feels it "writhing," 302/3; there is "a hot, sick swoop of anger in his stomach," 722/4; he has a "dull, sinking sensation in his stomach," 7/5, or his "insides were squirming" 343/5. He can also experience "a feeling of great gloom in his stomach" 22/3. See also 517/4, 782/5.

15. For example, 314/4, 319/4, and "soaring sensation of his stomach" 237/3.

16. 46/5. Sometimes Rowling offers more general reports of Harry's feelings, saying that he "had never suffered nerves like these" (313/4) or that his "insides went cold" (586/4), but these accounts are still more physiological than psychological.

17. Rowling herself has acknowledged that part of her material is based in occult beliefs (interview on *The Diane Rehm Show*, WAMU, National Public Radio, October 20, 1999, transcribed by Jimmi Thøgersen, http://www.accio-quote.org/articles/1999/1299-wamu-rehm.htm). See also Daniel Roland, "The Response of Mainline Protestant Clergy Members to the Moral Panic Regarding Harry Potter," *Journal of Religious & Theological Information* 12, nos. 3–4 (2013): 90–113. On the contemporary beliefs in witchcraft, paganism, and occult in the United States, see Helen A. Berger, *Witchcraft and Magic: Contemporary North America* (Philadelphia: University of Pennsylvania Press, 2006), 145, 148.

18. Harold Bloom, "Can 35 Million Book Buyers Be Wrong? Yes."

19. For a Harry Potter bibliography, see http://eulenfeder.de/hpliteratur.html. On Harry Potter fandom and Pottermania, see www.washingtonpost.com/wp-dyn/content/article/2007/07/13/AR2007071301730_2.html

20. On the Harry Potter style and its impact on the commodification of children though literature, see Jack Zipes, *Sticks and Stones: The Troublesome Success of Children's Literature from Slovenly Peter to Harry Potter* (New York: Routledge, 2001).

21. On Harry Potter as a bildungsroman, see Peter Appelbaum, "The Great Snape Debate" in *Critical Perspectives on Harry Potter*, 25–51.

22. Geordie Greig, "There would be so much to tell her . . . ," *The Daily Telegraph*, January 11, 2006, www.telegraph.co.uk/news/uknews/1507438/There-would-be-so-much-to-tell-her. . . . html

23. Even though the adjective "human" is still sometimes applied to wizards in her texts.

24. 122/4.

25. 99/1.

26. 15/1, 53/1.

27. 180/5. See also 115/2. On Muggles see Carmen Valero Garcés, "Translating the Imaginary World in the *Harry Potter* Series or How *Muggles, Quaffles, Snitches,* and *Nickles* Travel to Other Cultures," *Quaderns. Revista de traducció* 9 (2003): 121–34.

28. 242/7.

29. 19/1, 4/2.

30. 25/1, 47/1, 5/5.

31. 26/1.

32. 2–3/2, 16/3.

33. 5/5.

34. Pennington, "From Elfland to Hogwarts," 92.

35. Chris Suellentrop, "Harry Potter. Pampered Jock, Patsy, Fraud," *Slate*, November 7, 2002. Even these critics who discuss slavery and racism in the series (Claudia Fenske, *Muggles, Monsters and Magicians: A Literary Analysis of the Harry Potter Series* [New York: Peter Lang, 2008], or Peter Dendle, "Monsters, Creatures, and Pets at Hogwarts," 2011) have consistently overlooked antihumanism as a structural aspect of the series.

36. When he is exposed to the human aspects of his feelings, Harry "roars" at his favorite teacher, yelling that he does not want to be human. 824/5.

37. See chapter "The Muggle-born Registration Commission," in book 7.

38. For example: 145/4, 78/4, 142/4, 203/4, 31/2.

39. 65/1.

40. 49–50/4, 119/4.

41. Harry's nightmares, 270/3, 149/4, 101/5. Harry's nightmares are triggered by panic attacks. He cries in his sleep and wakes up at night in terror: 8/2; 15/5. For a rare instance in which Harry's nightmares have attracted scholarly attention, see Amy Christine Billone, "The Boy Who Lived: From Carroll's Alice and Barrie's Peter Pan to Rowling's Harry Potter," in *Children's Literature* 32 (2004): 178–202. Billone points out that Harry's dreams increase not only in quantity but also in severity as the series progresses. But she uncritically follows the plot thinking that Harry is a one-dimensional positive hero (178) who "fuses Peter Pan's and Alice's roles, participating in a dreamworld that is at once the product of his greatest joy and his most awful fears" (191). Finally, she makes the important point that Hermione has no recorded dreams, nor does anyone else in the series except Harry (179). Rarely, Harry's nightmares are mentioned with respect to the Harry Potter movie franchise. "When it comes to kids' entertainment, filmmakers are asked to walk a creative and commercial tightrope. They need to appeal to their audience's vivid sense of imagination but without causing nightmares or trauma. And in this arena, a little goes a long way. The third Harry Potter film, for instance, had a brooding, mythological potency that was too dark for young children." Vicky Roach, "Creepy Kid Flick," *Northern Territory News*, December 17, 2004.

42. Certainly, it would be too much of a stretch to argue that contemporary authors such as Rowling, Lisa Jane Smith, and Stephenie Meyer have been consciously inspired by any of the classics of European literature. But even direct proof, if such proof existed, that they have no familiarity with Nicholas Gogol, Charles Robert Maturin, Feodor Dostoevsky, or Thomas Mann would not necessarily preclude their having employed literary devices developed by those classical writers. What was once an innovative artistic tool created by great writers in their investigations of nightmare has been transformed, after two hundred years of use, into a recital of clichés. Now woven into the contemporary culture of night-

mare consumption, those clichés—substitutes for psychological complexity—have proven invaluable to the contemporary purveyors of nightmare.

43. 19/1.

44. 61/1.

45. 749/7.

46. For example, the cover blurb for *The Prisoner of Azkaban* says, "Harry Potter isn't safe, not even within the walls of his magical school, surrounded by his friends." See also 407/4.

47. 8/2, 179/5.

48. 635–36/5. He begins having nightmares after seeing his dead parents in a magical mirror: 215/1; 263/1.

49. 183–84/3, 494/4, 502/4.

50. For example: 9–10/5; 329/5.

51. For example, he sees his dreams and wakes up "sweating and shaking"; 130/1, 304/2, 324/3. On the relation of prophecies to "the turns of time" in Harry Potter, see Wolosky, *The Riddles of Harry Potter*, esp. chap. 3, "The Turns of Time: Memory, Prediction, Prophecy." On the temporality of nightmare, see Khapaeva, *Nightmare*, 76–79, 98, 119–37.

52. For example: 50/2. His vision goes "foggy" 320/2.

53. In another episode, believing that he is about to die, he watches the scene through lowered eyelids: 318/2.

54. 318/2.

55. His vision is "slightly blurred" and he squints: 388/3.

56. For example: 320/2, 475/5, 394/3, 302/2, 307/2.

57. For example: 49/2, 306/2.

58. 585/4.

59. "Our analysis leads us to conclude that Rowling's skillful introduction of minor details that later gain significance is a particular intratextual repetition that acts as a lure to her readers to read and reread the Harry Potter series." Eliza T. Dresang and Kathleen Campana, "Harry Potter Fans Discover the Pleasures of Transfiguration," in *Seriality and Texts for Young People: The Compulsion to Repeat*, ed. M. Reimer, N. Ali, D. England, M. Dennis Unrau, and Melanie Dennis Unrau (New York: Springer, 2014), 97. On repetition as a possible motivation for the young readers, see Colette L. Drouillard, "Growing Up with Harry Potter: What Motivated Youth to Read?" http://diginole.lib.fsu.edu/islandora/object/fsu:168822/datastream/PDF/view

60. 576/4. On happy dream, harmony, and their importance for nightmare hypnotics, see Khapaeva, *Nightmare*, 89–91.

61. 578/4.

62. 577–78/4.

63. Jerome K. Jerome, *Novel Notes* (London: Leadenhall Press, 1893), 41–42. On doubles in Jerome and Dostoevsky' works, see Khapaeva, *Nightmare*, 77–78, 113–18.

64. 52/7; also 376/7.

65. On the concept of literary reality, see Khapaeva, *Nightmare*, 67–71.

66. 70/1, 71/1, 134/1.

67. 429/3.

68. 187/3. The dementors and their "supply of human prey," 247/3.

69. "Giving Voldemort a French name connects him to the fear of foreigners in the novel. Rowling certainly seems to be taking a page from Stoker's book in this characterization, as his Dracula came from Transylvania to Britain, in an almost reverse colonization." Tracy Douglas, "Harry Potter and the Goblet of Colonialism," in *Phoenix Rising: Collected Papers on Harry Potter*, ed. Sharon K. Goetz (Sedalia, CO: Narrate Conferences, 2008), 282. Douglas makes the point that Voldemort needs Harry's blood to return to his body, which makes him comparable to a vampire. Annette Klemp also argues that Voldemort is an incarnation of xenophobia because of his Gallic-sounding name. Annette Klemp, "Evil and the Loss of Identity," in *Phoenix Rising*, 121.

70. 258–59/1, 653/4.

71. 298/1.

72. 642/4. See also Voldemort (through Quirrell) drinking unicorn's blood: "The cloaked figure reached the unicorn, lowered its head over the wound in the animal's side, and began to drink its blood." 256/1.

73. Klemp, "Evil and the Loss of Identity," 119–20. In addition to critics referenced elsewhere, Gail A. Grynbaum also discusses the vampire as an important theme in the series, but he considers Harry and Voldermort as protagonist and antagonist: Grynbaum, "The Secrets of Harry Potter," 17–48, 122. Annette Klemp also compares Voldemort to Dr. Faust and Victor Frankenstein in "Evil and the Loss of Identity," 121–22. She also uses Harry's ability to speak Parseltongue as an argument to prove Voldemort's vampiric nature (119). She draws no conclusions, however, on the cultural role of Rowling's main protagonist or on the series' significance in terms of the attitude toward human beings.

74. Klemp, "Evil and the Loss of Identity," 122.

75. Klemp, "Evil and the Loss of Identity," 121, 123.

76. 262–63/1.

77. 197/3.

78. This draught was first mentioned in *The Sorcerer's Stone* (138/1) but comes into its own in *The Half-Blood Prince* (189–91/6).

79. "I wanted Harry Potter's blood. I wanted the blood of the one who had stripped me of power thirteen years ago . . . for the lingering protection his mother once gave him would then reside in my veins too." 656–57/4.

80. 642/4.

81. 709/7.

82. As has been mentioned many times, especially by Rowling's Christian critics, there is no God in Harry Potter's world just as there is none in Tolkien's Middle Earth. The only hint at God's existence is the school's Christmas break and the associated shopping, gift giving, and lavish feasts. This gives good grounds to suggest that the series notion of immortality has little, if anything, to do with Christian dogma.

83. Harry, the main protagonist, receives this prize.

84. 310/4, 664/4. Also 85/1, and 697/4.

85. 720/7.

86. 724/7; see Hermione's earlier hint: 328/7.

87. 747–49/7.

88. 708/7.
89. 709/7.
90. 426/3.
91. 20/1.
92. See, for example, 217/1, 265/1, 213/3.
93. See, for example, 201/2, 577/4, 94/6, and 696/7.
94. 291/5.
95. 247/2, 593/5.
96. 242/2, 540/5.
97. 215/1, 213/3.
98. 260/1, 44/5.
99. "Rowling has spoken about depression as the loss of hope, how it has been her enemy, and how it has informed her depiction of the dementors here. [In] *Harry and Me,* (. . .) Rowling described the dementors as 'a description of depression . . . And entirely from my own experience. Depression is the most unpleasant thing I have ever experienced. . . . It is that absence of being able to envisage that you will ever be cheerful again. The absence of hope. That very deadened feeling, which is so very different from feeling sad. Sad hurts but it's a healthy feeling. It is a necessary thing to feel. Depression is very different." Roni Natov, "Harry Potter and the Extraordinariness of the Ordinary," *The Lion and the Unicorn* 25, no. 2 (April 2001): 310–27. See also Roni Natov, The Poetics of Childhood (New York: Routledge, 2012, 257.
100. 482/4, "barely controlled panic" (317/4), "a molten panic" that surges through his stomach (319/4).
101. 297/5.
102. For example: 706/4, 235/5, 327–28/5, 298/4 and 732/5. Harry being aggressive and impatient: 736/5, 823-824/5, 238/5, 733–734/5.
103. See, for example, 341/5, 495/5; and 535–36/5.
104. 823–24/5, 832/5.
105. 339/3.
106. 36/5, 23/2, 243/3, 670/4, 299/5.
107. 202/1, 381/5, 553/5.
108. 120/2.
109. 137–38/2.
110. 254/2.
111. 237–38/3.
112. 178/5.
113. 209/2.
114. For example: 248/2, 384–85/3.
115. "'It's going to kill someone!' he shouted [. . .]." "'Harry, *what* was that all about?' said Ron, wiping sweat off his face. 'I couldn't hear anything.'" 138/2.
116. See, for example, 262/1 and 284/4.
117. "[H]e had felt a spasm of horror, which had awoken him . . . or had that been the pain in his scar?" 17/4.
118. Among countless examples, see 298/1, 301/1.
119. See, for example, 144/4 and 148/4.
120. For example, 264/1.

121. 538/5, among multiple mentions.

122. 257/3.

123. 260/1, 301/4.

124. 54/3, 68/3.

125. 411–12/3.

126. 86/1.

127. 57–58/1. Critics often consider this sudden discovery a key to explaining the series' success, on the grounds that every teenager at some point has felt alienated from his or her family, has wondered who his or her "real" parents are, and has hoped they are *very* special people. The desire to wake up one morning rich and famous is surely common. These Cinderella-like motifs have been recycled countless times in literature but never to such acclaim.

128. Harry is described dreaming of "some unknown relation coming to take him away." 30/1.

129. 822/5. As we will see later, Harry also may be suspected of sharing something of Voldemort's experience, which Dumbledore describes as follows: "There he showed his contempt for anything that tied him to other people, anything that made him ordinary. Even then, he wished to be different, separate, notorious." 277/6.

130. 821/5.

131. 345/7. And that there are just two of them who matter. 322/2. See also "Riddle said I am like him," 332/2.

132. 686/7.

133. As Colman Noctor, who explores the series from a psychoanalytical perspective in "Putting Harry Potter on the Couch" (*Clinical Child Psychology and Psychiatry*, no. 11 (October 2006): 579–89, http://tinyurl.com/qzar8go, points out: "So in quite a concrete manner Voldemort is part of Harry! It is Harry's attempts at confronting his inner demons and his striving to integration that forms the crucial plot to the story" (583). Norton does not, however, see Voldemort as a product of Harry's hallucinations or of any mental disorder (584).

134. "Harry's voice was clear," 279/7; "Harry was laughing," 727/5, 531–32/5. For further examples see the section "Harry the Killer."

135. 711/7.

136. 815–16/5.

137. Amanda Cockrell, "Harry Potter and the Secret Password: Finding Our Way in the Magical Genre," in *The Ivory Tower and Harry Potter: Perspectives on a Literary Phenomenon*, ed. Lana A. Whited (Columbia: University of Missouri Press, 2002), 20. See also John Granger, *How Harry Cast His Spell: The Meaning Behind the Mania for J. K. Rowling's Bestselling Books* (Carol Stream, IL: Tyndale House, 2014), 87. On the special ties between Voldemort and Harry see also Ranita Chatterjee, "Gothic Half-Bloods: Maternal Kinship in Rowling's Harry Potter Series," in *Gothic Kinship*, ed. Agnes Andeweg and Sue Zlosnik (Manchester: Manchester University Press, 2013).

138. 17/4.

139. Renner also describes Tom as Dumbledore's "failure" (Karen J. Renner, "Evil Children in Film and Literature," in *The "Evil Child" in Literature, Film and Popular Culture*, ed. Karen J. Renner [New York: Routledge, 2013], 89) and states that "I

interpret Harry's similarity to Tom Riddle in light of other critics such as Michael Bronski, Tison Pugh and David Wallace, and Catherine Tosenberger, who have noted analogies between Harry's 'coming out' as a wizard to the queer child's experience. This understanding allows us, in turn, to regard the story of Tom Riddle in *Half-Blood Prince* as an unsuccessful coming-out story. If Harry's story in the series follows the paradigm of the coming-out story, and if Harry recognizes the similarities between his story and Tom's, then we have to ask *why* Tom's story is an aborted coming-out story in which a child is cast as a closeted monster that the school cannot exorcise. Tom's story is that of a neglected child aware of his 'difference' and left with little guidance" (89).

140. 317/2, 332/2, 704/7.

141. 199/2. "You can speak Parseltongue, Harry." 332/2.

142. 316–17/2, 646/4.

143. 212–15/6: the author implies that Harry feels sorry for both Tom and himself.

144. For example, in Giselle Liza Anatol, "Introduction," in *Reading Harry Potter: Critical Essays*, x–xiii. As we will see, however, the attraction of the plot cannot be explained by that alone.

145. 314/2.

146. 553/5.

147. Robert Freedman, *The Madness Within Us: Schizophrenia as a Neuronal Process* (Oxford: Oxford University Press, 2009), 3–4.

148. 466–68/5, 500/5.

149. 462–63/5.

150. 478/5.

151. 475/5.

152. 492–93/5.

153. "Sirius, I . . . I think I'm going mad. . . . Back in Dumbledore's office, just before we took the Portkey . . . for a couple of seconds there I thought I was a snake, I *felt* like one—my scar really hurt when I was looking at Dumbledore—Sirius, I wanted to attack him!" 480–81/5.

154. For example, 728/5, 593/5.

155. 586/5.

156. 541–42/5.

157. 577/4, 542/5, 85/3, 729/5.

158. 586/5.

159. 481/5.

160. As Deborah J. Taub and Heather L. Servaty-Seib point out, the description of Harry's "white-hot anger" (823/5) "is clearly in line with a frequently used journal for bereaved teens titled *Fire in my Heart: Ice in my Veins*." "Controversial Content: Is Harry Potter Harmful to Children?" in *Critical Perspectives on Harry Potter*, 26.

161. "In this article we review Harry Potter's headaches as described in the biographical series by JK Rowling. [. . .] Despite some quite unusual features, they meet all but one of the ICHD-II criteria for migraine, so allowing the diagnosis of 1.6 Probable migraine." Fred Sheftell, Timothy J Steiner, and Hallie Thomas,

"Harry Potter and the Curse of Headache," *Headache: The Journal of Head and Face Pain* 47, iss. 6, (June 2007): 911–16, abstract.

162. http://tinyurl.com/o3y8rv3

163. Melvin J. Konner, *The Tangled Wing: Biological Constraints on the Human Spirit*, 2nd ed. (New York: Times Books, 2002) (first publication 1982), 83.

164. Wikipedia entry, "Psychotic break," represents conventional wisdom about these symptoms: http://en.wikipedia.org/wiki/Psychotic_break

165. 85/3.

166. 663/4. See also Donald W. Mulder, Reginald G. Bickford, and Henry W. Dodge Jr., "Hallucinatory Epilepsy: Complex Hallucinations As Focal Seizures," *American Journal of Psychiatry* 113 (1957): 1100–1102. Also, in an interesting coincidence, "'Potter' Stars Doodle for Charity Auction to Benefit Epilepsy Action." www.mugglenet.com/app/category/show/37

167. https://www.britannica.com/science/epilepsy; www.epilepsy.com/learn/epilepsy-101/what-happens-during-seizure

168. Harry vomits, 463/5; he falls to the floor or to his knees, 84–85/3, 542/5; 247–48/2, 256/1, 589/5. Other examples of what appear to be hallucinatory fits are scattered throughout the books: 216/2, 239/3, 214/3, 670/4, etc.

169. 553–54/5. The point about Harry's seizures was made by Billone, who otherwise considers Voldemort a full-fledged antagonist: "As Book 5 advances, Harry's nights grow 'restless' and 'disturbed' (. . .); it seems he no longer has any good dreams at all. He believes he is being attacked by many-legged creatures with cannons for heads (a *normal* dream); he repeatedly thinks he is wandering down a windowless corridor and facing a locked door which he longs to enter (due to his own misjudgment these dreams will become *prophetic*); Hermione tells him to give Cho his Firebolt broomstick, which he can't do because the evil professor, Dolores Umbridge, has locked it up (a *normal*—and psychoanalytically fertile—dream); he turns into a snake who bites and nearly murders Ron Wesley's father (this dream is *factual*, although Voldemort was technically in the snake's body, not Harry); he has a long conversation, speaking in Voldemort's voice, and when he looks in the mirror he sees Voldemort rather than himself (another *factual* dream); he has a version of an epileptic seizure, and hears (even utters) Voldemort's maniacal laughter (again, a *factual* dream); he suffers from a terrible nightmare/seizure during an exam, brought on by his lack of sleep and his inability to remember names and dates from the real world—in this *implanted* dream, he once again has merged with Voldemort and is in the process of torturing Sirius." Billone, "The Boy Who Lived," 195.

170. 178–79/3.

171. 240/3.

172. 83–87/3. His friends are slapping his face to make him come to: 84/3.

173. 232–33/7, 278–80/7, 548–51/7.

174. His laughter is often called "mad" or "insane."

175. J. K. Rowling, "Harry Potter and Me: A Christmas Special Broadcast" (BBC) December 28, 2001, http://www.accio-quote.org/articles/2001/1201-bbc-hpandme.htm

176. The respect for situational good and absence of moral absolutes in the series has been a longstanding Christian criticism. See, for example, S. Brown, "Harry

Potter and the Fandom Menace," http://atheism.about.com/od/harrypotter/i/
witchcraft_2.htm. On Harry Potter and Christianity see also Greg Garrett, *One
Fine Potion: The Literary Magic of Harry Potter* (Waco, TX: Baylor University Press,
2010).

177. Susan Miller, "Turban Legend: A Different Perspective on P-p-poor P-p-
professor Quirrell," in *Phoenix Rising*, 137. According to Susan Miller, Rowling "built her pain and her experience into the character of Quirrell." (131).The
first key in John Granger's *Unlocking Harry Potter: Five Keys for the Serious Reader*
(Cheshire: Zossima Press, 2007) is "Narrative Misdirection," the implication being
that Rowling is an unreliable narrator. Granger argues that we have only Harry's
perspective on the story and that this increases the reader's identification with the
hero. See also Billone, "The Boy Who Lived," 196, and Phyllis D. Morris, "Tricked
or Fooled? Rowling's Mastery of the Art of Misdirection," in *Phoenix Rising*, 330–
49.

178. Pennington, "From Elfland to Hogwarts," 92.

179. "In effect, if Rowling would take the magic out of the Potter series with
some fine-tuning revision, her books would remain fundamentally the same, the
children attending a boarding school, getting into mischief, playing practical jokes,
and competing in various classroom and sporting events." Pennington, "From Elfland to Hogwarts," 91.

180. "On a fundamental level, Rowling is unwilling—or unable—to depart from
this consensus reality; her novels, for all their 'magical' trappings, are prefigured
in mundane reality, relying too wholly on the real from which she simultaneously
wants to escape" (Pennington, "From Elfland to Hogwarts,", 96).

181. 12/5.

182. 19/3, 11/5.

183. 28/3.

184. 26/3.

185. 299/5. See also 611–12/4, 705–6/4. Seamus does not "want to share a dormi-
tory with him anymore, he's a madman." 218/5.

186. 407/3.

187. 816/5.

188. 198/5. He sees "Sirius's head in the fire" where others might see "an oddly
shaped log or something." 300–301/5.

189. That image emerges as a visualization of the "spasm of horror" that grips
Harry as he tries to make sense of the nightmare from which he has just awoken.
At first, however hard he tries, Harry cannot picture Voldemort's horrible face but
gradually it resolves into a vaguely snake-like image (17/4).

190. 723/7. See also 28–29/7.

191. 661–69/4.

192. *The Diane Rehm Show*, WAMU Radio Washington, D.C., October 20, 1999,
http://www.accio-quote.org/articles/1999/1299-wamu-rehm.htm

193. Roger Highfield, *The Science of Harry Potter: How Magic Really Works* (New
York: Penguin, 2003). See also this comparison of the mechanisms behind the series
plot and a game: "Similarly, the driving force of the computer game consists in the
effects of suspense, curiosity, and surprise. A crucial difference is that in mainly

ludic works, including a computer game like *Harry Potter and the Philosopher's Stone*, these effects apply primarily to the user's activity." Anna Gunder, "As If By Magic: On Harry Potter as a Novel and Computer Game," www.digra.org/wp-content/uploads/digital-library/05150.57524.pdf. On the gaming aspect of Harry Potter, see Lisa S. Brenner, ed., *Playing Harry Potter: Essays and Interviews on Fandom and Performance* (Jefferson, NC: McFarland, 2015). See also http://harrypotter.wikia.com/wiki/Harry_Potter_%28video_game_series%29

194. See, for example, 94/5, or 166–67/5.

195. 10/5.

196. 74/5.

197. 614/5, 245/5, 265/5.

198. 782/5.

199. 485/4.

200. 693/4.

201. What the author consistently shows us is that his breaks or seizures usually begin with his scar hurting and that he has visions during these episodes.

202. 774–78/5, 380–81/5, 249–50/2.

203. 380–81/5.

204. Naturally, children have been observed creating games of their own based on the Harry Potter series. See Elizabeth Grugeon, "Listening to Children's Talk: Oral Language on the Playground and in the Classroom," in *Teaching Speaking and Listening in the Primary School*, ed. Lorraine Hubbard and Carol Smith (New York: Routledge, 2005), 72.

205. 717/4.

206. See, for example, 720–23/4. See also Peeves' taunt, "You're killing off students, you think it's good fun." 203/2. Early in the story Harry is suspected of murdering a cat, 140/2.

207. 572–73/6.

208. Renner, "Evil Children in Film and Literature," 89.

209. 828/5.

210. 727/5.

211. 232/7.

212. "Readers suspect Harry of killing Cedric" (www.cosforums.com/archive/index.php/t-122724.html). See also http://www.mugglenet.com/2003/06/dont-do-what-diggory-did/

213. Compare other killings: 11/4, and 15/4.

214. 693/4. Before being questioned by Dumbledore, Harry avoids his eyes. (694/4).

215. 8/5.

216. As it is the case with Cedric. It is, furthermore, unclear why Harry apologizes to those who have died: "'I didn't want you to die,' Harry said. These words came without his volition. 'Any of you. I'm sorry'" (700/7). What does "any of you" mean in this context—that some of them, such as Sirius, ended up dead because of him?

217. For example, 491/5 or 493/5.

218. 173/7.

219. Harry is described as having "the horrible impression that he was slowly turning into a kind of aerial that was tuned into tiny fluctuations in Voldemort's mood" (554/5). Psychologists and psychiatrists who are well aware of efforts to avoid stigmatization by sufferers from these diseases nevertheless recognize that people with such severe mental disorders may constitute a danger to themselves or to others, and that the patient may ultimately be endangered by his or her delusions. See, for example, Stephen Morse, "Blame and Danger: An Essay on Preventive Detention" (1996) *Faculty Scholarship*, Paper 798, http://scholarship.law.upenn.edu/faculty_scholarship/798, and Sara Gordon, "The Danger Zone: How the Dangerousness Standard In Civil Commitment Proceedings Harms People with Serious Mental Illness." http://scholars.law.unlv.edu/cgi/viewcontent.cgi?article=1934&context=facpub

220. 233–34/7.

221. 234/7, 727/5.

222. 234/7.

223. "'That job's jinxed. No one's lasted more than a year. . . . Quirrell actually died doing it. . . . Personally, I'm going to keep my fingers crossed for another death . . . .' 'Harry!' said Hermione, shocked and reproachful": 167/6.

224. 221/7.

225. Harry's sanity is questioned after the murder of Cedric: 703–6/4.

226. Graham dreams about the stag in episode 5/5 and he hallucinates it in episode 11/11.

227. In episode 22/9.

228. www.suicide.org/jk-rowling-considered-suicide.html

229. For example: "Ginny interpreted her experiences as evidence that she was going mad . . . In actuality, her body had been inhabited by the young Lord Voldemort through the medium of a diary . . . a perfectly rational explanation in the world of wizardry." Jessica Leigh Murakami, "Mental Illness in the World of Wizardry," 181, 185–87.

230. Colman Noctor (in "Putting Harry On The Couch") considers Harry's self-identification with Voldemort as potentially part of a program of "psychotherapeutic treatments." He interprets the series as a case study in the development of strength of and character (585) and also claims that books can have therapeutic effects (588).

231. On the series as a tool in furthering injury prevention, see Stephen Gwilym, Dominic P. J. Howard, Neve Davies, and Keith Willett, "Harry Potter Casts a Spell on Accident Prone Children." www.eena.org/ressource/static/files/1505.pdf

232. Elisa T. Dresang, "Hermione Granger and the Heritage of Gender," in *The Ivory Tower and Harry Potter*, 212–13.

233. "JK Rowling's World Book Day Chat, March 4, 2004," www.accio-quote.org/articles/2004/0304-wbd.htm

234. "[I]f a psychologist were ever able to get Voldemort in a room, pin him down and take his wand away, I think he would be classified as a psychopath (crowd laughs). So there are people, for whom, whatever you're going to call it—personality disorder or an illness—for whom redemption is not possible. They're rare": www.accio-quote.org/articles/2006/0801-radiocityreading1.html. In 2006, Rowling also told an interviewer that Voldemort at his core has a human fear—the fear of death.

Melissa Anelli and Emerson Spartz, "The Leaky Cauldron and MuggleNet interview Joanne Kathleen Rowling: Part Two," July 16, 2005.

235. 345/7. On Voldemort as a serial killer and psychopath, and Harry's true antagonist, see C. J. Patrick and Sarah K. Patrick, "Exploring the Dark Side: Harry Potter and the Psychology of Evil," in *The Psychology of Harry Potter*, 222, 230.

236. *The Diane Rehm Show*, http://www.accio-quote.org/articles/1999/1299-wamu-rehm.htm

237. *The Diane Rehm Show*.

238. "You know, they've been plotted very carefully since 1992. The larger plot has been in place. (. . .) As I was writing, I'm trying to do the thing properly—that needed to happen for plot reasons." *The Diane Rehm Show*.

239. "There would be so much to tell her," *The Daily Telegraph*, January 11, 2006.

240. For other possible interpretations, see Katrine Brøndsted and Cay Dollerup, "The Names in Harry Potter," *Perspectives: Studies in Translatology* 12 (2004): 56–72.

241. For example, 401/3, 640/4, 181/5, 183/5, 37/7, 639/4.

242. For example, 216/4.

243. 640/4.

244. For example, 106–7/3, 129/4, 110/3.

245. 142/4; see also note 68.

246. Inferi are described in the chapter "The Cave" of *Harry Potter and the Half-Blood Prince*.

247. 187/4. Ron and Hermione suspect that Dumbledore had sent him on a mission on which he was very likely to die. 302/1.

248. For example, 478–81/7, 646/4. Among several books interpreting the Harry Potter series as the Gothic novel, see John Granger, *Harry Potter's Bookshelf: The Great Books behind the Hogwarts Adventures* (New York: Penguin, 2009), who considers Voldemort as Rowling's "Gothic masterpiece"; June Cummins, "Hermione in the Bathroom: The Gothic, Menarche, and Female Development in the Harry Potter Series," in *The Gothic in Children's Literature: Haunting the Borders*, ed. Anna Jackson, Roderick McGillis, and Karen Coats (London: Routledge, 2013); and Ranita Chatterjee, "Gothic Half-Bloods: Maternal Kinship in Rowling's Harry Potter Series,." in *Gothic Kinship*, who considers the perverse kinship between heroic Harry and evil Voldemort the central theme of this Gothic story.

249. 12/1.

250. 216/4.

251. 15/4.

252. For the "disinterested" account of the deaths of secondary protagonists see, for example, 528/4 and 529/4. For images of the dead bodies of Ron and his family, see 174–75/5.

253. 638/4.

254. 670/4.

255. 596/6.

256. 605/6.

257. Indeed, a voyeuristic observation of the physicality of death is typical of every death, however important; curses or spells "hit" some body part or other, the character falls and it is all over ("Voldemort's curse hit Mad-Eye full in the face, he

fell backward off his broom and—there was nothing we could do, nothing, we had half a dozen of them on our own tail." 78/7).

258. 299/2.

259. 465/4.

260. 465/4.

261. June Cummins, "Hermione in the Bathroom: The Gothic, Menarche, and Female Development in the Harry Potter Series," 187.

262. 464/4.

263. 299/2.

264. Garcés, "Translating the Imaginary World in the *Harry Potter* Series," 122. For an analysis that contains not one word about the humiliation and murder of this girl Myrtle, see Alice Mills, "Harry Potter and the Terrors of the Toilet," *Children's Literature in Education* 37, iss. 1 (March 2006): 1–13.

265. For a discussion of Harry's death, see Fraser Los, "Harry Potter and the Nature of Death," *Alternatives* 34, iss. 1 (2008).

266. 321/2.

267. 384–85/3.

268. 83/3.

269. 660–62/4.

270. 646/4.

271. 670/4.

272. 703–4/7.

273. 703/7.

274. 704/7.

275. 738/7.

276. 744/7.

277. 691/7.

278. 687/7.

279. "You had accepted, even embraced, the possibility of death, something Lord Voldemort has never been able to do." 711/7.

280. Pennington, "From Elfland to Hogwarts," 92.

281. For Harry Potter as an incarnation of the Christian idea of sacrifice, see Nikolaus Wandinger, "'Sacrifice' in the Harry Potter Series from a Girardian Perspective," *Contagion: Journal of Violence, Mimesis, and Culture* 17, no. 2 (2010): 27.

282. 129/2.

283. 132/2.

284. 712/7.

285. On the danse macabre, see Ashby Kinch, *Imago Mortis: Mediating Images of Death in Late Medieval Culture* (Leiden: Brill, 2013).

286. 665–69/4. Another danse macabre is depicted in the lengthy scene in which Harry and Dumbledore destroy the last Horcrux. 573–79/6.

287. 699–701/7.

288. See also episode 7/1.

289. 566/6.

290. 321/2.

291. 699/7. "And again Harry understood without having to think. It did not matter about bringing them back, for he was about to join them. He was not really fetching them: They were fetching him." 698/7.

292. In episode 17/4.

293. Geordie Greig, "There would be so much to tell her . . ."; www.telegraph.co.uk/news/uknews/1507438/There-would-be-so-much-to-tell-her. . . . html

294. 297/1.

295. 302/1.

296. "The optimum age, I'd definitely say is 9+ for these books." *The Diane Rehm Show*, WAMU Radio Washington, DC, October 20, 1999.

297. 328/7. This quote from 1 Corinthians 15:26 should not mislead us.

298. 722/7.

299. 720–21/7.

300. Vladimir Propp, *Morphology of the Folktale* (1928), trans. Laurence Scott (Bloomington: American Folklore Society and Indiana University Press, 1968).

301. Colin Murray Parkes, "Conclusions II: Attachments and Losses in Cross-Cultural Perspective," in *Death and Bereavement Across Cultures*, ed. Colin Murray Parkes, Pittu Laungani, and William Young (London: Routledge, 2003), 234.

302. On early-medieval traits in the series, see Iver B. Neumann, "Pop Goes Religion: Harry Potter Meets Clifford Geertz," *Children's Literature in Education* 35, no. 1 (March 2004): 35–52.

303. With rare exceptions, such as Percy Weasley. On Harry Potter as "a Returning Prince who gets his worth 100% from heredity and genetics" see Andy Robertson, "Fictionmags" (quoted in Farah Mendlesohn, "Crowning the King," 163.

304. See, for example, Bettina Boldhauer, *Medieval Blood* (Cardiff: University of Wales Press, 2010).

305. Harry is made to write with his blood: 267/5, 274/5.

306. 118/3.

307. 118/3, 642/4.

308. 636/4.

309. See, for example, Hermione bleeding, 341/3; Harry bleeding, 632/4, a girl covered in blood; other children wounded and bleeding, 794–95/5.

310. Eagan Hunter, "Adolescent Attraction to Cults," *Adolescence* 33, no. 131 (1998): 709–14; "It is not the magic, but the morality of Harry Potter that is truly subversive." Jullian Sanchez, "Eichmann In Hogwarts: Harry Potter and the Banality of Evil," July 2, 2003, http://reason.com/archives/2003/07/02/eichmann-in-hogwarts

311. In addition to the examples quoted previously, see, for example, 215/4, 3/7, 7/7, 801–2/5, 648/4.

312. 84–85/7.

313. For example, 727/5.

314. 573/6.

315. 658/4.

316. 637–38/4.

317. For example, 602–3/4. Marc Bousquet points at the growing conviction in mass media that "torture can be 'good' when employed against 'evil people.'" Marc Bousquet, "Harry Potter, the War against Evil, and the Melodramatization of Public Culture," in *Critical Perspectives on Harry Potter*, 178. Bousquet also notices that Harry, "a victimized, misunderstood hero, who often appears paranoid or delusions to others—is a significant component of the success of the Harry Potter series," and that "one mode of reading the Harry Potter series, therefore, is in the mode of cultural pathology" (178).

318. In addition to previously cited, see: a pupil tortured by a teacher, 218/4, 232/4, 267/5.

319. 295/1.

320. 55/1.

321. 602/4.

322. *The Diane Rehm Show*.

323. On "invention" of childhood see Philippe Ariès, *L'Enfant et la vie familiale sous l'Ancien Régime* (Paris: Plon, 1960).

324. On uses of neomedievalism, new medievalism and various appropriations of medievalism in contemporary society, see Umberto Eco, "Dreaming of the Middle Ages," in *Travels in Hyperreality*, trans. W. Weaver (New York: Harcourt Brace, 1986), 61–72; Hedley Bull, *The Anarchical Society. A Study of Order in World Politics* (New York: Columbia University Press, 1977); Bruce Holsinger, *Neomedievalism, Neoconservatism, and the War on Terror* (Chicago: Prickly Paradigm Press, 2007); Frank Ankersmit, "Manifesto for an Analytical Political History," in *Manifestos for History*, ed. Keith Jenkins, Sue Morgan, and Alun Munslow (London, New York: Routledge, 2007), 179–96; Gabrielle M. Spiegel, "Getting Medieval: History and the Torture Memos," *Perspectives on History*, September 2008; Khapaeva, *Portrait critique de la Russie*, 127–42; Elise Impara, "Medieval Violence and Criminology: Using the Middle Ages to Understand Contemporary 'Motiveless' Crime," *Journal of Theoretical and Philosophical Criminology* 8, no. 1 (2016): 26–36.

325. "However, how children engage with this increasingly sensitive area of the books and films raises interesting questions for future research." A. Burn, "Potter-Literacy: From Book to Game and Back Again; Literature, Film, Game and Cross-Media Literacy," *Papers: Explorations into Children's Literature* 14, no. 3 (2005): 17. See also "Introduction: Fostering Insight Through Multiple Critical Perspectives," in *Critical Perspectives on Harry Potter*, 1–11. On Harry Potter as "escapist and consolatory fantasy," see Farah Mendlesohn, "Crowning the King: Harry Potter and the Construction of Authority," 167.

326. "[T]he trend in teen-age literature has been towards dark, reality-based fiction." Chris Crowe, "Young Adult Literature: The Problem with YAL," *The English Journal* 90, no. 3 (January 2001): 149.

327. On the contrary, the series was more often regarded as literature offering moral lessons and a new version of Bildungsroman: Nicholas Sheltron, "Harry Potter's World as a Morality Tale of Technology and Media," 47–65; and Peter Appelbaum, "The Great Snape Debate," 83–101.

328. Karl S. Rosengren, Isabel T. Gutiérrez, and Stevie S. Schein, "Cognitive Dimensions of Death in Context" in *Children's Understanding of Death: Toward a Contextualized and Integrated Account*, ed. Karl S. Rosengren, Peggy J. Miller, Isabel T. Gutierrez, Philip I. Chow, Stevie S. Schein, Kathy N. Anderson, and Maureen A. Callanan (Hoboken, NJ: Wiley-Blackwell, 2014), 60.

329. Peter Vardy, "Dead Reckoning," *The Times Higher Education Supplement*, August 18, 2011, 38.

330. On Harry as a "postmodern child," see Drew Chappell, "Sneaking Out After Dark: Resistance, Agency, and the Postmodern Child in JK Rowling's Harry Potter Series," *Children's Literature in Education* 39, no. 4 (2008): 281–93: "The Harry Potter series suggests to young readers that they can embrace qualities of postmodern

childhood—ambiguity, complexity, agency, resistance—rather than accept binaries promoted and constructed in traditional literature. These qualities facilitate the questioning of injustices established by and through the adult world of control" (292).

331. Natov, "Harry Potter and the Extraordinariness of the Ordinary," 310–27. Natov believes that Rowling's plot is heavily dependent on reality-grounded and plausible schema about a struggle between good Harry and evil Voldemort: "Rowling, I believe, is essentially a novelist, strongest when writing about the real world. Harry has a psychology; his problems need resolution in the real world" (314, 319, 321); and "Rowling attempts to humanize the demonic, rather than demonize the human" (322).

332. "Maurice Sendak on Children's Stories," http://wingfeathersaga.com/maurice-sendak-on-childrens-stories/. "The Harry Potter stories center on what children need to find internally—the strength to do the right thing, to establish a moral code." Natov, "Harry Potter and the Extraordinariness of the Ordinary," 324.

333. Anthony Gierzynski, *Harry Potter and the Millennials: Research Methods and the Politics of the Muggle Generation* (Baltimore: Johns Hopkins University Press, 2013).

334. Courtney B. Strimel, "The Politics of Terror: Rereading Harry Potter," *Children's Literature in Education* 35, no. 1 (2004): 35–52.

335. As the abstract of Strimel's article indicated.

336. http://www.mtv.com/news/1652609/emma-watson-felt-schizophrenic-shooting-harry-potter-and-the-deathly-hallows/

337. http://tinyurl.com/ozn2ltc

338. http://tinyurl.com/oxahedj

339. http://www.themarysue.com/daniel-radcliffe-harry-potter-quit/

340. http://tinyurl.com/obwjhh9

341. "The Return of Harry Potter," http://tinyurl.com/neobcb2

342. Taub, Servaty-Seib, "Controversial Content. Is Harry Potter Harmful for Children?" 18.

343. Taub, Servaty-Seib, "Controversial Content. Is Harry Potter Harmful for Children?" 22. For a view opposite to Taub and Servaty-Seib's, see Steven J. Kirsh, *Children, Adolescents and Media Violence: A Critical Look at the Research* (Thousand Oaks, CA: Sage Publications, 2006). "[C]hildren exposed to violent media can exhibit behavior changes ranging from sleep disturbances, academic struggles, and poor socialization to increases in anxiety, depression, and violent behavior" (Michael Rich, "Foreword," in *Media Violence and Children: A Complete Guide for Parents and Professionals*, 2nd ed., ed. Douglas A. Gentile [Santa Barbara: ABC-CLIO, 2014], xiii).

344. Jeffrey Michael Rudski, Carli Segal, and Eli Kallen, "Harry Potter and the End of the Road: Parallels with Addiction," *Journal of Addiction Research and Theory* 17, no. 3 (2009): 260–77.

345. Guy Dammann, "Harry Potter Breaks 400m in Sales," *The Guardian*, June 18, 2008, www.theguardian.com/business/2008/jun/18/harrypotter.artsandentertainment

346. Gillian Lathey, "The Travels of Harry: International Marketing and the Translation of J. K. Rowling's Harry Potter Books," *The Lion and the Unicorn* 29, no. 2 (2005).

347. *Harry Potter and the Philosopher's/Sorcerer's Stone* was translated by Il'ya Oransky (Moscow: Rosmen Publishing House, 2001). www.olmer.ru/hp/stat/23.shtml

348. See various translations at harrypotter.internetmagazin.ru or harrypotter.ru

349. http://hpclub.ru/. Compare with the Harry Potter Reading Club, http://hpread.scholastic.com/

350. On fandom sites and fanfics see, for example, http://ficbook.net/fanfiction/books/harri_potter and https://ficbook.net/readfic/2188314

351. http://tinyurl.com/o8s8yee

352. Dennis Karjala, "Harry Potter, Tanya Grotter, and the Copyright Derivative Work," *Arizona State Law Journal* 38 (2006) (also available at http://papers.ssrn.com/sol3/papers.cfm?abstract_id=1436760).

353. Dmitry Emets, *Tanya Grotter and the Magical Double Bass* (Moscow: Eksmo, 2002).

354. Emets, *Tanya Grotter*, 14.

355. Emets, *Tanya Grotter*, 44.

356. Emets, *Tanya Grotter*, 11, 18.

357. Emets, *Tanya Grotter*, 20, 32.

358. Emets, *Tanya Grotter*, 50.

359. Emets, *Tanya Grotter*, 4.

360. Emets, *Tanya Grotter*, 16, 18, 26, 28, 36.

361. Emets, *Tanya Grotter*, 41, 110.

362. Emets, *Tanya Grotter*, 21, 117.

363. Emets, *Tanya Grotter*, 111.

364. Emets, *Tanya Grotter*, 48.

365. Emets, *Tanya Grotter*, 124.

366. Emets, *Tanya Grotter*, 129.

367. Emets, *Tanya Grotter*, 126; 120; Van'ka, her friend, is injured, 124.

368. Emets, *Tanya Grotter*, 131.

369. Yury Tynyanov believed parody to be a fundamental principle of literature and art. Yury Tynyanov, "Dostoevsky and Gogol (Toward a Theory of Parody)," in *Poetics: A History of Literature* (Moscow: Kino, 1977).

370. Andrey Zhvalevsky and Igor' Mit'ko, *Porry Hatter and the Stone Philosopher* (Moscow: Vremya, 2002).

371. Harry Potter runs for president of Russia. http://nr2.ru/News/world_and_russia/garri-potter-tozhe-hochet-stat-prezidentom-rossii-14353.html

372. www.bbc.com/russian/russia/2015/05/150513_navalny_court_new

CONCLUSION

1. Khapaeva, *Nightmare*, 209–32; Khapaeva, *Portrait critique de la Russie*, 165–201.

2. This has been interpreted as an echo of the philosophical debates taking place at that time in England on the specificity of human nature in the chain of living organisms.

3. On the history of Gothic Aesthetic and the culture of nightmare consumption, see Khapaeva, *Nightmare*, 209–29.

4. David Rousset, *L'Univers concentrationnaire* (Paris: Pavois, 1946).

5. Theodor W. Adorno, *The Meaning of Working Through the Past* (1959), trans. Henry W. Pickford (New York: Columbia University Press, 1998), 95.

6. On the presence on the concentration camp universe in contemporary society, see Giorgio Agamben, *Homo Sacer*, trans. Marilene Raiola (Paris: Seuil, 1997). On the centrality of the memory of the Holocaust that holds "sacrosanct status" in American life, see Caroline J. Dean, *The Fragility of Empathy after the Holocaust* (Ithaca: Cornell University Press, 2005), 12.

7. Morton, *Trick or Treat*, 198.

8. *Understanding Dying, Death, and Bereavement*, 12.

Selected Bibliography

Adler, Margot. *Vampires Are Us: Understanding Our Love Affair with the Immortal Dark Side* (Newburyport: Weiser Books, 2014).

Adorno, Theodor W. "Culture Industry Reconsidered." *New German Critique*, no. 6 (1975): 12–19.

Adorno, Theodor W. *The Meaning of Working Through the Past* [1959]. Translated by Henry W. Pickford (New York: Columbia University Press, 1998).

Agamben, Giorgio. *Homo Sacer*. Translated by Marilene Raiola (Paris: Seuil, 1997).

Althusser, Louis. *For Marx* [1965]. Translated by Ben Brewster (London: Verso, 1990).

Anderson, Craig A., Douglas A. Gentile, and Katherine E. Buckley. *Violent Video Game Effects on Children and Adolescents: Theory, Research, and Public Policy* (New York: Oxford University Press, 2007).

Appelbaum, Peter. "The Great Snape Debate." In *Critical Perspectives on Harry Potter*, edited by Elizabeth E. Heilman (New York: Taylor & Francis, 2008), 83–101.

Ariès, Philippe. *The Hour of Our Death* (New York: Vintage Books, 1982).

Auerbach, Nina. *Our Vampires, Ourselves* (Chicago: University of Chicago Press, 1999).

Badmington, Neil. *Alien Chic: Posthumanism and the Other Within* (New York: Psychology Press, 2004).

Bakhtin, Mikhail. *Problems of Dostoevsky's Poetics*. Translated by Caryl Emerson (Minneapolis: University of Minnesota Press, 1984).

Bakhtin, Mikhail. *Rabelais and His World*. Translated by Helene Iswolsky (Bloomington: Indiana University Press, 2009).

Bannatyne, Lesley Pratt. *Halloween Nation: Behind the Scenes of America's Fright Night* (New Orleans: Pelican Publishing, 2011).

Barthes, Roland. "La mort de l'auteur" (1968), reprinted in Roland Barthes, *Le bruissement de la langue* (Paris: Seuil, 1984); English translation: "The Death of the Author," in *Barthes: Image, Music, Text*. Selected and translated by Stephen Heath (London: Fontana/Collins, 1977).

Baudrillard, Jean. *Fatal Strategies*. Translated by Phil Beitchman and W. W. J. Neisluchowski (Cambridge MA: MIT Press, 2008).

Baudrillard, Jean. *Symbolic Exchange and Death*. Translated by Ian H. Grant (New York: Sage Publications, 1993).

Baudrillard, Jean. *The Transparency of Evil* (London: Verso, 1993).

Becker, Ernest. *The Denial of Death* (New York: Free Press Paperbacks, 1973).

Belk, Russell W. "Halloween: An Evolving American Consumption Ritual." In *Advances in Consumer Research*, edited by Marvin E. Goldberg, Gerald Gorn, Richard W. Pollay (Provo: Association for Consumer Research), 508–17.

Best, Steven. "The Rise of Critical Animal Studies: Putting Theory into Action and Animal Liberation into Higher Education." *Journal for Critical Animal Studies* 7, no. 1 (2009): 9–52.

Beville, Maria. *The Unnameable Monster in Literature and Film: The 'Thing' as Itself* (London, New York: Routledge, 2013).

Billone, Amy Christine. "The Boy Who Lived: From Carroll's Alice and Barrie's Peter Pan to Rowling's Harry Potter." In *Children's Literature* 32 (2004): 178–202.

Black, Joel. *The Aesthetics of Murder* (Baltimore: Johns Hopkins University Press, 1991).

Bloom, Clive, ed. *Gothic Horror: A Guide for Students and Readers*, 2nd ed. (Basingstoke: Palgrave MacMillan, 2007).

Borenstein, Elliot. *Overkill: Sex and Violence in Contemporary Russian Popular Culture* (Ithaca: Cornell University Press, 2007).

Bousquet, Marc. "Harry Potter, the War against Evil, and the Melodramatization of Public Culture." In *Critical Perspectives on Harry Potter*, edited by Elizabeth E. Heilman (New York: Taylor & Francis, 2008), 177–95.

Bostrom, Nick. "A History of Transhumanist Thought." *Journal of Evolution and Technology* 14, no. 1 (2005): 1–25.

Botting, Fred. *The Gothic* (Cambridge: D. S. Brewer, 2001).

Bourke, Joanna. *What It Means to Be Human: Historical Reflections from the 1800s to the Present* (Berkeley, CA: Counterpoint, 2013).

Bouveresse, Jean. "L'objectivité, la connaissance et le pouvoir." In *L'infréquentable Michel Foucault: Renouveaux de la pensée critique*, edited by Didier Eribon (Paris: Actes du Colloque au Centre Georges Pompidou, 2000).

Bové, Paul A. *Intellectuals in Power: A Genealogy of Critical Humanism* (New York: Columbia University Press, 1986).

Brooks, Jeffrey. "Marvelous Destruction: The Left-Leaning Satirical Magazines of 1905–1907." *Experiment* 19, no. 1 (2013): 24–62.

Brooks, Jeffrey. *Thank You, Comrade Stalin! Soviet Public Culture from Revolution to Cold War* (Princeton: Princeton University Press, 1999).

Burke, Seán. *The Death and Return of the Author: Criticism and Subjectivity in Barthes, Foucault and Derrida* (Edinburgh: Edinburgh University Press, 1992).

Butler, Erik. *Metamorphoses of the Vampire in Literature and Film: Cultural Transformations in Europe, 1732–1933* (New York: Camden House, 2010).

Canguilhem, Georges. "The Death of Man, or, Exhaustion of the Cogito?" In *The Cambridge Companion to Foucault*, edited by Gary Gutting (Cambridge: Cambridge University Press, 2005).

Carroll, Noel. *The Philosophy of Horror: Or, Paradoxes of the Heart* [1990] (New York: Routledge, 2003).

Carver, Terrell. *The Postmodern Marx* (Manchester: Manchester University Press, 1998).

Chance, Jane. *Tolkien's Art* (Lexington: University Press of Kentucky, 2001).

Chartier, Roger. "Les arts de mourir, 1450–1600." *Annales: Économies, Sociétés, Civilisations* 31, no. 1 (1976): 51–75.

Chesnut, R. Andrew. *Devoted to Death: Santa Muerte, the Skeleton Saint* (Oxford: Oxford University Press, 2012).

Christie, Deborah. "Richard Matheson and the Modern Zombie." In *Better Off Dead: The Evolution of the Zombie as Post-Human*, edited by Deborah Christie, Sarah Juliet Lauro (New York: Fordham University Press, 2011), 67–80.

Cockrell, Amanda. "Harry Potter and the Secret Password: Finding Our Way in the Magical Genre." In *The Ivory Tower and Harry Potter: Perspectives on a Literary Phenomenon*, edited by Lana A. Whited (Columbia: University of Missouri Press, 2002), 15–26.

Colavito, Jason. *Knowing Fear: Science, Knowledge and the Development of the Horror Genre* (Jefferson, NC: McFarland & Company, 2008).

Crowe, Chris. "Young Adult Literature: The Problem with YAL." *English Journal* 90, no. 3 (2001): 134–51.

Cummins, June. "Hermione in the Bathroom: The Gothic, Menarche, and Female Development in the Harry Potter Series." In *The Gothic in Children's Literature: Haunting the Borders*, edited by Anna Jackson, Roderick McGillis, and Karen Coats (London: Routledge, 2013), 177–93.

Cusset, François. *French Theory: How Foucault, Derrida, Deleuze, & Co Transformed the Intellectual Life of the United States* (Minneapolis: University of Minnesota Press, 2008).

Davies, Douglas. *Death, Ritual and Belief* (London: Continuum International, 2002).

Davies, Douglas J., and Hannah Rumble. *Natural Burial: Traditional-Secular Spiritualities and Funeral Innovation* (London: Continuum, 2012).

Davis, Colin. *Haunted Subjects: Deconstruction, Psychoanalysis and the Return of the Dead* (London: Palgrave McMillan, 2007).

Davies, Tony. *Humanism* (London: Routledge, 2006).

Dean, Caroline. J. *The Fragility of Empathy after the Holocaust* (Ithaca: Cornell University Press, 2005).

Derrida, Jacques. *The Animal That Therefore I Am*. Translated by David Wills (New York: Fordham University Press, 2008).

Derrida, Jacques. "The Law of Genre." Translated by Avital Ronell. *Critical Inquiry* 7, no. 1 (1980): 55–81.

Derrida, Jacques. *Specters of Marx: The State of the Debt, the Work of Mourning, and the New International*. Translated by Peggy Kamuf (London: Routledge, 1994).

Derrida, Jacques. "Violence Against Animals." In *For What Tomorrow . . . A Dialogue*, edited by Jacques Derrida and Élisabeth Roudinesco. Translated by Jeff Fort (Stanford, CA: Stanford University Press, 2004).

Dosse, François. *History of Structuralism: The Rising Sign, 1945–1966* (Minneapolis: University of Minnesota Press, 1997).

Durkin, Keith F. "Death, Dying, and the Dead in Popular Culture." In *Handbook of Death & Dying*, edited by Clifton D. Bryant (Thousand Oaks, CA: Sage Publications, 2003), 1:43–49.

Elias, Norbert. *The Loneliness of the Dying* (1985) (London: Bloomsbury Publishing USA, 2001).

Ellis, Bill. "Safe Spooks: New Halloween Traditions in Response to Sadism Legends." In *Halloween and Other Festivals of Death and Life*, edited by Jack Santino (Knoxville: University of Tennessee Press, 1994), 22–44.

Elyutina, M. E., and S. V. Filippova. "Ritual Burial Practices: Substantive Changes" [Ritual'nye pokhoronnye praktiki: soderzhatel'nye izmeneniya]. *Sotsiologicheskie issledovaniya*, no. 9 (2010): 86–94.

Esposito, Roberto. *Bios: Biopolitics and Philosophy (Posthumanities)* (Minneapolis: University of Minnesota Press, 2008).

Evans, Caroline. *Fashion at the Edge: Spectacle, Modernity and Deathliness* (New Haven: Yale University Press, 2003).

Faust, Drew Gilpin. *This Republic of Suffering: Death and the American Civil War* (New York: Vintage Books, 2009).

Ferguson, Christopher J., Stephanie M. Rueda, Amanda M. Cruz, Diana E. Ferguson, Stacey Fritz, and Shawn M. Smith. "Violent Video Games and Aggression: Causal Relationship or Byproduct of Family Violence and Intrinsic Violence Motivation?" *Criminal Justice and Behavior* 35, no. 3 (March 2008): 311–32.

Ferry, Luc, and Alain Renaut. *La pensée 68: Essai sur l'anti-humanisme contemporain* (Paris: Gallimard, 1985).

Foley, Malcolm, and J. John Lennon. "JFK and Dark Tourism: A Fascination with Assassination." *International Journal of Heritage Studies* 2 (1996): 198–211.

Foltyn, Jacque Lynn. "Dead Famous and Dead Sexy: Popular Culture, Forensics, and the Rise of the Corpse." *Mortality* 13, no. 2 (2008): 153–73.

Foucault, Michel. *Archeology of Knowledge*. Translated by Rupert Sawyer (New York: Vintage Books, 2010).

Foucault, Michel. *The Order of Things* (New York: Vintage Books, 1994).

Freedman, Jonathan L. *Media Violence and Its Effect on Aggression: Assessing the Scientific Evidence* (Toronto: University of Toronto Press, 2002).

Friedländer, Saul. *Reflections of Nazism: An Essay on Kitsch and Death* (Bloomington: Indiana University Press, 1993).

Fukuyama, Francis. *Our Posthuman Future: Consequences of the Biotechnology Revolution* (New York: Farrar, Straus & Giroux, 2002).

Furet, François. *The Passing of an Illusion: The Idea of Communism in the Twentieth Century* (Chicago: University of Chicago Press, 2000).

Gabriel, S., and A. F. Young. "Becoming a Vampire Without Being Bitten: The Narrative Collective-Assimilation Hypothesis." *Psychological Science* 22 (2011): 990–94.

Gallagher, Catherine. *The Body Economic: Life, Death, and Sensation in Political Economy and the Victorian Novel* (Princeton: Princeton University Press, 2008).

Garces-Foley, Kathy. *Death and Religion in a Changing World* (Armonk, NY: M. E. Sharpe, 2006).

de Garis, Hugo. *Multis and Monos: What the Multicultured Can Teach the Monocultured: Towards the Creation of a Global State* (Palm Springs, CA: ETC Publications, 2010).

Garrett, Peter K. *Gothic Reflections: Narrative Force in Nineteenth-Century Fiction* (Ithaca: Cornell University Press, 2003).

Geary, Patrick J. *Living with the Dead in the Middle Ages* (Ithaca: Cornell University Press, 1994).

Gerbner, George, Larry Gross, Michael Morgan, and Nancy Signorielli. "Living with Television: The Dynamic of the Cultivation Process." In *Perspectives on Media Effects*, edited by Jennings Bryan and Dolf Zillman (Hillsdale, NJ: Lawrence Erlbaum Associates, 1986), 17–40.

Gierzynski, Anthony. *Harry Potter and the Millennials: Research Methods and the Politics of the Muggle Generation* (Baltimore: Johns Hopkins University Press, 2013).

Gilmore, David. *Monsters: Evil Beings, Mythical Beasts, and All Manners of Imaginary Terrors* (Philadelphia: University of Pennsylvania Press, 2002).

Girard, René. *The Scapegoat.* Translated by Yvonne Freccero (Baltimore: Johns Hopkins University Press, 1986).

Goldberg, Vicki. "Death Takes a Holiday, Sort Of." In *Why We Watch*, edited by Jeffrey Goldstein (New York: Oxford University Press, 1998), 27–52.

Good, Graham. *Humanism Betrayed: Theory, Ideology and Culture in the Contemporary University* (Montreal: McGill-Queen's University Press, 2001).

Goodrick-Clarke, Nicholas. *The Occult Roots of Nazism* (Wellingborough, Northamptonshire, UK: Aquarian Press, 1985).

Gorer, Geoffrey. "The Pornography of Death." *Encounter*, October 1955, 49–52.

Gottfried, Robert S. *The Black Death* (New York: Simon & Schuster, 2010).

Graham, Allen. *Roland Barthes* (London: Routledge, 2003).

Granger, John. *How Harry Cast His Spell: The Meaning Behind the Mania for J. K. Rowling's Bestselling Books* (Carol Stream, IL: Tyndale House, 2014).

Granger, John. *Unlocking Harry Potter: Five Keys for the Serious Reader* (Cheshire: Zossima Press, 2007).

Greek, Cecil, and Caroline Joan Picart. "The Compulsion of Real/Reel Serial Killers And Vampires: Toward A Gothic Criminology." *Journal of Criminal Justice and Popular Culture* 10, no. 1 (2003): 39–68.

Grimes, Ronald L. *Deeply into the Bone: Re-inventing Rites of Passage* (Berkeley: University of California Press, 2000).

Grixti, Joseph. *Terrors of Uncertainty: The Cultural Contexts of Horror Fiction* (London: Routledge, 1989).

Gros, François. "Foucault face à son œuvre" In *Lectures de Michel Foucault*, vol. 3 (Lyon: ENS Éditions, 2003), 93–101.

Gumbrecht, Hans Ulrich. *Atmosphere, Mood, Stimmung: On A Hidden Potential of Literature.* Trans. Erik Butler (Stanford, CA: Stanford University Press, 2012).

Gurdon, Meghan Cox. "Darkness Too Visible." *Wall Street Journal*, June 4, 2011.

Halliwell, Martin, and Andrew Mousley. *Critical Humanisms: Humanist/Anti-Humanist Dialogues* (Edinburgh: Edinburgh University Press, 2003).

Han, Béatrice. *L'ontologie manquée de Michel Foucault: Entre l'historique et le transcendantal* (Paris: Editions Jérôme Millon, 1998).

Hand, Richard J., and Joy McRoy, eds. *Monstrous Adaptations: Generic and Thematic Mutations in Horror Film* (Manchester: Manchester University Press, 2007).

Haraway, Donna J. "Cyborg Manifesto: Science, Technology, and Socialist-Feminism in the Twentieth Century." In *Simians, Cyborgs and Women: The Reinvention of Nature* (New York: Routledge, 1991), 149–81.

Haraway, Donna Jeanne, and Thyrza Nichols. *How Like a Leaf: An Interview with Thyrza Nichols Goodeve* (New York: Psychology Press, 2000).

Hart, Kylo-Patrick R., and Annette M. Holba, eds. *Media and the Apocalypse* (New York: Peter Lang, 2009).

Hayles, Katherine, and Niklas Luhmann. "Theory of a Different Order: A Conversation with Katherine Hayles and Niklas Luhmann." In *Observing Complexity: Systems Theory and Postmodernity*, edited by Carey Wolfe, William Rasch (Minneapolis: University of Minnesota Press, 2000).

Heessels, Meike. "Every Funeral Unique in (Y)our Way! Professionals Propagating Cremation Rituals." In *Emotion, Identity, and Death: Mortality across Disciplines*, edited by Douglas J. Davies and Chang-Won Park (Burlington: Ashgate, 2012), 125–45.

Hénaff, Marcel. *Claude Lévi-Strauss and the Making of Structural Anthropology* (Minneapolis: University of Minnesota Press, 1998).

Hertz, Robert. *Death and the Right Hand* (1907). Translated by Rodney and Claudia Needham (Glencoe, IL: The Free Press, 1960).

Herwig, Holger H. "The Cult of Heroic Death in Nazi Architecture." in *War Memory and Popular Culture: Essays on Modes of Remembrance and Commemoration*, edited by Michael Keren and Holger H. Herwig (Jefferson, NC: McFarland, 2009).

Hollinger, Veronica. "Apocalypse Coma." In *Edging into the Future: Science Fiction and Contemporary Cultural Transformation*, edited by Veronica Hollinger, Joan Gordon (Philadelphia: University of Pennsylvania Press, 2002).

Horkheimer, Max, and Theodor W. Adorno. "The Culture Industry: Enlightenment as Mass Deception." In *Dialectic of Enlightenment* (New York: Herder and Herder, 1972).

Housel, Rebecca. "The 'Real' Danger: Fact vs. Fiction for the Girl Audience." In *Twilight and Philosophy: Vampires, Vegetarians, and the Pursuit of Immortality*, edited by Rebecca Housel, J. Jeremy Wisnewski, and William Irwin (Hoboken, NJ: John Wiley & Sons, 2009), 177–92.

Howart, Glennys. *Death and Dying: A Sociological Introduction* (Cambridge: Polity, 2007).

Huizinga, Johan. *The Autumn of the Middle Ages*. Translated by Rodney J. Payton and Ulrich Mammitzsch (Chicago: University of Chicago Press, 1996).

Huntington, Richard, and Peter Metcalf. *Celebrations of Death: The Anthropology of Mortuary Ritual* (Cambridge: Cambridge University Press, 1979).

Hutton, Ronald. *The Stations of the Sun: A History of the Ritual Year in Britain* (Oxford: Oxford University Press, 1996).

Huxley, Julian. "Transhumanism." In *New Bottles for New Wine* (London: Chatto & Windus, 1957), 13–17.

Ingraham, Catherine. "What Is Posthumanism?" *Future Anterior* 7, no. 1 (Summer 2010): 96–103.

Jameson, Fredric. *Postmodernism or, The Cultural Logic of Late Capitalism* (London: Verso, 1991).

Jantzen, Grace M. *Foundations of Violence* (New York: Taylor & Francis, 2008).

Jay, Martin. *Songs of Experience: Modern American and European Variations on a Universal Theme* (Berkeley: University of California Press, 2005).

Jenkins, Catherine. "Life Extension, Immortality and the Patient Voice." In *The Power of Death: Contemporary Reflections on Death in Western Society*, edited by Maria-Jose Blanco and Ricarda Vidal (New York: Berghahn Books, 2014), 13–22.

Jenkins, Philip. *Using Murder: The Social Construction of Serial Homicide* (Chicago: AldineTransaction, 1994).

Jones, Steve. *Torture Porn: Popular Horror after Saw* (New York: Palgrave Macmillan, 2013).

Judt, Tony. *Past Imperfect: French Intellectuals, 1944–1956* (Oakland: University of California Press, 1994).

Judt, Tony. *Postwar: A History of Europe Since 1945* (London: Penguin Books, 2006).

Kearl, Michael C. "What Death Means." In *Endings: A Sociology of Death and Dying* (Oxford: Oxford University Press, 1989), 25–42.

Kearney, Richard. *Strangers, Gods, and Monsters: Interpreting Otherness* (London: Routledge, 2003).

Kellehar, Allan. *A Social History of Dying* (Cambridge: Cambridge University Press, 2007).

Kelly, Catriona. *St Petersburg: Shadows of the Past* (New Haven: Yale University Press, 2014).

Kern, Edmund M. *The Wisdom of Harry Potter: What Our Favorite Hero Teaches Us about Moral Choices* (Amherst, NY: Prometheus, 2003)

Khapaeva, Dina. *Dukes of the Republic in the Age of Translation: Humanities and the Conceptual Revolution* (Moscow: Novoe literaturnoe obozrenie, 2005).

Khapaeva, Dina. *Gothic Society: A Morphology of Nightmare* (Moscow: Novoe literaturnoe obozrenie, 2007) (2nd ed., 2008).

Khapaeva, Dina. "Historical Memory in Post-Soviet Gothic Society." *Social Research* 76, no. 1 (2009): 359–94.

Khapaeva, Dina. "The Vampire, a Hero of Our Time." *Novoe literaturnoe obozrenie* 109 (2011): 44–61.

Khapaeva, Dina. "Break of Language: A Russian French Comparison." *Journal of Russian Communications* 4, nos. 1/2 (2011): 94–113.

Khapaeva, Dina. *Portrait critique de la Russie: Essais sur la société gothique*, trans. from Russian by Nina Kehayan (La Tour d'Aigues: Éditions de l'Aube, 2012).

Khapaeva, Dina. "The International Vampire Boom and Post-Soviet Gothic Aesthetic." In *Gothic Topographies: Language, Nation Building and "Race"*, edited by P. M. Mehtonen and Matti Savolainen (London: Ashgate, 2013), 143–69.

Khapaeva, Dina. *Nightmare: From Literary Reality to Cultural Project*, trans. from Russian by Rosie Tweddle (Amsterdam: Brill, 2013).

Khapaeva, Dina. "Triumphant Memory of the Perpetrators: Putin's Politics of Re-Stalinization." *Communist and Post-Communist Studies* 49 (2016): 61–73.

Khapaeva, Dina, and Nicolaï Kopossov. "Les demi-dieux de la mythologie soviétique," *Annales: Economies, Sociétés, Civilisations* 47, nos. 4–5 (1992) 963–89.

King, C. Richard. "(Mis)uses of Cannibalism in Contemporary Cultural Critique." *Diacritics* 30, no. 1 (Spring 2000): 106–23.

Kirsh, Steven J. *Children, Adolescents and Media Violence: A Critical Look at the Research* (Thousand Oaks, CA: Sage Publications, 2006).

Klemp, Annette. "Evil and the Loss of Identity." In *Phoenix Rising: Collected Papers on Harry Potter*, edited by Sharon K. Goetz (Sedalia, CO: Narrate Conferences, 2008), 119–20.

Konner, Melvin. "Sacred Violence, Mimetic Rivalry, and War." In *Mimesis and Science: Empirical Research on Imitation and the Mimetic Theory of Culture and Religion*, edited by Scott R. Garrels (East Lansing: Michigan State University Press, 2011), 155–74.

Koposov, Nikolay. "L'Univers clos des signes: Vers une histoire du paradigme linguistique." In *De Russie et d'ailleurs: Mélanges Marc Ferro*, edited by Martine Godet (Paris: Institut d'études slaves, 1995), 501–13.

Koselleck, Reinhart. *The Practice of Conceptual History: Timing History, Spacing Concepts* (Stanford: Stanford University Press, 2002).

Kremleva, I. A. "Burial and Memorial Customs and Rituals" [Pokhoronno-pominal'nye obychai i obryady]. In *The Russians: Folk Culture, Then and Now* [Russkie: narodnaya kul'tura (istoriya i sovremennost')], vol. 3: *Family Life* [Semeiny byt] (Moscow: IEA RAN, 2000), 231–65.

Kübler-Ross, Elisabeth. *Questions and Answers on Death and Dying* (New York: Macmillan, 1974).

Kumar, Krishan. "Apocalypse, Millennium and Utopia Today." In *Apocalypse Theory and the Ends of the Earth*, edited by Malcolm Bull (Oxford: Blackwell, 1995).

Kurzweil, Ray. *The Singularity Is Near: When Humans Transcend Biology* (New York: Viking, 2005).

Lacroix, Paul. *Manners, Custom and Dress During the Middle Ages and During the Renaissance Period* [1878] (New York: Kessinger Publishing, 2010).

Lane, Christel. *The Rites of Rulers: Ritual in Industrial Society* (Cambridge: Cambridge University Press, 1981).

Latour, Bruno. *Reassembling the Social: An Introduction to Actor-Network-Theory* (Oxford: Oxford University Press, 2005).

Laqueur, Thomas W. *The Work of the Dead: A Cultural History of Mortal Remains* (Princeton: Princeton University Press, 2015).

Lathey, Gillian. "The Travels of Harry: International Marketing and the Translation of J. K. Rowling's Harry Potter Books." *The Lion and the Unicorn* 29, no. 2 (2005): 141–51.

Leming, Michael R., and George E. Dickinson, eds. *Understanding Dying, Death, and Bereavement*, 6th ed. (Belmont, CA: Thomson Publishing, 2007).

Leskin, Vladimir. "To Die in Russia" [Umeret' v Rossii]. *Mir v Rossii*, no. 4 (2010): 124–61.

Lévi-Strauss, Claude. *The Savage Mind* (Chicago: University of Chicago Press, 1966).

Lévi-Strauss, Claude. *Structural Anthropology*. Translated by Monique Layton (Chicago: University of Chicago Press, 1983).

Lipovetsky, Marc. *Russian Postmodernist Fiction: Dialogue with Chaos* (Armonk, NY: M. E. Sharpe, 1999).

Llored, Patrick. *Jacques Derrida: Politique et éthique de l'animalité* (Paris: Sils Maria, 2012).

Lloyd-Smith, Allan, and David Punter, eds. *A Companion to the Gothic* (Oxford: Blackwell, 2000).

Lyotard, Jean-François. *Le Tombeau de l'intellectuel, et autres papiers* (Paris: Galilée, 1984).

Lyotard, Jean-François. *The Inhuman: Reflections on Time*, trans. Geoffrey Bennington and Rachel Bowlby (Cambridge: Polity Press, 1991).

Magliocco, Sabina. *Witching Culture: Folklore and Neo-Paganism in America* (Philadelphia: University of Pennsylvania Press, 2004).

Malin, Irving. *New American Gothic* (Carbondale: Southern Illinois University Press, 1962).

Marchi, Regina M. *Day of the Dead in the USA: The Migration and Transformation of a Cultural Phenomenon* (New Brunswick, NJ: Rutgers University Press, 2009).

McCauley, Clark. "When Screen Violence Is Not Attractive." In *Why We Watch*, edited by Jeffrey Goldstein (New York: Oxford University Press, 1998), 144–62.

Megill, Allan. *Prophets of Extremity: Nietzsche, Heidegger, Foucault, Derrida* (Berkeley: University of California Press, 1985).

Metcalf, Peter, and Richard Huntington, eds. *Celebrations of Death: The Anthropology of Mortuary Ritual*, 2nd ed. (Cambridge: Cambridge University Press, 1991).

Miah, Andy. "A Critical History of Posthumanism." In *Medical Enhancements & Posthumanity*, edited by Bert Gordijn and Ruth Chadwick (New York: Routledge, 2007), 71–94.

Mighall, Robert. *Geography of Victorian Gothic Fiction: Mapping History's Nightmares* (New York: Oxford University Press, 1999).

Miles, Robert. *Gothic Writing 1750–1820: A Genealogy*, 2nd ed. (Manchester: Manchester University Press, 2002).

Mitford, Jessica. *The American Way of Death* (1963) (New York: Buccaneer Books, 1993).

Moeller, Susan D. *Compassion Fatigue: How The Media Sell Disease, Famine, War, and Death* (New York: Routledge, 1999).

Mongin, Olivier. *Face au scepticisme: Les mutations du paysage intellectuel (1976–1998)* (Paris: Hachette, 1998).

Montillo, Roseanne. *Halloween and Commemorations of the Dead* (New York: Infobase Publishing, 2009).

Morton, Lisa. *Trick or Treat: A History of Halloween* (London: Reaktion Books, 2013).

Natov, Roni. *The Poetics of Childhood* (New York: Routledge, 2012).

Nel, Philip. "Is There a Text in This Advertising Campaign? Literature, Marketing, and Harry Potter," *The Lion and the Unicorn* 29, no. 2 (2005): 236–67.

Nietzsche, Friedrich. *"On the Genealogy of Morality" and Other Writings*. Edited by Keith Ansell-Pearson. Translated by Carol Diethe (Cambridge: Cambridge University Press, 2007).

Nikolaejeva, Maria. "Harry Potter and the Secrets of Children's Literature." In *Critical Perspectives on Harry Potter*, edited by Elizabeth E. Heilman (New York: Taylor & Francis, 2008), 230–45.

Noctor, Colman. "Putting Harry Potter on the Couch." *Clinical Child Psychology and Psychiatry*, no. 11 (2006): 579–89.

Nora, Pierre. "L'Ère de la commémoration." In *Les Lieux de mémoire*, vol. III, edited by Pierre Nora (Paris: Gallimard, 1992), 346–93.

Norris, Christopher. *Derrida* (Cambridge, MA: Harvard University Press, 1987).

Nussbaum, Martha. "Mortal Immortals: Lucretius on Death and the Voice of Nature." *Philosophy and Phenomenological Research* 50 (1989): 303–51.

Paglia, Camille. *Vamps & Tramps: New Essays* (New York: Knopf Doubleday, 2011).

Paik, Peter Yoonsuk. *From Utopia to Apocalypse: Science Fiction and the Politics of Catastrophe* (Minneapolis: University of Minnesota Press, 2010).

Parasecoli, Fabio. *Bite Me: Food in Popular Culture* (Oxford: Berg Publishers, 2008).

Parkes, Colin Murray. "Conclusions II: Attachments and Losses in Cross-Cultural Perspectives." In *Death and Bereavement Across Cultures*, edited by Colin Murray Parkes, Pittu Laungani, and William Young (London: Routledge, 2003).

Patrick, C. J., and Sarah K. Patrick. "Exploring the Dark Side: Harry Potter and the Psychology of Evil." In *The Psychology of Harry Potter: An Unauthorized Examination of the Boy Who Lived*, edited by Neil Mulholland (New York: Smart Pop Books, 2007), 210–25.

Patterson, Diana, ed. *Harry Potter's World Wide Influence* (Cambridge: Cambridge Scholars Publishing, 2009).

Pennington, John. "From Elfland to Hogwarts, or the Aesthetic Trouble with Harry Potter," *The Lion and the Unicorn* 26, no. 1 (2002): 78–97.

Petersen, Jesper Aagaard, ed. *Contemporary Religious Satanism: A Critical Anthology* (Controversial New Religions). (London: Ashgate, 2009).

Platt, Kevin M. F. *History in a Grotesque Key: Russian Literature and the Idea of Revolution* (Stanford: Stanford University Press, 1997).

Plumwood, Val. "Tasteless: Towards a Food-Based Approach to Death." *Environmental Values* 17, no. 3 (2008).

Propp, Vladimir. *Morphology of the Folktale* [Morfologiya volshebnoi skazki] (1928). Translated by Laurence Scott (Bloomington: American Folklore Society and Indiana University Press, 1968).

Punter, David. *The Literature of Terror: A History of Gothic Fictions from 1765 to the Present Day*, 2 vols. (Harlow, Essex: Longman, 1996).

Punter, David, and Glennis Byron. *The Gothic* (London: Wiley, 2004).

Renner, Karen J. "Evil Children in Film and Literature." In *The "Evil Child" in Literature, Film and Popular Culture*, edited by Karen J. Renner (New York: Routledge, 2013).

Rogers, Nicholas. *Halloween: From Pagan Ritual to Party Night* (Oxford: Oxford University Press, 2002).

Rorty, Richard. "Moral Identity and Private Autonomy: The Case of Foucault." In *Essays on Heidegger and Others: Philosophical Papers*, vol. 2 (Cambridge: Cambridge University Press, 1991), 193–98.

Santino, Jack. "Introduction: Festivals of Life and Death." In *Halloween and Other Festivals of Death and Life*, edited by Jack Santino (Knoxville: University of Tennessee Press, 1994).

Sax, Boria. *Animals in the Third Reich: Pets, Scapegoats, and the Holocaust* (London: A & C Black Publishers, 2000).

Schaeffer, Jean-Marie. *La Fin de l'exception humaine* (Paris: Seuil, 2007).

Schmid, David. *Natural Born Celebrities: Serial Killers in American Culture* (Chicago: University of Chicago Press, 2005).

Senf, Carol. *Bram Stoker* (Cardiff: University of Wales Press, 2010).

Sewell, William H. *Logics of History: Social Theory and Social Transformation* (Chicago: University of Chicago Press, 2005).

Sharpley, Richard, and Philip R. Stone, eds. *The Darker Side of Travel: The Theory and Practice of Dark Tourism* (Bristol: Channel View Publications, 2009).

Shea, Brendan. "To Bite or Not to Bite: Twilight, Immortality and the Meaning of Life." In *Twilight and Philosophy: Vampires, Vegetarians, and the Pursuit of Immortality*, edited by Rebecca Housel, J. Jeremy Wisnewski, and William Irwin (Hoboken, NJ: John Wiley & Sons, 2009), 79–93.

Shillabeer, Rebecca. "The Fascination with Torture and Death in Twenty-First-Century Crime Fiction." In *The Power of Death: Contemporary Reflections on Death in Western Society*, Maria-Jose Blanco and Ricarda Vidal (New York: Berghahn Books, 2014), 102–15.

Shippey, Tom A. *The Road to Middle-Earth: How J. R. R. Tolkien Created a New Mythology* (New York: HarperCollins, 2005).

Simpson, Philip. *Psycho Paths: Tracking the Serial Killer Through Contemporary American Film and Fiction* (Carbondale: Southern Illinois University Press, 2000).

Singer, Peter. *Animal Liberation: A New Ethics for our Treatment of Animals* (New York: Random House, 1975).

Singer, Peter. *Rethinking Life and Death: The Collapse of Our Traditional Ethics* (Melbourne: Text Publishing, 1994).

Skal, David J. *Death Makes a Holiday: A Cultural History of Halloween* (New York: Bloomsbury USA, 2002).

Slocum, Joshua, and Lisa Carlso. *Final Rights: Reclaiming the American Way of Death* (Hinesburg, VT: Upper Access Books, 2011).

Sobchack, Vivian. *Carnal Thoughts: Embodiment and Moving Image Culture* (Berkeley: University of California Press, 2004).

Sokolova, Tatyana. "'Funerals Without a Corpse': Transformations in the Traditional Burial Ritual" ['Pokhorony bez pokoinika': transformatsii traditsionnnogo pokhoronnogo obryada]. *Antropologicheskii forum*, no. 15 (2011): 187–202.

Spiegel, Gabrielle M. *The Past as Text: The Theory and Practice of Medieval Historiography* (Baltimore: Johns Hopkins University Press, 1997).

Suny, Ronald Grigor. *The Soviet Experiment: Russia, the USSR, and the Successor States* (New York: Oxford University Press, 1998).

Taub, Deborah J., and Heather L. Servaty-Seib. "Controversial Content: Is Harry Potter Harmful to Children?" In *Critical Perspectives on Harry Potter*, edited by Elizabeth E. Heilman (New York: Taylor & Francis, 2008), 13–32.

Todorov, Tzvetan. *The Fantastic: A Structural Approach to a Literary Genre*. Translated by Richard Howard (Cleveland, OH: Case Western Reserve University Press, 1973).

Tumarkin, Nina. *Lenin Lives: The Lenin Cult in Soviet Russia* (Cambridge, MA: Harvard University Press, 1983).

Tynyanov, Yury. "Dostoevsky and Gogol (Toward a Theory of Parody)" [Dostoevsky i Gogol' (k teorii parodii)]. In Yury Tynyanov, *Poetics: A History of Literature* [Poetika Istoriia literatury] (Moscow: Kino, 1977).

Van Brussel, Leen, and Nico Carpentier, eds. *The Social Construction of Death: Interdisciplinary Perspective* (London: Palgrave, 2014).

Vanderstraeten, Raf. "Burying and Remembering the Dead." *Memory Studies* 7, no. 4 (2014): 457–71.

Vardy, Peter. "Dead Reckoning." *The Times Higher Education Supplement*, August 18, 2011.

Vatsuro, Vadim. *Goticheskii roman v Rossii* [The Gothic Novel in Russia] (Moscow: Novoe literaturnoe obozrenie, 2002).

Vidal, Ricarda. "Death and Visual Culture." In *The Power of Death: Contemporary Reflections on Death in Western Society*, edited by Maria-Jose Blanco and Ricarda Vidal (New York: Berghahn Books, 2014), 115–26.

Vieira, Mark A. *Hollywood Horror: From Gothic to Cosmic* (New York: Harry N. Abrams, 2003).

Vinitsky, Ilya. *Ghostly Paradoxes: Modern Spiritualism and Russian Culture in the Age of Realism* (Toronto: University of Toronto Press, 2009).

Walter, Nicolas. *Humanism: What's in the Word* (London: Rationalist Press Association, 1997).

Walter, Tony, Rachid Hourizi, Wendy Moncur, and Stacey Pitsillides. "Does the Internet Change How We Die and Mourn?" *Omega* 64 no. 4 (2011–12): 275–302.

Walter, Tony, Jane Littlewood, and Michael Pickering. "Death in the News: The Public Invigilation of Private Emotion." In *Death, Dying, and Bereavement*, edited by Donna Dickenson, Malcolm Johnson, and Jeanne Samson Katz (London: Sage, 2000).

Wells, Paul. *The Horror Genre: From Beelzebub to Blair Witch* (London: Wallflower Press, 2000).

Wheeler, Michael. *Heaven, Hell, and the Victorians* (Cambridge: Cambridge University Press, 1994).

White, Hayden. *The Content of the Form: Narrative Discourse and Historical Representation* (Baltimore: Johns Hopkins University Press, 1990).

Williams, Bernard. "The Human Prejudice." In *Philosophy as a Humanistic Discipline*, edited by A. Moore (Princeton: Princeton University Press, 2005), 135–54.

Wilson, Natalie. *Seduced by Twilight: The Allure and Contradictory Messages of the Popular Saga* (Jefferson, NC: McFarland, 2011).

Wittgenstein, Ludwig. *Philosophical Investigations* [1953]. Translated by G. E. M. Anscomb (Oxford: Blackwell Publishing, 2009).

Wolin, Richard. *The Seduction of Unreason: The Intellectual Romance with Fascism from Nietzsche to Postmodernism* (Princeton: Princeton University Press, 2006).

Wolfe, Cary. *What Is Posthumanism?* (Minneapolis: University of Minnesota Press, 2010).

Wolosky, Shira. *The Riddles of Harry Potter: Secret Passages and Interpretive Quests* (New York: Palgrave Macmillan, 2010).

Zillmann, Dolf. "The Psychology of the Appeal of Portrayals of Violence." In *Why We Watch*, edited by Jeffrey Goldstein (New York: Oxford University Press, 1998), 179–211.

Zimmerman, Andrew. "Foucault in Berkeley and Magnitogorsk: Totalitarianism and the Limits of Liberal Critique." *Contemporary European History* 23, no. 2 (2014): 225–36.

Zipes, Jack. *Sticks and Stones: The Troublesome Success of Children's Literature from Slovenly Peter to Harry Potter* (New York: Routledge, 2001).

Index

Printed and bound by CPI Group (UK) Ltd, Croydon, CR0 4YY

09/06/2025

14686099-0003